Jewish Cookery
from Boston to Baghdad

Malvina W. Liebman

Jewish Cookery from Boston to Baghdad

E. A. SEEMANN PUBLISHING, INC.
Miami, Florida

Library of Congress Cataloging in Publication Data

Liebman, Malvina W
   Jewish cookery from Boston to Baghdad.

   Includes index.
   1. Cookery, Jewish. I. Title.
TX724.L46   641.5   75-2186
ISBN 0-912458-52-6

Manufactured in the United States of America

*This book is dedicated to my husband,
Seymour, whose encouragement, help, and devotion
make every undertaking — and all of life
a joyous pursuit.*

Contents

Glossary

Burghul: Cracked wheat.

Chanukah: Dedication; commemorates the re-dedication of the Temple by the Maccabees after it was defiled by Antiochus Epiphanes in 165 B.C.E.

Hoummus: A thick, creamy sauce made of chick peas, sesame seeds, and seasoning. (This may be purchased in cans, exported by Israel).

Kasha: Buckwheat groats. This is sold in supermarkets or stores catering to Jewish customers. It comes packaged in whole grain, medium, or fine grind. For the recipes in this book which include *kasha* as an ingredient, the whole grain is preferrable.

Pesach: Passover; commemorates the releasing of the Jews from bondage in Egypt.

Phyllo Leaves: Paper thin sheets of dough, sometimes called *strudel dough.*

Purim: Lots; celebration of the deliverance of the Jews from extermination by Haman of Persia, *circa* 485 B.C.E., who was the chief minister of King Ahasueras. The date for the mass killing was to be chosen by casting lots.

Rosh Hashanah: New Year; begins ten days of worship meditation, atonement, and reconciliation.

Sabbath: From sundown on Friday to after sunset on Saturday.

Shavuoth: Weeks; celebrates the first fruits and grains of spring and the anniversary of the giving of the Torah to Moses on Mount Sinai, after the exodus from Egypt, *circa* 1250 B.C.E.

Succot: Tabernacles; commemorates the forty years of wandering in the desert and celebrates the harvest season. *Succahs* (booths) are built of slats or boards and decorated with flowers, fruits, and vegetables. Meals are eaten in the succah during the week of Succot.

Talmud: Comprehensive term which includes the Mishnah and Gemara, commentaries, and interpretations of the Bible.

Tehina: A thick, creamy sauce made of sesame seeds, chick peas, spices, and seasoning. (This may be purchased in cans, exported by Israel).

Torah: The Law; the five books of the Bible.

Yom Kippur: Day of Atonement; ends the ten day period of prayer and meditation; a day of fasting, and solemnity, and prayer.

Jewish Communities
and Food Customs

Jewish Communities and Food Customs

What has come to be known as "Jewish food" in the United States includes such well known dishes as *gefillte* fish, bagels and lox, chicken soup with *matzo* balls, pickled herring, and chopped liver. However, these foods, and many others, are the result of Jewish interpretations of the cooking styles prevalent in the various countries in which Jews lived. Russian Jews cooked and ate *borsht,* Hungarian and Austrian Jews became experts with strudel, and German Jews developed a taste for red cabbage and *sauerbraten.* Just as Jews spoke the languages of their native lands, they cooked as did the majority population except that adaptations were made for the sake of observing the religious dietary laws which are enumerated in Leviticus XI and called *kashrut.* The words kashrut and *kosher* are derived from the Hebrew *kasher,* which means "suitable" or "fit". Certain foods and their manner of preparation must be suitable or fit (according to Jewish law) for consumption.

Jews have always lived in parts of the world other than Eastern Europe. There are Sephardic and Oriental Jews as well as those of other derivations who have never eaten gefillte fish, *latkes* or pickled herring but whose regular diet may have included *couscous, borekas, mishmishiya, risotto, arroz con pollo, chiles rellenos,* and many other dishes unfamiliar to most East European and American Jews, the majority of whom are Ashkenazim.

The Sephardim inhabited the Iberian Peninsula and southern France; Mediterranean Jews lived in Italy and Greece; Levantine Jews (some of whom are referred to as Oriental Jews) are from Turkey, Iraq, Iran, Syria, Lebanon, and Yemen. The Jews of North Africa are identified as North African Jews. (These specific designations are now becoming blurred because of political developments in Israel. All non-Ashkenazim are increasingly included in the general classification, Sephardim).

Indian Jews have lived in several areas of India since pre-Christian times and, from the time of the Sung Dynasty in 979 until the end of the nineteenth century, a small but distinguished Chinese Jewish community flourished in K'aifeng-fu, China. All of these people cooked kosher food in the styles of their culture groups.

Some foods, such as the thin, filled pancake, seem to have achieved universality. Whether called *blintzes, crepes,* egg roll, *blini, pannukakku, ataif, palacsinta, enchiladas,* or *cannelloni,* these delicious morsels are enjoyed in their native lands by all the residents.

Variations of a dish which used to be served on the Sabbath in Eastern Europe, and there called *cholent,* or *shalet,* can also be found in places as diverse as North Africa, Spain, and the Yucatan Peninsula of Mexico. Cholent, (a word which is said by some to be a corruption of the French word *chaud,* which means hot), consists of lima beans, potatoes, onion, meat, and water. Although there are several versions, this basic combination of ingredients was placed in an earthenware crock and left in the oven from Friday until Saturday evening because of the prohibition against cooking during the Sabbath. This dish, warm and tantalizingly fragrant, was so much part of the Sabbath and so greatly savoured that in 1850 Heinrich Heine included the following in his poem, "Princess Sabbath", (a parody of Schiller's "Hymn to Joy"):

> "Schalet, ray of light immortal!
> Schalet, daughter of Elysium!"
> So had Schiller's song resounded,
> Had he ever tasted Schalet,
> For this Schalet is the very
> Food of heaven, which, on Sinai,
> God Himself instructed Moses
> In the secret of preparing."

When the Inquisition in Spain was trying to formulate a list of the mores, customs, and observances by which Jews could be identified, they sought, among other things, to ferret out food or food habits which distinguished Jews from others of the population. One of the foods listed as being characteristically eaten by Jews was *adafina,* the recipe for which was found in a tenth-century document. Adafina was made of meat, rice, and eggs in the shell, cooked together until the eggs were brown both inside and outside. The liquid was used as soup and the other ingredients were served as separate courses. This was prepared prior to the Sabbath and left in the oven until after sundown on Saturday. Variations of adafina (sometimes called *ani, dfina* or *hamim)* are still made in Spain, Portugal, North Africa, and some parts of the Middle East.

However, it is surprising that presently in Yucatan, Mexico, a similar (non-kosher) dish of meat, beans, and other vegetables is cooked from

Friday to Saturday evening, although there is no purpose in doing so since Judaism is not practiced by the people of Yucatan. It is also notable that, except for a few bakers in Jewish or formerly Jewish neighborhoods of Mexico City or Monterrey, the only braided bread, (called *pan trenza* in Spanish and *challah* in Hebrew), in Mexico is found in Merida, Yucatan.

An explanation of these two not unrelated circumstances lies in the fact that in the sixteenth, seventeenth, and eighteenth centuries there were Jews in Yucatan, as well as other parts of Latin America, who had fled the persecution in Spain and Portugal. They had servants who, over a period of time, acquired the eating habits of their masters. Even after the absence of Jews for about two centuries, the descendants of those who had contact with Jews still maintain some of the culinary customs. Another of these customs is practiced by the bakers. They pinch off a piece of bread dough and throw it into the fire. When questioned about the reason for doing this the reply was, "It's a tradition". It is interesting to note that Jewish women, baking their own challah, threw a piece of the dough into the fire as a symbol of the sacrifices made at the Temple of Solomon. During the days of the Temple, the sacrifice itself was called challah, from which the Sabbath loaf derives its name.

The Inquisition, having been established subsequently in some parts of the New World, continued its relentless pursuit of the adherents to the "dead Law of Moses". The Jews had suffered expulsion from the Iberian Peninsula, where they had lived since the time of King Solomon, rather than forsake their faith. Again, in the unfamiliar and difficult setting of the New World, the people of "the Hebrew Nation" persisted in their religious observance although the earnestness of Inquisitorial effort was unmistakably indicated by the series of *autos-da-fe* covering three centuries. The conditions precluded any open admission of Judaism and, ostensibly, the Jews were Catholic. The necessity for clandestine observance gave rise to many strange and interesting practices.

Slaughtering of fowl was carried out at night by the women of the households in order to hide from the eyes of the servants the fact that this was done according to the laws of kashrut. Although orthodox observance forbids the eating of pork or even food prepared in utensils which had been used for non-kosher products, Jews were frequently forced to violate these laws. Eating with neighbors or Christian friends could not be avoided. Some Jews pretended that they couldn't eat pork for health reasons. Some picked out the pieces of pork from a stew and left them on the plate until all else was consumed, then claimed that they could eat no more. Others, to avert suspicion, served pork to guests, but didn't use the dishes for their own food when they were alone. If they

couldn't avoid eating forbidden foods, some families would forcibly re-
gurgitate the food after the guests had departed.

In 1641, a pious Jewish woman of Mexico and her daughter, were sur-
prised by a Catholic neighbor while they were preparing *matzot* for passover. They had to concoct a story to allay suspicion, although the neighbor insisted upon tasting the dough.

On religious fast days, some couples would pretend to have a big argu-
ment at the table which gave them the excuse to leave the table without
eating. Others ostentatiously walked in the Alameda holding toothpicks
in their mouths, giving the impression that they had eaten.

The mainstays of the diet were fish, eggs, vegetables, fruits, and olives.
It is not difficult to see that this was more expedient since these foods fall
neither into the category of "milk" foods nor of "meat" foods, thus re-
quiring no special preparation or separation.

The style of cooking was the only one known to them, Spanish or
Portugese. To the extent that the necessary ingredients were available,
the dishes were prepared in the manner of their ancestors. However,
changes were gradually introduced through the influence of Indian servants and availability of formerly unknown products, notably chocolate,
chile peppers, and tomatoes.

As is still practiced today, hard-boiled eggs were eaten upon return
from a funeral. The egg and its shape represent the cycle of life and, being
cooked hard, is a reminder of life's trials and tribulations. Fried eggs and
chocolate were sent by friends to the mourning family. For the first week
of mourning, friends delivered and served all meals to the family of the deceased. Wedding meals usually included poultry and started with a first
course of honey cake. The Friday evening meal usually consisted of fish;
a meat course; small breads, sprinkled with salt; a sweet, and wine. One
of the special treats during the early seventeenth century was a combination of almonds, walnuts, honey, and spices, called *alfojor*. A similar dish
is almost universally eaten during Rosh Hashanah, the observance of the
New Year.

Among the places to which Jews fled from Spain in the fifteenth century was Salonica, then under Turkish rule. Some of the refugees
founded small towns in Turkey to which they gave Spanish names and
where they maintained the old customs and food habits. So isolated were
some of these villages that in recent years it was discovered that the
people living in them spoke Spanish as it was spoken in no other place,
because the purity of the old Spanish had undergone no change. Similarly, the women were cooking in the manner of the original settlers,
using recipes handed down from one generation to the next.

One dish was made originally as a delicacy for women who had just given birth. Such a woman was called a *parida*. Thus, the concoction is called *fritas de parida*. It is very similar to what is generally called french toast and is covered with an orange flavored syrup and cinnamon.

Sesame and olive oils were common ingredients of many foods. As in Spain, green beans, for reasons not known, were called *judias,* Jewesses. They were frequently served with sauteed onion and oil. This dish was eaten on Tuesdays and prior to the Sabbath on Fridays. On Saturdays, religious or family holidays or celebrations, a special breakfact was served. This consisted of *bureques,* (also spelled *bourekas* and *burekes*), or turnovers, filled with chopped meat or cheese or vegetables such as spinach, eggplant, or squash combined with meat or cheese. This was accompanied by eggs cooked in oil, with onion skins for flavor and pungent odor. *Raki,* or *arak,* a brandy made from dates, was drunk, too. After a hard day's work the men sometimes had a drink of raki, but with these exceptions, the liquor was drunk only in connection with religious observances. Afternoon tea for the children took the form of thick slices of bread smeared with oil and sugar or honey.

It was the custom of the housewives to arise before dawn on Fridays to start the baking of bread for the week. In addition, cakes were baked for the Sabbath, and for visitors who might come to call at the close of the Sabbath. In winter, after the baking was finished and while the oven was still hot, almonds, walnuts, and hazelnuts were placed inside to toast for a Saturday night treat. Flour was costly and much work was involved in baking. Therefore, baked goods were valued intrinsically as well as a symbol of the good things of life. No bread or cake was ever thrown out or stepped upon. If a piece fell to the floor it was picked up, kissed, and put aside to be fed to domestic animals. Stale bread was used as a porridge when cooked with water and sprinkled with cheese and oil.

With "Operation Ezra-Nehemia" in 1950, the Jewish population of Iraq ended a residence in that country which began in the eighth century B.C.E. They brought with them to Israel such customs as baking small cakes or cookies during the first eight days of the Hebrew month of Ab (July-August) for members of a family in which a death had occurred that year. This symbolized forgiveness of the sins of the deceased. Similarly, during Chanukah of the same year, another kind of cake was offered by the family to anyone to whom the deceased had been in debt.

Passover, always a time preceded by hectic household preparations often resulting in the exhaustion of the housewife, was called *az frihli,* the holiday of falling apart. Part of the Seder service consisted of showering all present with green onions. A custom peculiar to the Jews of Morocco and other North African countries is, during the first Seder, placing a fish on a plate and lifting it over the heads of those present, saying, "We have gone forth in haste from Egypt". After reading the Haggadah, the men take a staff in their hands, and a pack on their backs, and go into the street crying, "Thus did our ancestors go forth from Egypt in haste with packs upon their backs." The evening after Passover is dedicated to the memory of Maimonides. During the day, families and friends go out into the woods to recite "The Blessing of the Trees." Upon their return, a table is decorated with flowers and stalks of wheat, and set with milk, flour, five dates, five eggs, and five green bean pods, also honey, fruits, nuts, cakes, and wine. It is a time for prospective bridegrooms to present gifts to their fiancees during the dinner at the home of the bride's parents. The meal includes a kind of crepe dipped in honey (for a sweet life together), and fish, the symbol of fertility. In Tunisia, on the Sabbath preceding the wedding, the bridegroom ate at the home of the bride's parents. The main dish of the meal was a stuffed chicken which was hidden somewhere in the house. The bridegroom had the responsibility of finding it and carrying it to the table.

Even now among the Jews of North Africa, after the marriage contract is drawn up, some families maintain the custom of having festivities that go on for three weeks during which time there are exchanges of food between the bride and bridegroom as well as their families. In this area, the circumcision of a child occasions a meal of hard-boiled eggs with pancakes, nuts, and cake. The father of the child shares a meal with his friends in the synagogue at which is served adafina—hard-boiled eggs, potatoes, and meat—followed by the *oriza* or rice pudding. A feast is also given at the appearance of the first tooth and an offering is made of wheat and chickpeas. Another feast is celebrated for the first haircut at which time sweetmeats are distributed among the children. After the speech-making, singing, and praying at a *bar-mitzva,* the newly initiated member of the congregation is showered with bonbons.

In Libya, one of the foods which the bridegroom presents to his fiancee is a roasted lamb's heart dipped in sugar. (Can this have been the origin of the word sweetheart?) Also in Libya, on Shavouth, the celebration of the Giving of the Law, Jews baked cookies in such shapes as the Tablets of Moses, Mount Sinai, and ladders, presumably with which to climb Mount Sinai.

The custom of the traditional Rosh Hashanah meal of the Persian Jews is still maintained by the Jews of Kabal and Herat, Afghanistan. The meal begins with the blessing of the ten foods, each suggestive of a hope for the coming year. Served are meat from the head of a lamb, "that he may put us at the head and not the tail;" apples cooked in honey, "that the new year may be prosperous and happy;" pomegranates, "that our merits may be as numerous as its seeds;" fish, "that we may be fruitful and multiply". Other foods included are squash, bread, beets, beans, strawberries, cucumbers, and wine. Nuts were never included as one of the ten foods since translation of the numerical value of the Hebrew letters which comprise the word for nut; *egoz,* results in the same sum as that of the word for sin, *het.*

Ashkenazim, Jews of East European origin, also use foods in much the same way, to dramatize the hopes and prayers of the people on this day of reflection. Bread is dipped into honey in hope of a "sweet year." A whole fish is served so that we may remember the dignity of wholeness and the opportunity of being leaders—the heads. Carrots are eaten as a sweet dessert to denote prosperity. On the first day of Rosh Hashanah the ceremony of *Tashlich* is performed. It consists of carrying crumbs in the pockets to a flowing stream and there emptying them into the water. It is symbolic of the resolve to free ourselves from our sins.

In some Arabic countries, Rosh Hashanah is the time for consuming great quantities of small, fried turnovers, filled with a variety of stuffings.

Chanukah is the holiday characterized, in Israel, by the jelly doughnut. This is a much anticipated treat. The bakeries have difficulty keeping up with the demand for the delicious *soofganiyot* during these eight days. The Chanukah delicacy in other parts of the world takes the form of crisp latkes, served with apple sauce or sour cream.

In some North African communities, the precariousness of the Jewish condition was thought to be counteracted by the promise of continuity symbolized in an unusual food practice. Cookies baked for Rosh Hashanah were saved to be eaten on Purim; others, baked for Purim, were eaten on *rosh hodesh* Nissan, (the first day of the Hebrew month of Nissan, April-May); the first matzo baked for Passover was saved until the following Passover.

Although the earliest history of the Jews in India is shrouded in the mystic veils of the pre-Christian era, it is undisputed fact that from the fifteenth to the fifth centuries *B.C.E.,* the Jews in Cranganore had a virtually independent principality, ruled over by a Jewish chief.

It is also known that the oldest word in the Tamil (Indian) language found in any written record is the word for peacock, *toki.* In the Hebrew text of the Book of Kings and in Chronicles, the word for peacock is *tuki.* (According to a widely accepted theory, this is the origin of the English word, turkey. It is known that a Hebrew-speaking sailor on the Santa Maria, Luis de Torres, was acting as an aide and translator to Columbus. It is said that upon seeing a wild, spread-tailed gobbler for the first time, he called it tuki, which later became turkey. In Spanish the word for turkey is *pavo.* A peacock is a *pavo real,* a royal turkey).

The religious observances of the *bene Yisrael,* (the sons of Israel) of

India, and the food associated with the holidays, are different from that of most other Jewish communities of the world. This can be attributed to long periods of isolation from other communities and teachers, fear of open religious practice because of political persecution, and the usual acculturation.

Three days after Rosh Hashanah, *kiru-sha-san* is observed by arranging a cloth covered tray, set with porridge made of cereal and coconut milk, and some sweetmeats. The family, sitting around the tray, repeats the *Shema* while incense burns. Passover is observed by excluding two staples from the diet, bread and a syrup called *anas*. Before and after the fast commemorating the destruction of the Temples, a dish made of beans, spices, and herbs is eaten. The beans are previously layered with fabric and soaked in water. Food on this occasion is served on leaves rather than on dishes, to recall the loss suffered in Jerusalem's fall.

Thanksgiving and sacrificial offerings are made of foods frequently mentioned in the Bible—wine, bread, oil, and meat. Rice has come to be a basic part of the diet, especially when seasoned with condiments.

Because the dominant culinary heritage of most Jews in the United States consists of the delicious and varied dishes of Eastern Europe, which are so familiar and accessible, less has been said about it. However, recipes from that wealth of gustatory delights are included in the text.

Jewish cooking has influenced and, in turn, has been influenced by the food customs of people on all the continents. The availability of ingredients far from their places of origin and the development of sophisticated tastes as a result of travel, has broadened the opportunity for internationalizing our cuisine. Appreciation for a wide variety of food styles has developed. This trend has caused obliteration of many lines between "Jewish food" and foods of other ethnic groups, to their mutual benefit.

The recipes in this book are formulated to conform to the laws of kashrut, which prohibit the use of pork, certain cuts of beef, lamb and veal, shellfish, and other fish which do not have fins and scales; as well as a mixture of dairy foods with meat or meat products. All ingredients mentioned are available as kosher products.

Some foods are neither "dairy" nor "meat". They are called *"parve"* and may be used with either dairy or meat foods. They include fruits, vegetables, fish, and eggs. In recent years there have been produced kosher non-dairy substitutes for such things as whipped cream, cream, milk, butter, and other items. These, too, are parve.

Any cookbook is an individual's limited selection of recipes from a far larger number of possibilities. In this book, the selection was made on the basis of those, which in the author's judgment, seemed interesting, practical, and representative of a variety of culture groups.

It has been said that man does not live by bread alone. While nourishing our bodies we can also enrich our understanding of the varied customs, culture, and experiences, of that diverse group of people who call themselves Jews. Though separated geographically and culturally, they are united by a common faith which finds expression in many areas of life, including food customs.

In our sophisticated society the availability of foods originating in any part of the world does not seem remarkable, nor does the excellent quality of fruits, vegetables, and meats. Yet, it was not always so. Many centuries were required for man to acquire the skills of agriculture and animal husbandry, and many more passed before cooking became one of the creative arts. It is interesting to learn where some of our foods originated and how wars, explorers, crusades, and merchants spread them from their sources. Changes in geographical location frequently caused change in their uses and names and added to them religious or superstitious significance.

There is a welcome resurgence of interest in cookery as a creative art. It is obvious that one cannot starve as long as food is available, but man does not live—in the fullest sense—simply by eating to nourish the body. Eating throughout the ages has been more than a physical experience. It has taken the form of the Greek symposium, the purpose of which was to use the meal as a setting for serious discussion. It has been used as an occasion symbolic of religious events and meanings. It has been the festival catalyst for celebrating such important milestones as birth, religious affirmation, and marriage, and even as part of an event to mark the passing from this life. Most of all, however, food and eating are associated with good fellowship and cordiality. It is therefore worthy of thought, creativity, and artistic presentation.

One of the first axioms for creative cooking is, "Don't be afraid to experiment!" The first time you try the recipes, follow them as suggested. After that, change them to suit your taste or desire for invention. Create and invent with verve, courage, and joy.

It is hoped that this volume will offer the reader opportunities for the degree of culinary pleasure and challenge that the author experienced in years of travel and research and in adapting the recipes for American tastes and kitchens.

Hors d'Oeuvres and Appetizers

Hors d'Oeuvres and Appetizers

Melon of the Pure and True Temple

From the time of the Sung Dynasty (949) or possibly earlier, until the middle of the nineteenth century, in the city of K'aifeng-fu, there was a flourishing community of Chinese people who were Jews. They had an elaborate synagogue, built in oriental design but authentically Jewish. It was called the Pure and True Temple. The men wore blue *yarmulkas* (skull caps) and prayed facing west, toward Jerusalem. In the Temple there was a table on which were placed bowls of crystallized ginger, sweetmeats, flower vases, and a candlestick.

honeydew melon balls	**crystallized ginger**
orange liqueur	

Marinate the melon balls in the liqueur, in the refrigerator, for an hour. Sprinkle with crystallized ginger before serving.

Bourekas

Bourekas, also called boyos and bulemas, are eaten by Sephardic Jews of many countries. They are eaten for *desayuno,* which is the Spanish word for breakfast. However, in this sense, the desayuno is a small meal which may be a holiday breakfast, a late supper, or an afternoon tea, for almost any time is a good time for eating these savoury delights. They may be accompanied by olives, grapes, melons, cheese, coffee, or wine.

The Jews of Tunisia serve them on the evening preceding a *bris,* (circumcision).

Dough:	*Filling:*
2-1/4 cups flour, sifted	**sauteed onions and**
1 teaspoon salt	**mushrooms or**
1/2 cup shortening	**chopped liver**
1 egg, beaten	**or**
2 tablespoons water	**mashed potatoes and cheese or**
1 egg plus 1 teaspoon water	**spinach and cheese or tuna salad**

Sift together the flour and the salt. Use a pastry blender to cut in the shortening until the mixture has the consistency of coarse sand. Add the egg and work it into the dough. Add the water and mix the dough gently until it forms a ball and "cleans" the bowl. Handle it as little as possible. Cover with plastic wrap and let it rest in a cool place for an hour or two.

Roll the dough out thinly on a lightly floured board or between pieces of wax paper. Cut into three-inch rounds. Put a spoonful of filling on each round and fold over to form half-moons. Pinch the edges together securely. Brush the tops with the egg beaten with water.

Place on ungreased baking sheets and bake in a preheated 375 degree oven for about 30 minutes, or until golden.   Makes about 20 bourekas

Chicken Livers on Toast

This is an American adaptation of the more traditional chopped liver, as a first course. The liver is grilled to conform to the laws of kashrut.

3 tablespoons margarine	1/2 lb. mushrooms, sliced
12 chicken livers, cut in	salt and pepper
halves, grilled	1 cup cooked peas
1/2 teaspoon ground laurel	2 tablespoons flour
or basil	1/2 cup chicken broth
1 onion, chopped	1/2 cup red wine
2 cloves garlic, minced	6 slices toasted white bread

Saute the onion in the margarine. Add the mushrooms, laurel, garlic, salt and pepper. Sprinkle with the flour and cook, stirring, for 3 minutes. Add the wine, broth, and chicken livers. Stir over moderate heat. Cover and cook for 5 to 7 minutes, or until cooked through.

Cut each slice of toast diagonally. Place two points of toast, slightly apart, on each plate. Spoon liver mixture over. Garnish with peas.

Serves 6.

Cheese Balls Taj Mahal

Between 960 and 1126 C.E. Jews, coming from India, brought the first products from the Western World to China as gifts for the Chinese Emperor. Among them were spices formerly unknown in that land.

1 lb. cream cheese	2 tablespoons pickle relish,
1 teaspoon curry powder	well drained
	chopped peanuts

Soften the cheese. Add the curry powder and relish. Blend well. Add a small amount of relish liquid, if necessary. Form into balls and roll in the chopped nuts. Serve on crackers, with picks, or in tiny fluted cups.

Earth and Moon Balls

"Say among the nations: 'The Lord reigneth . . . Let the heavens be glad, and let the earth rejoice.'"

1 can tuna, drained and flaked	1/2 teaspoon hot pepper sauce
1 small package cream cheese	chopped parsley
1 tablespoon lime juice	chopped nuts
1 teaspoon prepared white horseradish	

Beat the cream cheese, lime juice, horseradish, and pepper sauce until smooth. Add the tuna and blend thoroughly. Form into bite-sized balls. Dip one side of each ball into the chopped parsley and the other side into the chopped nuts. The green half represents the earth and the "rocky" side, the moon.

Seeded Cheese Diamonds

The origins of caraway are prehistoric. The aroma and flavor are so well-liked that these small, crescent-shaped seeds are used in bread, soup, with cabbage or noodles, and as the flavoring of the liqueur, Kummel. A candy is also made of it. Chestnuts sold by Italian street vendors are sometimes boiled with caraway seeds. Holland grows caraway for export. When dry, the seeds fall from the plants at a touch. They are, therefore, gathered before dawn when the dew causes them to adhere more firmly.

A soup made of caraway seeds was thought by some European Jews to have great benefits for new mothers.

2-1/4 cups flour, sifted	1/3 cup water
1 teaspoon ground caraway seeds	1-1/4 cups grated Cheddar cheese
1/2 teaspoon salt	2 tablespoons poppy seeds
3/4 cup shortening	1 egg white, slightly beaten

With a pastry blender cut the shortening into the flour which has been sifted with the salt and ground caraway. When the mixture has the consistency of coarse sand, add the water and toss lightly with a fork. Make a ball of the dough and divide it in half. Chill.

Roll out half of the dough, between pieces of wax paper, to a rectangle about 1/8 inch thick. Place on a lightly-greased cookie sheet. Spread the grated cheese on it.

Roll out the remaining half of the dough and place over the cheese layer. Roll the rolling pin over the top once, lightly.

Brush the whole surface with the egg white and sprinkle rather thickly with the poppy seeds.

With a sharp knife score the dough about halfway through into diamond shapes about 1-1/2 inches long. Bake in a preheated 400-degree oven for about 20 minutes or until golden. While still warm, cut through to separate the diamonds. Cool on a rack.

Aegean Tyropites
(Cheese Puffs)

Phyllo dough lends itself with grace to desserts, main dishes, and finger foods. This paper-thin dough is called strudel dough in Austria, Hungary, and Germany where many different kinds of fillings are used. It is rolled up, jelly-roll fashion, and cut into slices after it is baked. Tyropites are popular wherever they are served. Ground meat, spinach or mashed potatoes are alternate fillings.

1/3 lb. Feta cheese, crumbled	6 tablespoons butter, melted
1/4 lb. cottage cheese	1/3 lb. phyllo dough sheets
2 eggs	

Blend the Feta cheese and cottage cheese very thoroughly. Add the eggs. Mix well. Set aside.

Cut off the bottom third of the package of folded phyllo sheets. (Save the two-thirds section for future use. It can be stored in the refrigerator indefinitely if carefully wrapped and sealed). Unfold the third to be used, but keep it covered with a slightly damp tea towel. It dries out very quickly and becomes hard to work with. Work with one sheet at a time.

Brush one sheet of dough with melted butter and fold it to a two inch width. Place one tablespoon of the cheese mixture near the left hand end of the strip. Bring that lower left hand corner to the top edge of the strip to form a triangle. Continue folding, keeping the edges parallel and maintaining the triangular shape. Repeat the process until all the ingredients have been used. Brush the tops with melted butter. Bake on a greased cookie sheet in a preheated 425-degree oven for about 20 minutes, or until golden. Serve warm.   Makes about 25 triangles.

Liptauer Cheese

From the most ancient times the people of what is now called Hungary used dairy products extensively. This culinary taste probably originated with the advent into the area of barbaric tribes from Asia who were horsemen. They carried a perpetual food supply with them in the form of the milk of their mares which they used fresh and which they permitted to sour or curdle into cheese.

1/2 lb. cottage cheese	1/2 teaspoon salt
4 anchovy filets	3 tablespoons capers
1 teaspoon dry mustard	1 (8 oz.) package cream cheese

2 tablespoons caraway seeds	2 tablespoons gin
2 tablespoons paprika	4 tablespoons chopped chives
1/2 teaspoon white pepper	

Blend the cottage cheese in the blender with the anchovies, mustard, caraway seeds, paprika, salt, and pepper. Add the capers and blend for 2 seconds. In a bowl blend the softened cream cheese, the butter, and gin. Combine the two cheese mixtures and mix until smooth. Cover and let ripen in the refrigerator for about a week. Add the chives just before serving. Serve on very thin slices of pumpernickel bread.

Makes about 2-1/2 cups.

Parmesan Cocktail Cookies

Parma, the city in Italy where Parmesan cheese was first made, is also the location of the Palazzo della Pilotta in which is contained the extensive and valuable de Rossi collection of Hebrew manuscripts and books. The library is named for its collector, Giovanni Bernardo de Rossi, who died in 1831. Although Christian, de Rossi was a great Hebraist. The collection includes the only copy extant of the first book printed in Hebrew. It is Rashi's *Commentary on the Pentateuch,* 1475.

6 tablespoons butter	1/4 lb. Parmesan cheese, grated
2 cups flour	1 egg white
1 teaspoon salt	1/2 cup finely-chopped pecans
1 egg yolk, beaten	

Cream the butter until light. Gradually add the flour, mixing well. Add the cheese, salt, and beaten egg yolk. Work into a smooth dough.

Roll out on a lightly floured board to 1/4 inch thickness. Cut with a small cookie cutter. Place on an ungreased cookie sheet. Beat the egg white slightly and brush cookie tops. Sprinkle with chopped nuts. Bake in a pre-heated 375-degree oven for 8 to 10 minutes or until golden.

Makes about 5 dozen cookies.

Felafel

The Copts of Egypt, who claim to be descendents of the Egyptians of the Pharoanic age, make *ta'amia (felafel)* differently from the Israelis. They claim that the dish originated with them in ancient times and was made with broad white beans, *(ful nabed)* and onions. That is the way they make it today. It is a special dish for religious holidays and especially used during Lent when it substitutes for meat. Felafel is one of the national dishes of Israel and sold from kiosks on many streets. It is served in pita, the bread pockets of the Middle East, garnished with any or all of the following, depending upon the digestive fortitude of the consumer: sauerkraut, *tehina,* pickle relish, salad or a spicy, chutney-like relish.

1/2 lb. chick peas	1/4 teaspoon cayenne pepper
3 tablespoons fine buckwheat groats	1/2 teaspoon ground coriander
	1/2 cup chopped parsley
3 cloves garlic, minced	1 egg
4 tablespoons flour	fat for deep frying
1 teaspoon cumin	

Soak the chick peas overnight, then put them into a blender just long enough to chop finely rather than to grind into a powder. Soak the groats for 45 minutes in 4 tablespoons of water. Combine all the ingredients and blend well. Shape into balls 1 inch in diameter. Fry in hot fat for a minute or two or until lightly browned. Serve on picks with or without a tehina dip. (An excellent prepared mix is made in Israel and available in some supermarkets, gourmet shops or Middle East grocery stores.)

Makes about 20 balls.

Boston Tricorns

After the American Revolution, housewives of the colonies made tricorn pastries of various sorts to honor their heroes through their headgear. It was said that they copied the idea from the much older Jewish custom of making triangular filled cookies to represent the hat of Haman, the villain of the Purim observance.

Dough:	*Filling:*
2-1/2 cups flour, sifted	2 cans tuna, well drained
3/4 cup shortening	1/4 lb. mushrooms, coarsely chopped
3/4 teaspoon salt	1/2 cup finely chopped celery
1/4 lb. grated Cheddar cheese	1 teaspoon onion juice
2 egg yolks, beaten	2 tablespoons finely-chopped dill
2 tablespoons water	mayonnaise

Combine the flour and salt. With a pastry blender cut the shortening into the flour until the mixture has the consistency of coarse sand. Add the cheese and blend. Add the egg yolks, blend well. Add the water, a little at a time. You should have a stiff dough. Roll out to 1/8 inch thickness. Cut into 3 inch rounds. Place each round on previously cut rounds of foil and gently shape the foil and dough into tricorn cases to hold the filling. Prick the dough several times and, on a baking sheet, bake in a preheated 425-degree oven for 10 minutes or less, until lightly browned. Combine all the filling ingredients with just enough mayonnaise to hold them together. Carefully remove the foil from the cooled bases. Fill the tricorns.　　　　　Makes about 18 tricorns.

Ethiopian Fish Balls

"Are ye not as the children of the Ethiopians unto Me, O Children of Israel?" (Amos 9:7)

A sect of Black Jews, who call themselves Beta Israel or Falashas, have lived in Ethiopia since the destruction of the Second Temple in Jerusalem in the year 70 C.E. Their religious customs remain unchanged since that time because the Bible was their only reference. Until recently they still offered animal sacrifices in front of their synagogues or *mesjids*. They do not observe the holidays of Chanuka or Purim, since those holidays are of post-Biblical origin.

1 lb. white fish filets, cooked and flaked	1/2 teaspoon dry mustard
	1/4 cup pickle relish, drained
1/2 cup onion, chopped	2 cups mashed potatoes
4 tablespoons butter	1-1/2 teaspoons lemon juice
3 tablespoons flour	1 egg
1/2 cup milk	bread crumbs
1-1/2 teaspoons salt	oil for frying
1/4 teaspoon pepper	

Saute the onion in the butter until soft. Add the flour, salt, pepper, and mustard. Stir. Add the milk and stir until smooth. Add the relish, lemon juice, fish, and potatoes. Blend. Form into balls.

Dip into beaten egg and then into breadcrumbs. Fry in hot oil to cover until golden. Serve accompanied by a dip made of

1 cup mayonnaise	1 tablespoon sherry
1 teaspoon curry powder	

Prague Domes

In Prague, the building called the Jewish Town Hall was once, in the sixteenth century, just that. In a section of Prague there was an autonomous Jewish city, with its own officials and town hall. Today the building houses offices of Jewish organizations and records of the community, dating from its inception. There is a kosher restaurant in the basement which serves a variation of this dish as an appetizer. An interesting feature is a pair of clocks. One, with Hebrew letters for numerals, has hands that run backwards. The other, having Arabic numerals, has hands that move conventionally.

hard-boiled eggs	salt
scallions, about 1 to every three eggs	mayonnaise
	salami, thinly sliced

While the eggs are still hot, finely dice them. Add the scallions, finely diced, with the salt. Toss lightly. Cover and let stand until cool. Add enough mayonnaise to make a moist mixture. On each salami slice place a mound of egg salad. Garnish with a sprig of dill, a pimento-stuffed olive, or a gherkin slice.

Isfahan Cabbage Rolls

These stuffed cabbage leaves are served by the Persian Jews during the Succoth Festival.

1 large cabbage	2 tablespoons fresh dill
1 cup rice	2 tablespoons fresh mint, chopped
2-1/4 cups water	2 tablespoons parsley, chopped
2 small tomatoes, peeled,	1/4 cup lemon juice
seeded, chopped	1 or 2 teaspoons sugar
1/4 teaspoon cinnamon	1/2 cup olive oil
1/4 teaspoon allspice	1 cup water
salt and pepper	1/4 teaspoon saffron
1 cup pine nuts	2 cloves garlic, minced
4 scallions, finely chopped	1 cup raisins

Cut the core out of the cabbage and place in a large pot of simmering water until the leaves are wilted but not cooked. Drain and cool. Separate the leaves. Boil the water and add the rice. Cook, covered until the rice is tender. In a bowl put the rice, tomatoes, scallions, dill, parsley, mint, cinnamon, allspice, salt and pepper and pine nuts. Mix.

If some cabbage leaves are too large, cut them in half (the finished rolls should be about 3 inches long and 1 inch in diameter). On each leaf place about 1 tablespoon of the rice mixture. Roll up, tucking in the sides. Place the rolls snugly in a large saucepan. Combine the water, olive oil, garlic, lemon juice, sugar, and saffron. Pour the mixture over the cabbage rolls. Sprinkle the raisins over the top. Simmer, covered, for 2 or 3 hours, adding very small amounts of water, if necessary. There should be enough liquid to moisten the rolls when served. Serve hot.

Stockholm Whitefish

In Stockholm there is a police station on Sjalagardsgatan, which translates to Soul Guarding Street. The building was the original synagogue of the city. The women's balcony is still to be seen but no other indication of its original use remains.

smoked whitefish	toast slices
butter	1/2 cup white wine (approximately)
onion rings	fresh dill
basil	

Filet the whitefish and, with a sharp knife, cut into serving size pieces. Saute the onion rings in the butter until very lightly browned, adding a pinch of basil. Remove from the pan and reserve. Place the whitefish in the pan and saute lightly, being careful not to break the pieces. Add the wine and baste for one minute.

On each slice of toast place some of the onion, topped with a serving of whitefish. Spoon a little liquid over and garnish with a sprig of dill.

Tehina Dip

For the Sabbath in Morocco, fish is cooked with *tehina* or *hommus*. It is said that through this dish "the souls of the righteous pass prior to their ascent to heaven."

6 oz. sesame seeds	juice of 2 lemons
1 cup water	1 teaspoon salt
2 cloves garlic	1/8 teaspoon cayenne

Place all ingredients in a blender to make a sauce of mayonnaise-like consistency, or slightly thinner. (This may be purchased in cans, ready for use. It is exported by Israel and can be found in some supermarkets, gourmet shops, or Middle East groceries).

This dip is used with *felafel* or raw vegetables. Tehina may also be used as a salad dressing by adding more lemon juice, vinegar, or water.

Guacamole

Among the fruits brought to Europe by early explorers and conquerors of the New World was the avocado. The English word is a corruption of the Nahuatl Indian word for testicle, *ahuacatl*. It was so called, presumably, because of its shape.

Luis de Carvajal el Mozo, incarcerated for adhering to Judaism in the secret cells of the Inquisition in Mexico in 1596, wrote his Last Will and Testament on the nut of an avocado. It was stolen from the Mexican National Archives in 1932.

1 avocado, mashed	2 teaspoons grated onion
1/4 teaspoon salt	1 tablespoon mayonnaise
1/2 peeled, seeded tomato, chopped	1/4 teaspoon hot pepper sauce

Combine all the ingredients to make a smooth paste. Serve as a dip with cornmeal chips or other crackers.

Baba Ghanouj
(Eggplant and Tehina)

The name of this dish is also spelled Baba Gannoy, Baba Ganoush, and in other similar ways, depending upon which Arabic-speaking person spells it. Many of the sounds associated with the Arabic alphabet cannot easily be represented by the Roman alphabet. Thus, some of the differences in spelling result from attempts to approximate the correct pronunciation. A similar difficulty exists in translating words from the Hebrew.

The name of this dish means "indulged father," said to derive from a doting son's preparation of it for his toothless father. The dish is popular all through the Middle East.

1 small eggplant
3 cloves garlic, minced
1/2 teaspoon salt
1/2 teaspoon cumin
3 tablespoons finely-chopped
   parsley

1 cup tehina (or enough
   to make a creamy consistency)
juice of 2 lemons
1 tablespoon olive oil

Broil the whole eggplant, turning frequently until the skin is black and blistery and the eggplant feels soft and juicy. Under cold running water, remove all the skin. Squeeze the juice out of the eggplant. Cut it into pieces and put it into a blender with the garlic, salt, cumin, and parsley. Blend until smooth. Add the tehina and lemon juice a little at a time to achieve desired taste and consistency. Add olive oil. Blend for 2 or 3 seconds. Pour into a bowl. Garnish with black olives or a little cayenne sprinkled on top. Serve with pieces of *pita,* Arab flat bread.

Molded Vermouth Pate

The word vermouth is from the German *wermut,* meaning absinthe. Vermouth is a wine flavored with ingredients such as coriander, peel of bitter orange, absinthe, cinnamon, quinine, and anise.

1 teaspoon unflavored gelatine
2/3 cup sweet vermouth
1 hard-boiled egg
pimento strips
1/2 cup margarine
1/2 onion, chopped
1/2 lb. chicken livers
   (grilled to conform to the
   rules of kashrut)
1/2 cup consomme

pinch nutmeg
pinch cloves
pinch salt
pinch curry powder
1/4 cup sherry
1-1/2 teaspoons unflavored
   gelatine
1/3 cup consomme
3/4 cup chopped walnuts

Sprinkle the gelatine over the 2/3 cup sweet vermouth to soften. Heat to dissolve gelatine. Pour into a 4-cup mold and tilt so that gelatine mixture coats sides as well as bottom. Set aside, but tilt mold from time to time as gelatine cools. Refrigerate until gelatine in the bottom is sticky and beginning to set. Cut slices of hard-boiled egg. Arrange these and pimento strips in a design. Press lightly into gelatine. Refrigerate.

Saute onion in the margarine until soft. Add the cut-up chicken livers and cook until no longer pink inside. Add the consomme, nutmeg, cloves, salt, curry powder, and sherry. Bring to a boil and remove from heat. Whir in a blender until smooth. Remove the liver mixture to a bowl.

Soften 1-1/2 teaspoons of gelatine in the 1/3 cup of consomme and dissolve over medium heat. Add to the liver mixture. Mix well. Add the chopped walnuts. Pour into the prepared mold. Chill for several hours or overnight.

Zakuski

Zakuski is the Russian appetizer tray of a variety of fishes, cheeses, and vegetables. The custom of having this "little meal" encourages the consumption of vodka—and vice versa. Thinly-sliced meats may be substitued for the dairy products.

The aristocrat of caviars is the roe of the beluga white sturgeon found in the Black and Caspian Seas. (It is from the air sac of this fish that isinglass, a transparent gelatine, also is obtained). The *Dictionnaire du Commerce,* 1741, says of "kavia," "It is beginning to be known in France where it is not despised at the best tables."

thinly-sliced Nova Scotia
 smoked salmon
caviar, garnished with sieved
 hard-boiled egg yolks and
 very finely-chopped onion
smoked whitefish, fileted and
 cut into inch wide slices
sauteed mushrooms and whole,
 very small onions

matjes herring in wine
sliced pickled beets
chopped cucumber and dill in
 sour cream
sliced Swiss cheese
cream cheese
black olives
cherry tomatoes
parsley sprigs for garnishing

Arrange one large or several small trays or platters with the above or similar foods. Serve with thinly-sliced pumpernickel, thin slices of toast or crackers, or thinly-sliced Danish or Swedish dark bread.

Manna Sandwiches

This and similar "sandwich" dishes are said, in Libya, to represent manna between two layers of dew.

1 large eggplant
salt
1/2 lb. fresh mushrooms, chopped
1 medium onion, finely minced
2 tablespoons butter
1/2 lb. cream cheese, softened

1 eggyolk, beaten
flour
matzo meal
salt and pepper
oil

Peel and cut eggplant into slices less than 1/2 inch thick. Cut each slice into rectangles about 1-1/2 by 2 inches. Put them in a colander and sprinkle with salt. Let them stand for about 30 minutes.

Saute the onion in the butter until transparent. Add the mushrooms and saute lightly. Cool. Add the cream cheese and a pinch of salt. Blend well. Add the egg yolk. Mix.

Rinse the eggplant pieces and pat dry with paper towels. Dredge in flour. Fry lightly in oil until soft and just golden, but retaining their shape.

Spread half of the eggplant pieces with the cheese mixture. Cover with another piece to make a sandwich.

Beat the remaining eggs and dip each sandwich into the egg and then into the seasoned matzo meal, completely covering. Fry in deep, hot oil for about 3 minutes or until crisp but not too brown. Drain on paper towels. Serve hot.

Balkan Cornucopias

There is a five-hundred-year-old fountain in Dubrovnik called Fountain Kosher. Originally called *Fontana per gli Ebrai* (Hebrew Fountain), it was probably so designated because it stood just outside the old ghetto.

caviar (not necessarily of sturgeon)	hard-boiled eggs
	lemon juice
thin slices of smoked salmon	finely chopped onion

Sieve the yolks of the eggs. To the caviar add the lemon juice and finely-chopped (or grated) onion to taste. Roll small rectangles of salmon into cornucopias and fasten with a toothpick. Fill the cornucopias with the seasoned caviar. Sprinkle with the sieved egg yolk.

Tongue and Cranberry Spread

Mustard has been known since prehistoric times. Being of Asiatic origin, it was used for millenia by the Chinese. Our name for it, however, stems from the early Roman use of the seeds. Dry mustard has little odor or flavor. The Romans learned to release its pungency by mixing it with the juice pressed from grapes. This liquid, prior to fermentation, was called "must." Thus, the seeds were called must seeds, later corrupted to mustard.

1/2 can jellied cranberry sauce	1/2 cup chopped black olives
1 lb. pickled or smoked tongue	1/2 cup very finely-chopped parsley
1/2 cup margarine	1 tablespoon brandy
1 clove garlic, crushed	1/2 teaspoon dry mustard
1 tablespoon grated orange rind	1/4 teaspoon pepper

Melt the cranberry sauce over low heat. Chop the tongue finely. In a bowl soften the margarine only until smooth, not runny. Beat in the crushed garlic. Add the tongue, orange rind, olives, parsley, brandy, mustard, and pepper. Mix. Add the cranberry sauce. Blend well.

Refrigerate for several hours. Mound on a plate and garnish with black olives and threads of orange rind.

Herring Katarina

This combination of foods is said to have been one of the favorites of Catherine the Great of Russia. It was she who broke from the policies of her predecessors by encouraging Jewish merchants to develop Riga and other areas on a basis equal with other Russians.

1-1/2 cups sour cream	2 cups sliced herring in
2 tablespoons dry sherry	wine sauce
2 cups pickled beets and onion,	2 sieved hard-boiled egg yolks
well drained	

Add the sherry to the sour cream. Mix well. Toss together, lightly, the beets, herring, and sour cream mixture. Serve in lettuce leaf cups, garnished with sieved egg yolks.

Tuna on Toast Rounds

In about the year 1260, an Egyptian physician called El Beithar, wrote of the protective properties against pestilence of the herb *tarkhun,* which is the Arabic word for dragon. This is the first known reference to the herb we call tarragon. Tarragon is native to Siberia and made its way slowly to the Middle East and thence to Europe in the sixteenth century. It is called *estragon,* little dragon, by the French. The only reason given for this odd name for such a pleasant, aromatic herb is that its roots grow in snakelike undulations.

2 (7 oz.) water packed cans of tuna	1 tablespoon chopped parsley
6 shallots of scallions, finely	1/4 cup grated Swiss cheese
chopped	
3 tablespoons butter	*Topping:*
1-1/2 tablespoons cornstarch	2 egg whites, beaten
1/2 cup white wine	1/8 teaspoon cream of tartar
1 cup light cream	1/2 cup grated Parmesan cheese
1/2 teaspoon pepper	
3/4 teaspoon dried tarragon	*Toasted Rounds:*
1/4 teaspoon dried thyme	6 slices white bread
1/2 teaspoon dry mustard	butter for frying
2 tablespoons chopped pimento	

Lightly saute shallots or scallions in the butter until soft but not brown. Dissolve the cornstarch in the wine and add to the shallots, stirring. Add the cream, pepper, tarragon, thyme, mustard, pimento, parsley, and Swiss cheese. Stir until thickened. Add the flaked tuna. Heat through.

With a biscuit cutter, cut rounds out of slices of white bread. Fry in butter until golden. Beat egg whites with the cream of tartar until stiff. Combine the Parmesan cheese with the mayonnaise. Fold the egg whites into this mixture.

Place toasted rounds on an ungreased cookie sheet. Spoon some of the tuna mixture on each. Cover each with a mound of the egg white mixture. Brown under the broiler for just 2 or 3 minutes, or until golden.

Serves 6.

Coquille de Paris

A coquille, though actually a container to hold charcoal for roasting meats, is a name also given to little sauced dishes serve in shells.

Jews have lived in France since the years prior to the reign of Charlemagne. As in most European countries, intermittent expulsions took place, as exemplified by Marie de Medici. Acting as Regent for her son, Louis XIII, she decreed, in 1615, that Jews be expelled from the kingdom because they were "sworn enemies of the Christian religion."

1 lb. white fish filets	1/3 cup heavy cream
6 tablespoons vegetable bouillon	3 tablespoons butter
6 tablespoons dry white wine	1 small onion, finely diced
1-1/2 teaspoons lemon juice	1/4 lb. mushrooms
1/8 teaspoon salt	1/2 avocado
2 teaspoons cornstarch	slivered almonds
2-1/2 tablespoons water	

In a saucepan, combine the bouillon, wine, lemon juice, and salt. Add the fish filets and simmer for 10 minutes, or until the fish flakes easily with a fork. Do not overcook. Remove the fish from the liquid, cool and cut into 1-inch dice. Dissolve the cornstarch in the water and add to the wine mixture. Stir. Remove from the heat when the mixture is clear. Saute the onion and mushrooms in the butter. Puree the avocado. Add the cream to the wine mixture, stirring. Add the sauteed onion and mushrooms. Add the fish and pureed avocado.

Pour into shells or ramekins. Sprinkle with slivered almonds. Bake in a preheated 450-degree oven for 5 to 7 minutes or until almonds are lightly toasted.

Serves 6.

Soups

Soups

Chicken Soup with Matzo Balls

Chicken soup, long associated with Jewish cooking, was until recent times, a dish for special occasions or needs—the celebration of the Sabbath or religious holidays, the nourishment of invalids or new mothers, or to honor the presence of distinguished guests.

The pattern of immigration of Jews from Eastern Europe frequently took the form of the husband leaving for America with funds saved and borrowed. In the new country he worked to establish a home for his family and to save enough money to send them the cost of their passage. Everyone travelled in the dark bowels of the ship called the steerage, carrying his own food for the journey of two weeks, and sleeping on the floor. Horrible stories of seasickness and other illnesses were told and retold by the new arrivees who were processed at the huge immigration centers of Castle Garden and, later, at Ellis Island. The confusion, chaos, and noise there has caused a phrase to become part of the Yiddish vocabulary. When there is confusion, milling crowds or loud talk, it is described as a "kessel gart" (Castle Garden).

However, wives and children eagerly looked forward to the day when they would be reunited with husbands and fathers in the "golden land," where, according to a song, "even on weekdays white bread is eaten and where, little son, I'll cook chicken soup for you whenever you want it."

1 large chicken, cut into
   serving pieces
2 to 3 quarts cold water
2 carrots, quartered
1 large onion, cut in half
1 large parsnip, quartered
2 stalks celery, with leaves,
   cut into 3 inch pieces
several sprigs parsley
several sprigs dill
salt and pepper

Matzo balls:
3 egg whites, beaten
3 egg yolks
3/4 cup matzo meal
1/2 teaspoon salt
pinch of pepper
1 teaspoon very finely-chopped parsley

Put the chicken and water in a large pot. Add the carrots and onion. Tie the parsnip, celery, parsley, and dill into a piece of new cheesecloth and add to the pot. Add salt and pepper. Cover and bring to a boil. Reduce heat to a simmer and cook until chicken is tender. Cool, skim and strain.

Matzo balls: Beat the egg whites with salt until stiff. Add the yolks, one at a time, beating continuously. Combine the matzo meal, salt, pepper, and chopped parsley and very gently fold it into the egg mixture until well blended. Let is rest for 20 minutes. With hands repeatedly rinsed with cold water, form the batter into balls the size of small walnuts. It is most important not to press on the batter. Just take up a spoonful and use the water to smooth the shape gently. They do not have to be perfectly smooth. Lower them into slowly boiling salted water. Cook, covered, for about 20 minutes or until the matzo balls come to the top and are very light.   Serves 6.

Vegetable and Zitti Soup

In the Middle Ages (and currently in some places), the generic term for all pasta was macaroni. During the eighteenth and nineteenth centuries, it was symbolic of sophistication and wealth to make the Grand Tour of Europe. One of the most important areas on the tour was Italy. The tourists often returned displaying foppish fashions and manners which frequently caused them to be ridiculed and called "macaronis." The following well-known American ditty reflects this feeling:

"Yankee-doodle went to town
Riding on a pony.
Stuck a feather in his hat
And called it macaroni!"

Zitti is a pasta similar to elbow macaroni.

1/2 cup butter
1 large onion, chopped
2 cloves garlic, finely minced
1/2 lb. frozen green beans,
    thawed and cut into inch lengths
1/2 lb. diced zucchini
1/2 lb. frozen chopped broccoli,
    thawed

1/4 lb. frozen chopped spinach,
    thawed
4 cups vegetable bouillon
1/2 lb. zitti or elbow macaroni
1 teaspoon rosemary
1 tablespoon chopped dill
salt and pepper
1/2 cup sherry
1-1/2 cups sour cream

Saute the onion and garlic in the butter.

To 3 cups of bouillon add the beans, zucchini, and broccoli. Place the spinach and the remaining cup of bouillon in the blender and whir for

3 seconds. Add to the other vegetable mixture. Bring to a boil. Add the
zitti and the rosemary and dill. Cook until the zitti is at the *al dente*
stage. Add the sherry, stir. Just before serving add the sour cream and
heat, but do not boil.   Serves 6 to 8.

Hot Borsht

Borsht, the Russian beet soup made in many variations, has long been
part of Jewish cuisine. Sholom Aleichem writes of the making and enjoyment of borsht in his town of Kasrilovka. Borsht appears on the menus
of Jewish restaurants around the world, and the Catskill Mountain re-
sort area, made famous by Jewish hostelries, is known as the Borsht
Belt.

3 lbs. flanken, or short ribs,	5 cloves garlic, crushed
cut into serving pieces	1 bay leaf
1 large soup bone	1 teaspoon paprika
6 cups water	3 tablespoons sugar
3 stalks celery, with leaves	1 teaspoon salt
2 cups diced beets	1/8 teaspoon pepper
4 cups shredded cabbage	boiled potatoes
3 cups canned tomatoes	chopped dill
1/2 cup lemon juice	

Cover the bone and meat with 5 cups of water. Bring to a boil. Add the
celery. Reduce heat and simmer in a covered pan until meat is half done.
Tie the garlic and bay leaf in a piece of cheesecloth, to remove later.
Add to the pot along with the beets, cabbage, tomatoes, lemon juice, pap-
rika, salt, pepper, sugar. Cover and simmer until meat is very tender.
Remove bone and cheesecloth packet.

Serve in deep soup bowls over small, whole, boiled potatoes. Sprinkle
with dill.   Serves 8.

Gazpacho Madrileno

The Spanish gazpacho is usually thought of as a cold, tomato-based
soup. But there are probably as many as twenty-five different dishes by
this name. Some are made without tomatoes. Some are not even liquid.
And none of them are made in northern Spain.

The gazpacho given here is made as a cool, refreshing summer soup
in Madrid.

2 cloves garlic	salt and pepper
6 ripe tomatoes, coarsely chopped	1/2 cup white vinegar
4 green peppers, coarsely cut	6 cups ice water
1/4 cup olive oil	2 cucumbers, diced
1 cup ice water	2 green peppers, diced
6 slices of day old bread, crumbled	2 tomatoes, peeled, seeded and diced
1/2 teaspoon cumin seed	

Put into a blender the garlic, tomatoes, peppers, oil, 1 cup water, bread, cumin seed, salt and pepper. Whir until pureed. Pour into a bowl and stir in 6 cups of ice water and the vinegar. Chill.

Combine the 2 cucumbers, 2 green peppers, and 2 tomatoes. Add some to each individual serving.   Serves 8.

Pomegranate Soup

Granada was known, until the Decree of Expulsion in 1492, as the Jewish City. Almost every facet of its history, for centuries, was linked with Jewish learning and influence. Even its typically Spanish name had an interesting evolution. Early in its history, the Arabs referred to the city as Gharnatha al-Yahud (Gharnatha of the Jews). Gharnatha was corrupted to Granata which, in Spanish, means pomegranate. During one period, the Jews called the city Rimmon, which is the Hebrew word for pomegranate.

3/4 lb. lean ground beef	salt and pepper
1 onion, finely grated	1-3/4 cups pomegranate juice
1/2 cup cooked rice	(cranberry juice may be
1/4 teaspoon cinnamon	substituted)
1/2 teaspoon salt	1/3 to 1/2 cup sugar (omit if
1/4 teaspoon pepper	using cranberry juice)
8 cups water	2 teaspoons lime juice
1/2 cups chopped parsley	1/2 teaspoon cinnamon
1 cup chopped celery	1/8 teaspoon nutmeg
1/2 cup chopped green onions	1/8 teaspoon ground cardamom

In a bowl, combine the meat, onion, rice, cinnamon, salt, pepper, and ¼ cup water. Blend very well and form into walnut size balls.

In a large pot put the water, parsley, celery, and green onion. Bring to a simmer and add the meat balls. Simmer for 20 minutes. Add the salt and pepper, pomegranate juice, sugar, and lime juice. Cook until meatballs are tender and flavors have blended. Just before removing from heat, rub the mint between the palms of the hands and add. Also add the cinnamon, nutmeg and cardamom.   Serves 6 to 8.

Apple Vichyssoise

The Pletzel, the Jewish Quarter in Paris, has existed since the thirteenth century, although Jews have been in France since the fourth century. The word *pletzel* is the Yiddish diminutive for *platz,* or place. Therefore, the Pletzel would be the little place, probably implying intimacy as well as size. At one time the population of the quarter was largely Yiddish-speaking. Recently there has been an influx of Jews from North Africa, which has brought other tongues and mores. The kosher foods sold are different from those used by people of European origin. The shops sell items in demand by a new culture. The maze of alleys has a different look.

In the Quarter lives a Chassidic rabbi who spends the night reciting the Psalms and is said to eat only one meal a day, but he provides bed and board for the needy.

3 large eating apples
6 cups vegetable bouillon
3/4 teaspoon salt
2 teaspoons sugar

3/4 cup light cream
2 teaspoons lemon juice
chopped mint

Peel and core apples and cut into small pieces. Cook the apples in the bouillon until just tender. Whir in a blender until smooth. Add the salt and sugar. Chill. Add the cream and lemon juice. Chill again. Mix well. Serve cold garnished with finely chopped fresh mint leaves.   Serves 6 to 8.

Latin-American Fish Soup

This soup is especially popular in Mexico. Fish is a welcome adjunct to the Mexican diet. Even during the pre-Columbian era, it is said that Moctezuma, in Tenochtitlan (Mexico City), was supplied with fresh fish daily by runners who brought it from the coast, three hundred miles away.

8 to 10 cups water
1-1/2 lbs. red snapper
2 large fish heads
2 bay leaves
2 whole cloves
1 onion, cut in half
1 clove garlic
1 onion, chopped
1/4 cup olive oil

3 tomatoes, peeled and chopped
1 Jalapena pepper, chopped
  (optional)
1 teaspoon thyme
1/2 teaspoon oregano
1/2 teaspoon marjoram
salt and pepper
lime wedges

Boil the fish, fish heads, bay leaves, cloves, and onion in the water. When the fish is cooked, remove all the fish and strain the liquid. Discard the heads and shred the fish.

Saute in the oil the remaining onion. Add the tomatoes, pepper, thyme, oregano, marjoram, salt and pepper. Cover and simmer for 5 to 10 minutes. Add to the strained liquid. Add the shredded fish. Heat. Serve accompanied by lime wedges.   Serves 8 to 10.

Dried Fruit Soup

After the Roman destruction of the Temple in Jerusalem, it was no longer possible to bring sacrifices or foods to feed the needy. On the holiday of Tu B'Shvat, the New Year of the Trees, dried fruits representative of fruits grown in Israel are eaten in commemoration of the sacrifices and the tithes.

Sephardic Jews celebrate the holiday, which they call *Frutas,* by presenting children with little bags, embroidered with their names, containing dried fruits. In Baghdad, the festival was celebrated by friends and family feasting on many varieties of dried fruit, nuts, bread, and wine. The guests took turns reading from the book, "The Goodly Tree."

In Greece and Bulgaria, celebrations took place in the form of picnics in the woods.

3/4 lb. ground lean beef	1 cup dried apricots
4 saltines, soaked in water	1/3 cup walnuts, coarsely chopped
1/2 onion, finely grated	1/2 cup finely-chopped parsley
1 egg, beaten	1/3 cup cooked chick peas
salt and pepper	salt
1/4 teaspoon nutmeg	1/2 cup lime juice
3 tablespoons margarine	1/3 cup sugar
10 cups water	1 tablespoon dried mint leaves
1/2 cup pearl barley	1/4 teaspoon cinnamon
1-1/2 cups pitted prunes	1/4 teaspoon pepper

Combine the meat, crumbled soaked saltines, onion, salt and pepper, and nutmeg. Blend thoroughly and form into walnut size balls. Saute in the margarine. In a large pot put the water and barley. Cook for 15 minutes. Add the meat balls, prunes, apricots, walnuts, parsley, chick peas, and salt. Simmer about 20 minutes. Add lime juice and sugar. Cook to blend flavors. Just before serving, rub the mint between the palms of the hands into the pot. Add the cinnamon and pepper.   Serves 6 to 8.

Pottage of Lentils

"And Jacob gave Esau bread and a pottage of lentils; and he did eat and drink, rose up and went his way. So Esau despised his birthright." (Genesis 25:34)

1/2 cup margarine	1 large tomato, peeled,
6 onions, chopped	seeded, chopped
1 lb. ground beef	1-1/2 cups water
2 carrots, finely diced	1 lb. lentils
1 parsnip, finely diced	salt and pepper
2 stalks celery, finely chopped	

Saute the onions in the margarine. Add the ground meat and stir until no pink is visible in the meat. Add the carrots, parsnip, celery, tomato, water, lentils, salt and pepper. Cook about 1-1/2 hours or until lentils are tender.

Chicken Liver and Pea Soup

The Hebrews were among the first to cultivate peas as food. As noted in the accounts of Herodotus and in those of the Sumerians and Egyptians, this delicate vegetable was known to them and prized as a banquet food.

5 cups chicken consomme
2 celery stalks, with leaves,
    chopped
1 large carrot, finely diced
2 (10 oz.) packages frozen peas
3 teaspoons salt
1/4 teaspoon pepper

1/2 teaspoon powdered ginger
2 tablespoons margarine
1 small onion, diced
1/2 lb. chicken livers, (grilled to
    conform to the laws of kashrut)
1/3 cup sherry

Put the consomme in a saucepan. Add the celery and carrot and cook until tender. Add the peas and cook about 7 minutes. Add salt, pepper and ginger.

Saute the onion in the margarine. Add the chicken livers and cook, stirring, until livers are no longer pink. Slice rather fine.

Put the consomme, pea mixture into a blender. Whir until mixture is smooth. Pour into a saucepan. Add the liver mixture and the sherry. Heat but do not boil.   Serves 6.

Salmon Bisque

In medieval times, fish was an important part of the European diet. In France, fish-breeding enclosures were built in the Seine. Trout, salmon, carp, and sturgeon were often served at feasts for the king or noblemen.

Jews have always used fish as a staple since it is a *parve* food (in neither the meat nor dairy category) and can be used at any meal.

1 (1 lb.) can red salmon, drained
liquid from canned salmon and
    water to make 3 cups
1/4 teaspoon pepper
1/2 teaspoon salt
1/2 teaspoon basil
1/4 teaspoon thyme

2 tablespoons uncooked rice
1 carrot, diced
2 tablespoons butter
1 small onion, diced
2 egg yolks, beaten
2 cups light cream
1/2 cup sherry

In a saucepan combine the salmon liquid and water, pepper, salt, basil, thyme. Bring to a boil. Add the carrot and rice. Cook until carrot and rice are tender.

Saute the onion in the butter until soft. Remove the skin and bones from the salmon and flake with a fork. Add to the onion and stir for about 2 minutes.

Put the seasoned liquid mixture, salmon, and onion into a blender. Whir on low speed for 30 seconds or until very smooth. Add a little of this mixture to the beaten egg yolks. Stir vigorously. Pour the contents of the blender into a saucepan. Add the egg mixture. Stir to blend. Add the cream and sherry. Stir, heat, but do not boil.

Serve garnished with diced avocado or croutons.   Serves 6 to 8.

Cold Yogurt Soup

Elie Mechnikov was a Russian bacteriologist living in France who won the Nobel prize for medicine in 1908. He visited Bulgaria and was impressed by the health and longevity of the population. He noted with interest their daily consumption of a soured milk called yogurt. He thought there might be some cause-and-effect relationship, so he began investigating the properties of yogurt. This led to his identification of the strain of bacteria which provides the characteristic yogurt flavor. He named it *Lactobacillus bulgaricus,* to link it to Bulgaria. However, no connection could be found between the eating of yogurt and longevity.

The use of yogurt is common in the Near and Middle East. This Persian yogurt soup, relished by Jews of Iran, is a variation of the Bulgarian Tarator soup.

3/4 cup raisins	2-1/2 teaspoons salt
4 cups yogurt	1/2 teaspoon pepper
3/4 cup light cream	1-1/2 tablespoons dill, chopped
2 small cucumbers, chopped	2 stalks celery, chopped
2 hard-boiled eggs, chopped	3/4 cup walnuts, chopped
1/3 cup green onions, chopped	1-3/4 cups water

Soak raisins in cold water for 15 minutes. Drain. In a large bowl combine all the ingredients. Mix well. Refrigerate for at least 3 hours. Garnish with chopped parsley or mint leaves.   Serves 6 to 8.

Cranberry and Cabbage Borsht

For many years a man, working in the garment district of New York, patronized the same restaurant each day for lunch. Of course, he was well-known and treated with special consideration. One day, seating himself at his usual table, he ordered borsht. After the greeting and small talk, the waiter brought a large bowl of borsht. After a moment, the customer called the waiter back and said, "Taste the borsht."

The waiter, anxious to please, said, "What's wrong? You don't like it? I'll take it back. No problem."

The customer merely said, "Taste the borsht!"

"I take your word for it. There's not enough cream, maybe? I'll bring you another bowl. Just let me take it back."

"No, taste the borsht!"

"Look, I want you to be happy. Whatever it is you want, tell me. I'll bring it."

"Taste the borsht!"

"O.K., so I'll taste the borsht. Where's the spoon?"

The customer, lifting a finger said, "Aha! Now you've got it!"

1 cup cranberries	1/2 cup brown sugar
1 cup cold water	2 tablespoons white sugar
2 cups shredded white cabbage	1 teaspoon salt
3 cups water	1 egg yolk, beaten
3 tablespoons lemon juice	sour cream

Cook the cranberries in 1 cup of water for a few minutes until they pop. Whir in the blender until smooth. Put into a saucepan with the cabbage, remaining water, lemon juice, brown sugar, white sugar, salt. Cook for about 15 minutes or until the cabbage is tender. Pour a little of the hot liquid into the beaten egg yolk, stirring vigorously. Add the egg mixture to the saucepan and stir. Cook to thicken slightly.

Serve hot or chilled with dollops of sour cream.   Serves 4 to 6.

Beef

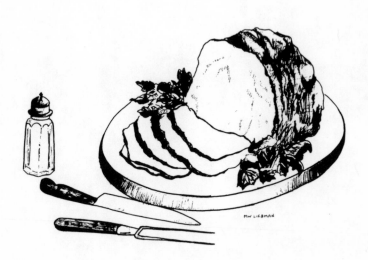

Beef

Holishkes
(Stuffed Cabbage)

Stuffed cabbage leaves probably originated in the Middle or Near East as an alternative to using grape leaves. The idea spread and became popular with Jews in Eastern Europe. Although served all through the year, many people make a point of serving it during the Sukkot holiday. It is commanded in the Torah that for seven days during the Hebrew month of Tishri (October) Jews should live in a *sukkah,* or outdoor booth made of lattices or boards, covered with branches and greenery. Inside is hung a variety of fruits and vegetables and flowers. Today, "living" in the sukkah is interpreted to mean taking all the family meals in the booth. It is customary to invite guests to the festivities held there. The holiday celebrates the harvest season, and the sukkah is a reminder that the Jews wandered in the desert for forty years, unable to build permanent homes.

1 large or 2 medium cabbages	1/2 teaspoon salt
2 lbs. ground beef	1/2 oz. citric acid crystals (sour salt)
3/4 teaspoon garlic powder	1-1/2 cups dark brown sugar
3/4 teaspoon salt	1 cup fine ginger snaps crumbs
2 cups water	2 (8 oz.) cans tomato sauce
3/4 cup rice	3 cups water

Cut the core out of the cabbage and put the cabbage into a very large pot of simmering water to wilt, but not cook, the leaves. Cool and carefully separate the leaves. Cut the middle vein of each leaf so that it is no thicker than the rest of the leaf.

Cook the rice in the two cups of water, with the salt, until about half done. Put the meat in a bowl and add the rice and the water in which it was cooked. Add the garlic powder and 1/2 teaspoon of salt. Beat the meat mixture until it is light and spongy.

In a very large pot put the two cans of tomato sauce and two cups of water, the crumbs, and sugar. In a small saucepan dissolve the sour salt in the remaining cup of water over low heat. Add to the tomato sauce mixture. Stir well.

On each opened cabbage leaf place a heaping tablespoon of the meat mixture. Roll up firmly but not too tightly, starting at the stem end and folding the sides in. Place each cabbage roll, seam side down, in the pot, fitting them rather closely together. Spoon the liquid over the top ones several times during the cooking. Place pot cover over 3/4 of the top of the pot. Cook for two hours over moderate to low heat. The flavor improves with slow reheating.   Makes about 35 rolls.

Baked Marinated Brisket

Rashi, who lived in the eleventh century, was Judaism's greatest Talmudist and commentator on the Bible. He was born and lived all of his life in Troyes, France, which was a great center of Jewish learning. It is said that a butcher shop was established on the old site of Rashi's synagogue, and that it was the only food shop in which flies could never be found.

5 lb. brisket of beef	3 cloves garlic, chopped
8 potatoes, peeled and cut	1 bay leaf
into quarters	2 teaspoons dried thyme
1-1/2 lbs. carrots, cut into	2 teaspoons dried marjoram
1 inch pieces	1/2 cup parsley, finely chopped
3 tomatoes, peeled and chopped	1 cup dry red wine
	10 peppercorns
Marinade:	2 teaspoons sugar
1/4 cup salad oil	1 teaspoon lemon juice
2 onions, chopped	

Combine all the marinade ingredients in a saucepan and simmer for 25 minutes. Cool. Place meat in a pan just large enough to hold it and pour the marinade over it. Pierce the meat all over with a large tined fork and turn from time to time during a 24 hour period. It need not be refrigerated the whole time.

Place the meat in a casserole with the strained marinade. Arrange the potatoes and carrots around the meat. Cover and bake in a preheated 350-degree oven for about two hours. Add the chopped tomatoes and continue baking uncovered for another hour or until very tender.

Serves 10 to 12.

Chiles Rellenos
(Stuffed Peppers)

The Old-World cuisine was greatly enhanced by the new additions brought back by the conquerors and explorers of the New World. Almost all of the novelties were quickly cultivated and used. The many varieties of hot chile pepper, however, had only limited acceptance. This recipe is made in Mexico using Chiles Poblanos, a hot green pepper which most Americans find a little too formidable. The tomato, another of the New World products, was not only enjoyed in Europe, but was also credited with romantic attributes. It was called a Venus Apple or Love Apple and was said to have aphrodisiacal powers.

Luis de Torres, a Jew, was the first-known explorer to set foot on the North American continent. He was the first man off the Santa Maria. He and his compatriots brought chile and tomato seeds back to Europe.

8 Italian peppers (Bell peppers are not suitable)	2 (8 oz.) cans tomato sauce
	1 can water
1-1/4 lbs. ground beef	1/2 teaspoon salt
1/2 teaspoon cayenne	1/4 teaspoon hot pepper sauce,
1 tablespoon flour	or more, to taste. It
oil	should be spicy.
2 egg whites	1/2 teaspoon sugar
2 egg yolks	oil for frying
flour	

Char the whole peppers over a gas flame or by holding over the coils of an electric stove set at moderately high heat. Turn so that all sides are blistered, but do not let the peppers cook or get soft. Strip the skin off immediately under cold, running water. Handle carefully. Do not break the peppers. Set aside.

Heat a little oil and add the meat, browning and breaking up lumps and stirring until no pink is visible. Sprinkle with 1 tablespoon of flour and the salt. Mix and remove from the heat.

In a large skillet, combine the tomato sauce, water, sugar, salt and hot pepper sauce. Place over low heat.

Make a slit in each pepper for about 2/3s of it length. Carefully remove the seeds but leave the stem on. Beat the egg whites until stiff. Add the yolks, one at a time, continuing to beat the mixture.

Fill each pepper with the meat mixture and place on a plate containing flour. Cover the pepper with flour so that a thin coating remains on the pepper. Holding the pepper slit side up, dip it into the egg mixture to cover. Place it immediately into a skillet of hot oil, turned down to moderate heat. Fry until golden on all sides. It usually takes about three turns to fry all sides, giving the finished pepper a rather triangular shape. As each pepper is fried, place it in the tomato sauce mixture. Bring to a simmer. Do not boil.

Serve peppers in a deep platter with the sauce.   Serves 8.

Short Ribs and Lentils

In the Municipal Archives in Amsterdam are notarial records which indicate that during the first half of the eighteenth century many Dutch ships involved in world trade were not only owned by Jewish shippers but were manned by Jewish captains and crews. These crews carried livestock and insisted upon having a *shochet* (ritual slaughterer) aboard so that kosher meat would be available.

5 lbs. flanken or short ribs, cut into serving pieces	**1 large onion, chopped**
5 cups water	**2 stalks celery with leaves, chopped**
1-1/2 teaspoons salt	**1 teaspoon dried thyme**
1 bay leaf	**1 tomato, peeled, seeded, and chopped**
2 cloves garlic, minced	**2 cups lentils**

In a large, heavy saucepan place the meat, water, salt, bay leaf, garlic, onion, and celery. Bring to a boil. Turn the heat down and simmer, covered, for about 2 hours, or until the meat is very tender. Add the thyme, tomato, and lentils. Cook about 35 minutes, stirring often, but gently, until lentils are tender but not disintegrated.   Serves 6 to 8.

Greek Meat Souffle

Jews have lived in Greece since Biblical times. There are records of a Jewish community in Chalkis in the year 200 *B.C.E.* After the Expulsion from Spain in 1492, many Jews went to Greece, giving Jewish culture in and around Salonica a distinctly Spanish influence, evidenced even today.

1 onion, finely minced	**1/2 teaspoon cinnamon**
1/4 cup oil	**1/2 lb. ground lamb**
1/2 cup finely chopped parsley	**1/2 lb. ground beef**
1/2 cup finely chopped celery leaves	**1/4 cup matzo meal**
	salt and pepper
1/2 teaspoon allspice	**6 egg yolks**
1/2 teaspoon coriander	**6 egg whites**

Saute the onion in the oil until lightly browned. Add the parsley, celery, allspice, coriander, and cinnamon. Stir for 1 minute. Add the lamb and beef, salt, and pepper. Stir until the meat is brown. Cool. Add the matzo meal and mix to incorporate. Beat the egg yolks and add to the meat, blending thoroughly, then beat the meat mixture until it is light and spongy. Beat the egg whites until stiff and fold into the meat mixture. Pour into a greased 9x9 inch baking dish. Bake in a preheated 350-degree oven for about 1 hour.   Serves 4 to 6.

Cholent

"Ye shall kindle no fire throughout your habitations upon the Sabbath day. (Exodus 35:3)

In many Jewish homes, *cholent* was prepared on Friday, prior to sundown, and placed in an oven so that the Sabbath meal would be hearty and hot without violating the religious precept quoted above. In European *shtetls* (small villages), families usually did not have large ovens in their homes. They used the baker's ovens. On Fridays, around noon, a regular parade of teenagers and housewives could be seen carrying the large, earthenware pots of cholent to the bakery. Each pot was distinctively marked. Twenty-four hours later, upon returning from synagogue services, the pots were picked up for the noonday meal. Snacking then went on as long as any cholent remained.

The house in which Heinrich Heine was born in Dusseldorf, Germany, was destroyed by bombs during World War II. It has now been restored but part of the space is used as a bakery. It was Heine who wrote so lyrically about shalet (cholent), as quoted on page 14. He also spoke of it as "God's kosher ambrosia."

In Aramaic the word for this type of dish is *khamin,* from which is derived the Arabic word, *hamim,* used by Jews from North Africa. The words *adifina* or *d'fina* are used by some Sephardim for a similar dish. (See page 14).

3 lbs. flanken or brisket	1/4 teaspoon ground ginger
1 lb. dried lima beans	4 large potatoes, peeled and
3 or 4 onions, coarsely diced	cut into 1 inch cubes
1/4 cup chicken fat	3 tablespoons flour
2 teaspoons salt	1 tablespoon paprika
1/4 teaspoon pepper	boiling water

Soak beans overnight. Drain. Lightly brown the onions in the fat. Remove from the pan and brown the meat in the same fat. Put the meat in a Dutch oven. Sprinkle with the salt, pepper and ginger. Add the beans, onions and potatoes in alternating layers. Sprinkle with the flour and paprika. Add enough boiling water to cover. Cover with a tightly-fitting lid. Bake for 24 hours in a 250-degree oven or cook over very low heat (or on an asbestos pad) for 3 to 4 hours. Add a little more boiling water, if necessary. All the liquid should be absorbed. The cholent should have the consistency of moist pudding.   Serves 8 to 10.

Malabar Pepper Steak

From earliest times, civilized man placed a high value on spices. His relentless and often dangerous search for them led to inadvertent land discoveries, colonization of new areas, changes in national economies, and other events of world importance.

While traveling, Pedro de Covilhao, an agent of the Portugese king, discovered the Malabar coast of India as a spice center. This opened the area to traders. Peppercorns were so valuable that they were used as legal tender in exchange for everything from gold coins to slave girls. Jews were among the early spice merchants of India, having lived in Malabar since arriving with King Solomon's merchant fleet in 963 B.C.C.

6 fairly thick, small steaks	3/4 teaspoon instant beef
1-1/2 teaspoons salt	broth powder
3 tablespoons crushed peppercorns	1/2 cup hot water
1-1/2 tablespoons oil	1 teaspoon prepared mustard
1 tablespoon flour	1 teaspoon Worcestershire Sauce
1 tablespoon margarine	1/4 cup brandy

Salt the steaks and press each side on the crushed peppercorns. In a small pan, melt the margarine. Add the flour and mix to a smooth paste. Cook for 2 or 3 minutes, stirring. Add the powdered beef broth to the hot water to dissolve. Add all at once to the flour mixture. Beat vigorously with a wire whisk until smooth. Add Worcestershire Sauce and mustard. Keep warm. Put brandy in a small pan to warm.

In a large skillet, heat the oil and saute the steaks for two or three minutes on each side. Transfer to a warm platter and place in the oven at the lowest setting.

Pour the flour mixture into the skillet and mix to incorporate the pan juices. Stir and bring quickly to a boil. Turn down immediately and simmer for 1 minute. Light the warmed brandy and add. Stir and pour over the steaks.   Serves 6.

Hamim

Many years ago, in the mountains of Morocco, some tribes were discovered which called themselves by such names as Ait Isaac and Ait Meriem. They were a primitive, untutored people practicing a unique kind of Judaism. They said that they were descended from Berbers but converted to Judaism during the reign of the Queen of Sheba. They made a dish similar to this which they, also, called *hamim*.

The d'fina:
2 lbs. of fat beef
1 lb. calf's foot
1/2 lb. dried lima beans
1/2 lb. dried chick peas
3 large onions, chopped
oil
3 cloves garlic, minced
8 eggs in their shells
1 teaspoon hot pepper sauce
salt and pepper

The kouclas:
1 cup breadcrumbs
2 tablespoons flour
1/4 cup parsley, finely chopped
3/4 teaspoon allspice
salt and pepper
3 eggs
1 large onion, finely chopped

The d'fina: Soak the lima beans and chick peas overnight, drain. Blanch the calf's foot in boiling water. Saute the garlic and onions in a little oil, until golden. Scrub the eggs. Put a layer of chick peas and lima beans in the bottom of an earthenware pot or Dutch oven which has a tight cover. Add the meat, onions, garlic, and calf's foot. Place the eggs in carefully and cover with the remaining chick peas and lima beans. To 2 cups of water add the hot pepper sauce, salt and pepper. Pour over casserole contents. Add more water, if necessary, to cover.

The kouclas: Combine the breadcrumbs, flour, salt, pepper, allspice, and parsley. Add the eggs and mix thoroughly. Add the chopped onion. Mix again and shape into a ball. Place this in the casserole. Cover and place in a 250-degree oven overnight, or simmer over very low heat for several hours, or until meat is very tender.

Instead of the kouclas, rice can be used. Cook 1-1/2 cups of rice until about half done. Tie it up in a new handkerchief or clean piece of muslin and lower it into the d'fina.

The hamim is usually served in separate courses. If more liquid is used, the first course is a soup, following are the eggs, the meat and the beans, chick peas, and kouclas.

Serves 10.

Matambre
(Stuffed Flank Steak)

The word matambre is derived from two Spanish words, *matar* to kills, and *hambre,* hunger. Thus, the name of this South American dish is "to kill hunger." This is a kosher version of the original.

3 pounds flank steak, pounded
  very thin

Marinade:
1 onion, chopped
2 cloves garlic, crushed
1/2 cup chopped parsley
1 bay leaf
1/2 teaspoon thyme
1/2 teaspoon rosemary
4 peppercorns
1 cup dry red wine
1/4 cup salad oil

Stuffing:
3 or 4 slices white bread
1/4 cup chopped celery leaves
3/4 cup cooked, chopped spinach
4 scallions, chopped
1 egg
1/4 lb. salami, ground or finely chopped
4 hard-boiled eggs, coarsely
  chopped
1-1/2 cups hot water
2 teaspoons powdered beef broth
1/2 teaspoons powdered beef broth
1/2 teaspoon hot pepper sauce
flour
oil

Combine all the marinade ingredients in a flat glass or enamel container. Pound the steak into a rectangular shape and place in the marinade for three or four hours, turning from time to time.

Soak the bread in water, squeeze out and tear into bits into a bowl. Add the spinach, celery leaves, scallions, salami, and raw egg. Mix well. Remove the steak from the marinade and spread it with the stuffing to within 1 inch of the edges. Spread the chopped hardboiled eggs over the top. Carefully, but firmly, roll up the steak, jelly-roll fashion. Secure with toothpicks or skewers so that the stuffing will not come out. Dust with flour and brown on all sides in a little oil. Place seam side down in a Dutch oven or skillet with a tight cover. Dissolve the powdered beef broth in the hot water. Add the hot pepper sauce and pour over. Add the strained marinade. Cover and cook over moderate heat about 2 hours, or until tender. This may be served sliced, hot or cold.   Serves 10 to 12.

Italian Deviled Roast

A variation of this recipe was found in an Italian cookbook of the eighteenth century. However, it is unlikely that many Jews in Italy at that time were faring well enough to dine so sumptuously. Jews were confined to ghettoes except during the daytime.

Although the importation of books in Hebrew was prohibited, Jews smuggled them in. Despite the hardships, serious efforts were made to keep Jewish learning alive and some scholars were produced, among them the famous Rabbi Leon of Modena.

5 lb. beef roast	1-1/2 teaspoons dry mustard
1-3/4 cups dark brown sugar	1 tablespoon catsup
2 tablespoons lemon juice	1/2 teaspoon salt
1/2 cup orange juice	1/2 cup dry red wine
1/2 teaspoon ginger	

Combine the sugar, juices, ginger, mustard, catsup and salt. Rub all over the raw meat, leaving a generous layer on top. Place in a shallow pan and add 1 cup of water. Place in a preheated 425-degree oven. After 30 minutes reduce heat to 350 degrees and roast for about 1-1/2 hours or until tender. Add 1/2 cup of dry red wine and baste frequently for 30 additional minutes.   Serves 8 to 10.

Polish Beef Tongue in Wine

Jews were inhabitants of Poland from the twelfth century. Some date their presence from the ninth century. In the thirteenth century, they were in charge of the Polish mint and designed the coins of the realm, many of which bore Biblical inscriptions. However, beginning with the fifteenth century, Polish persecution of Jews began and continued until the Nazi occupation in 1939. Needless to say, the Nazis destroyed the Warsaw ghetto and all of its occupants, and continued the mass exterminations at Auschwitz and Treblinka. The Polish Jewish population of three and a half million is no more. Despite the continuous harassment, centers of Jewish learning had produced great scholars whose influence on Jewish culture is still manifest.

Polish style cooking also persists, having come to this country with the Jewish immigrants of the late nineteenth and early twentieth centuries.

A large, smoked beef tongue	1 bay leaf
1/4 cup oil	4 tomatoes, peeled and chopped
3 large, chopped onions	1/2 lb. parsnips, sliced
2 tablespoons chopped parsley	1/2 lb. carrots, sliced
2 tablespoons celery leaves,	salt and pepper
chopped	1-1/2 cups dry red wine

In a large pot place the tongue and enough water to cover. Cover and boil gently for about an hour. Change the water and repeat the process. Remove the tongue from the water and remove and discard the skin. Place in a casserole which has a tightly fitted lid.

Saute the onions in the oil and add all the other ingredients, except the wine. Stir for one minute and add to the casserole. Pour the wine over. Cover and bake in a preheated 350-degree oven for an hour or until the tongue is very tender. Remove tongue from casserole and keep warm. Pour the contents of the casserole into a blender. Blend until it makes a smooth gravy. Reheat, if necessary. Slice tongue and pour gravy over.   Serves 6.

Israeli Meat Balls

A variation of this recipe was used when beef was not easily available in Israel, and other ingredients were used to extend it. However, the combination of fruit, nuts and meat proved so popular that now, even when there is no necessity for extending the beef, the meatballs are enjoyed.

1-1/2 lbs. lean beef, ground
1 tablespoon oil
2 cloves garlic, minced
1/2 cup finely chopped onion
4 cups apples, peeled and
    cut into 1/2 inch dice
1 egg
1/2 teaspoon allspice
1/2 teaspoon cinnamon
1 teaspoon salt
1 slice rye bread
1 cup pecans, chopped
1/2 cup water (approximately)

cornstarch
oil

Tehina Sauce:
1 cup pecans
1 clove garlic
1/4 cup water
1/4 teaspoon salt
2 tablespoons lemon juice
4 tablespoons parsley, chopped
1 (11 oz.) can tehina sauce
8 oz. medium noodles, cooked

In the oil, saute the onion and garlic. Add the apples and stir just until crispness diminishes. Do not overcook.

In a large bowl combine meat, egg, allspice, cinnamon, salt, soaked and crumbled rye bread, pecans, and water. Beat the mixture with a large spoon until light and spongy. Form into balls 1—1-1/2 inches in diameter. Roll in the cornstarch. Fry in oil in a large skillet, browning on all sides.

Make the sauce by putting into a saucepan the tehina, water, lemon juice, and salt. Place over low heat. In the blender put the nuts and garlic. Blend until nuts are chopped rather than ground. Add to the tehina mixture. Simmer for 15 minutes.

Serve the meat balls on the noodles, pouring the sauce over.   Serves 8.

Beef and Noodles

It is popularly believed that Marco Polo brought noodles from China to Italy from which place it spread to other parts of Europe. But records which predate Marco Polo's voyage indicate that a dough product called *sevika* (thread) was used in Arab countries and one called *rishta* (thread) was popular in Persia. Logically, the Italian word should have been *filo* (thread). Instead it was named spaghetti, or little string. Regardless of the origin, spread it did. What Jewish mother fails to use chicken noodle soup as a reward, caress, a celebration, or the most effective panacea for mortal ills?

2 lbs. lean beef, ground	6 tablespoons flour
3 tablespoons oil	1/2 teaspoon salt
3 onions, chopped	2 teaspoons powdered beef
1 clove garlic, crushed	broth
1/2 cup celery leaves,	2 cups hot water
chopped fine	3/4 cup non-dairy coffee
1 teaspoon dried oregano	lightener
1/2 teaspoon dried marjoram	1/2 cup white wine
1/2 lb. sliced mushrooms	8 oz. medium noodles, cooked
1/3 cup margarine	

In a skillet, saute the onions and garlic. Add the celery leaves, oregano, marjoram, and mushrooms. Stir for 2 minutes. Add the meat to the skillet and brown, stirring until no pink is visible. Add the salt and pepper. Mix to blend.

In a greased casserole, layer the cooked noodles and the meat mixture.

In a saucepan melt the margarine. Add the flour and salt and stir until golden. Add, all at once, the hot water in which the powdered beef broth has been dissolved. Stir with a wire whisk until smooth. Add the coffee lightener and wine. Cook, stirring continuously until the mixture is smooth and thickened and comes to a boil. Pour over and around the sides of the noodle-meat mixture. Bake in a preheated 375-degree oven about 40 minutes or until golden and bubbly.   Serves 8 to 10.

Picadhino
(South American Stew)

This Portugese dish was brought to Brazil by Jews fleeing the Inquisition of the Iberian Peninsula in the sixteenth century. Local products were introduced to the original recipe but the name, meaning stew or hash, was unchanged.

2 lbs. ground beef	salt and pepper
1/4 cup oil	1 teaspoon oregano
3 onions, coarsely chopped	2 tablespoons flour
2 cloves garlic, chopped	2-1/2 cups beef broth
4 large tomatoes, peeled,	2 cups rice
seeded, chopped	5 hard-boiled eggs
2 green peppers, seeded and	2 cups pimento-stuffed olives
cut into small pieces	

Lightly saute the onion and garlic in the oil. Add the green pepper, Add the meat and stir until no pink is visible. Add the tomatoes, salt, pepper, oregano. Sprinkle with the flour and stir for 2 minutes. Add the broth. Stir and cover tightly. Cook about 25 minutes over low heat.

Add rice to about 4-1/2 cups of salted, boiling water. Stir, cover, and cook over low heat until tender.

Serve the meat mixture over the rice. Garnish with chopped eggs and olives.   Serves 10.

Beef T'iao-Chin

The people of the Chinese Jewish community of K'aifeng-fu called themselves T'iao-chin Chiao (The Plucked-Sinew People) because, in strict adherence to the religious requirement, they removed the thigh sinew from all meat. The law originates with the story of Jacob wrestling with the angel. When the angel touched Jacob's thigh, the sinew shriveled and left him lame.

It is interesting to note the names of some of the people of that Chinese community as recorded on a synagogue stone dated 1489. Some of them were: A-tan (Adam), A-wu-lo-han (Abraham), Ai-tzu-la (Ezra), Lieh Wei (Levi), Miesh-she (Moses or Moshe), Yi-tz'u-lo-yeh (Israel), Yush-shu-wo (Joshua), Nu-wo (Noah).

Pearl Buck's novel, *Peony,* is a fictionalized account of this community.

2 lbs. lean beef, very
   thinly sliced
	2 green peppers, cut into
	   3/4 inch squares

1/4 cup oil	1 cup bean sprouts
2 onions, thinly sliced	1 cup bamboo shoots, sliced
2 slices fresh ginger root or 1/2 teaspoon ground ginger	1 cup water chestnuts, sliced
salt	2 cups beef bouillon
1 lb. snow peas	1/4 cup cornstarch
4 stalks celery, cut in diagonal slices	2 tablespoons soy sauce
	1/2 cup chicken bouillon
	1/2 cup sherry

In a *wok* or skillet heat the oil and add the meat and onions, stirring until they are lightly browned. Add the ginger, salt, snow peas, celery, green peppers, bean sprouts, bamboo shoots, and water chestnuts. Stir over high heat until everything is coated with oil, about 2 minutes. Add the beef bouillon and cover tightly. Cook over moderate heat for 10-15 minutes. The vegetables should be crispy tender. Do not overcook.

In a saucepan combine the cornstarch, soy sauce, chicken bouillon, and wine. Stir to dissolve cornstarch and cook over moderate heat until clear and thickened. Add to the meat mixture and stir over low heat for five minutes. Serve over rice or Chinese noodles.   Serves 6 to 8.

Lamb

Lamb

Mishmishiya
(Lamb Stewed with Apricots)

Mishmish is the Arabic word for apricot. Most Eastern people cook various dishes which combine meat and fruit. Also, in Central and Eastern Europe, a cholent was made as a regular Sabbath dish which consisted of beef, vegetables, prunes, or apricots.

An account of foods cultivated in China during the first century lists twelve varieties of apricots.

3 lbs. lean lamb, cut into cubes	3/4 teaspoon cinnamon
2 onions, chopped	1/8 teaspoon pepper
1/2 teaspoon salt	1 lb. dried apricots
oil	1/3 cup ground almonds
1 tablespoon flour	1/2 teaspoon saffron
1 teaspoon ground coriander	1 tablespoon sugar
1/2 teaspoon ground ginger	2 teaspoons rose water

Soak apricots in water to cover overnight. Saute the onion in the oil. Add the meat and stir to brown on all sides. Sprinkle with flour, coriander, ginger, cinnamon, pepper, and salt. Stir. Add enough boiling water just to cover. Cover the pot and simmer.

Put almonds into a blender and whir for 2 seconds on high speed to grind the nuts. Add to the meat. Remove apricots from the water. Put half of them into the blender and whir at low speed for 2 or 3 seconds. Cut the remaining half coarsely. Add to the meat. Reserve the water in which the apricots soaked.

Place pot cover over 3/4 of the pot and simmer mixture until meat is almost finished. Add sugar. Add some of the apricot water if more liquid is necessary. Cook until meat is very tender. Add rose water. Stir. Serve over rice.   Serves 8.

Lamb With Kumquats

Lamb with fruit is often served on Rosh Hashanah (New Year). It recalls the substitution of the ram for Isaac as a sacrifice. Meat from the head of a lamb is also served in some Eastern countries to "help us to be the head, and not the tail."

12 preserved kumquats	oil
3/4 cup of kumquat liquid	2 cloves garlic, minced
1/4 cup orange liqueur	1 teaspoon rosemary
3-1/2 lbs. shoulder of lamb,	1 teaspoon thyme
cut into large cubes	1 tablespoon tomato paste
flour	2 cups beef broth
salt and pepper	salt

Combine the kumquats, liquid, and orange liqueur. Set aside for an hour.

In a bag containing seasoned flour, shake a few pieces of lamb at a time. Brown on all sides in the oil. Remove from the oil and keep warm. In the remaining oil stir the garlic, rosemary, and thyme for 1 minute. Dissolve the tomato paste in the beef broth and add to the pan. Bring to a simmer. Return the meat to the pan. Cover and cook over low heat for about 1-1/2 hours, or until meat is tender. Remove meat to a serving platter and keep warm. To the pan juices add the combined kumquat liquid and liqueur, reserving the fruit. Heat but do not boil. Pour over the meat. Garnish with the kumquats.　　　　　　　　　　Serves 8 to 10.

Layered Kibbeh

"Thus shall they prepare the lamb, and the meal offering, and the oil. . .". (Ezekiel 46:15)

Kibbeh:	*Filling:*
1-1/2 lbs. ground lamb	2 onions, finely chopped
1 large onion, finely grated	1/4 cup oil
2 cups fine burghul	1 lb. ground lamb
(cracked wheat)	1 egg plus 2 tablespoons water
salt and pepper	1/2 teaspoon thyme
2 tablespoons ice water	1 teaspoon cinnamon
	salt and pepper
	1/2 cup pine nuts
	6 tablespoons margarine

Kibbeh: Combine the onion and the lamb and knead until smooth. Put the burghul into a sieve and rinse with cold water. Immediately squeeze out the moisture and add, with salt and pepper, to the meat mixture. Knead firmly to form a very smooth, moist paste, adding the ice water.

Filling: In the oil, saute the onion. Add the meat and stir until no pink is visible. Cool. Beat the egg with the water and combine with the meat mixture, blending very well. Add cinnamon, thyme, salt, and pepper. Mix.

Grease a shallow baking dish. Press and smooth half of the kibbeh in the bottom. Spread the filling over the kibbeh and sprinkle with pine nuts. Cover with the remaining kibbeh. Smooth the top.

Score into diamond shapes, cutting about halfway through. Drizzle melted margarine over the top. Bake in a preheated 400-degree oven for about 30 minutes, until top is brown and crisp.

This can be served hot or cold. Cut into smaller pieces, it can be used for hors d'oeuvres.   Serves 8.

Beer-Sheba Lamb Chops

"And Abraham set seven ewe lambs of the flock by themselves. And Abimelech said unto Abraham: 'What mean these seven ewe lambs which thou hast set by themselves?' And he said; 'Verily, these seven ewe lambs shalt thou take of my hand, that it may be a witness unto me, that I have digged this well.' Wherefore that place was called Beer-Sheba, the well of the seven (lambs)."

In Hebrew the words beer and sheva (or sheba) mean well and seven. Until very recently a large gathering of desert people held a sheep and camel market at Beer-Sheba each Thursday.

8 thick shoulder lamb chops	1/2 teaspoon cayenne
1/2 cup lemon juice	2 teaspoons dried mint leaves
1/2 cup dry wine	salt and pepper
1/4 cup oil	1 teaspoon cornstarch
1 teaspoon powdered ginger	1 teaspoon brown sugar

Combine the lemon juice, wine, oil, ginger, cayenne, mint leaves, salt, and pepper in a shallow pan large enough to hold all the chops in a single layer. Add the chops. Turn at least twice in a 2-hour period. Remove the chops, reserving the marinade. Brush the chops lightly with a little oil and broil, being careful not to overcook. Dissolve the cornstarch and sugar in the strained marinade. Heat in a saucepan, stirring until clear and slightly thickened. Pour over the chops.   Serves 8.

Curried Lamb Shanks

Moses, feeding the flocks of Jethro, went in search of a little lamb which had strayed from the flock. He found it drinking from a brook. *"Had I known that thou wast thirsty I would have taken thee in my arms and carried thee thither"*, said Moses upon finding the lamb. Then *"the bush burned with fire, and the bush was not consumed"* and *"out of the midst of the bush a Heavenly voice resounded, 'As thou livest, thou art fit to shepherd Israel.'"* (Exodus 3:1)

6 lamb shanks, cut into serving pieces	2 teaspoons turmeric
flour	1/2 teaspoon pepper
1/2 cup oil	1/4 teaspoon cayenne
1 large onion, chopped	2 teaspoons salt
2-1/2 tablespoons ground coriander	3 cloves garlic, minced
1-1/2 teaspoons cumin seed	4 cups boiling water
2 teaspoons ground ginger	1 cup non-dairy coffee lightener
2 teaspoons ground cardamom seed	juice of 1/2 lemon

Dredge shanks in flour and brown in the oil in a large skillet. Remove from the oil and set aside but keep warm. In the oil saute the onion until golden. Add all the spices and the garlic. Stir over low heat for 1 minute. Return the shanks to the skillet, turning the pieces to coat with the spice mixture. Pour the boiling water over. Cover and cook over moderate heat for an hour, or until meat is tender. Before serving, remove the shanks from the pan, add the coffee lightener and lemon juice. Stir over low heat. Pour over the shanks.   Serves 6.

Oriental Coxcombs

About three thousand years ago the Chinese held spring festivals in which they roasted lamb with garlic and herbs. They offered it as a symbolic sacrifice to their gods.

Filling:	1/4 cup flour
2 lbs. lean, ground lamb	1/2 cup chopped green olives
1 onion, chopped	1/2 cup walnuts, chopped
1/4 cup oil	1/2 cup raisins
1 teaspoon dried mint leaves	
2 teaspoons ground coriander	*Pastry:*
1/2 teaspoon ground ginger	3 cups sifted flour
1/4 teaspoon cinnamon	1-1/2 teaspoons salt
1 clove garlic, minced	1 cup shortening
salt and pepper	1/2 cup water (scant)

Filling: Saute the onion in the oil until soft and transparent. Add the mint, coriander, ginger, cinnamon, garlic, salt, and pepper. Stir for 2 minutes. Add the lamb and stir until no pink is visible. Sprinkle with flour and continue stirring. Add the olives, nuts and raisins. Stir. Remove from heat.

Pastry: Cut the shortening into the flour until it has the consistency of coarse sand. Add the water and toss to form a sticky dough. Handle lightly to form a ball which "cleans" the sides of the bowl. Roll out between pieces of wax paper to a very thin sheet. Cut circles about 5 inches in diameter. Place a rounded tablespoon of filling in a stripe down the middle of each circle, keeping well away from the edges. Moisten the rims of the circles and bring them together at the top of the filling. Pinch them into coxcombs. Bake on an ungreased baking sheet in a preheated 400-degree oven for about 15 minutes or until golden.   Serves 8 to 10.

Stuffed Shoulder of Lamb

According to Jaime Vicens Vives, a Spanish economic historian who advanced some revisionist theories, one of the most important motivations for the Spaniards pushing the Moors out of Spain was the need to regain the *mesta* (the central plain), so that it would be available to their flocks of sheep for grazing. The wool trade helped to make Castile a maritime power, according to Vives, and contributed to the birth of the textile industry. Despite this economic promise, the luxury loving monarchy had economic needs greater than its resources. Jews, some of whom were money lenders to whom nobles and churchmen were in debt, soon incurred the hatred of the debtors who incited the common people against the conservative and industrious Jewish residents. This economically-based antagonism and the desire to achieve a homogeneous Catholic State contributed, ultimately, to the Expulsion of 1492.

A (5 to 6 lb.) boned,
   shoulder of lamb
salt and pepper
2 cloves garlic, crushed
1 teaspoon grated lemon rind
2 teaspoons oil

Stuffing:
1/4 lb. liverwurst
2 tablespoons non-dairy coffee
  lightener
2 tablespoons oil
1/2 lb. mushrooms, chopped

4 shallots, finely chopped
1/2 large onion, chopped
1-1/4 cups breadcrumbs
1 teaspoon dried marjoram
1/2 teaspoon dried chervil
1 tablespoon chopped parsley
1 egg, beaten
1 cup beef broth
1 cup white wine
2 carrots, thinly sliced
1/2 onion

Rub the inner surface of the lamb with a mixture of the salt, pepper, garlic, oil, and lemon rind.

Stuffing: Mix the liverwurst and coffee lightener to a smooth paste. Spread over the inner surface.

Saute in the oil the mushrooms, shallots, and onion. Add to the bread-crumbs the marjoram, chervil, and parsley. Add the beaten egg and mushroom mixture and blend well. Spread over the liverwurst mixture. Roll the meat and tie firmly. Melt the margarine in a skillet and brown the meat on all sides, adding the 1/2 onion, to saute. Add the beef broth and carrots. Cover and put into a preheated 375-degree oven for 1 hour. Pour in the cup of wine and continue cooking, uncovered, for another 30 to 40 minutes, or until done. Slice and spoon gravy over.   Serves 8 to 10.

Ethiopian Lamb Shanks

The Black Jews, or Falashas, claim descent from King Menelik I, the son of King Solomon and the Queen of Sheba. Menelik is credited with bringing the Ark of the Covenant to Ethiopia. A legend has it that a Falasha queen, Gudit (Judith), once reigned over all of Ethiopia.

1 cup double-strength coffee	1/2 teaspoon dry mustard
1 cup dry red wine	1 teaspoon rosemary
1/2 cup oil	2 teaspoons grated orange rind
3 onions, diced	6 lamb shanks
2 cloves garlic, crushed	3 tablespoons oil
1/2 teaspoon ground ginger	

In a saucepan combine all the ingredients except the last two—the lamb shanks and 3 tablespoons of oil. Simmer for 5 minutes. Cool. Pour the marinade into a shallow pan large enough to hold the shanks in one layer. Add the shanks, and marinate for 12 hours, turning several times. Remove the shanks from the marinade and pat dry with paper towels. Brown in oil. Add the strained marinade and cook over moderate heat for about 1-1/2 hours or until tender.   Serves 6.

Moussaka

The fat-tailed sheep of the Middle East were valued for the amount and quality of the fat contained in the huge tails. The tails sometimes constituted as much as ten percent of the total body weight. Cookbooks of the ancient world of the Middle East refer repeatedly to *alya,* the fat rendered from the tail of this breed of sheep.

3 lbs. eggplant	1/2 cup dry red wine
olive oil	
2 tablespoons margarine	*Bechamel Sauce:*
2 lbs. ground, lean lamb	2 tablespoons margarine
3 tomatoes, peeled and chopped	2 tablespoons flour
1/2 onion, finely chopped	3 cups non-dairy coffee
1/4 cup flour	lightener
2 tablespoons chopped parsley	salt and pepper
1/4 teaspoon allspice	pinch of nutmeg
1/4 teaspoon cinnamon	3 eggs, beaten

Slice the eggplants (peeled or unpeeled) about 1/2 inch thick. Salt and set to drain in a colander for 30 to 45 minutes. Rinse in cold water and pat dry. Fry lightly in the oil until browned. Remove from the pan and keep warm.

In another pan, saute the meat in the margarine. Add the onion and tomato. Sprinkle with the flour and stir until no pink is visible in the meat. Add the wine, parsley, allspice, cinnamon. Cover and cook over low heat for about 15 minutes, stirring from time to time. If excess liquid accumulates increase the heat and cook uncovered, stirring constantly, for 5 minutes.

Make the bechamel sauce by melting the margarine in a saucepan, adding the flour, and stirring for 2 minutes. Add the coffee lightener and stir briskly with a wire whisk until smooth and thickened. Add 3 tablespoons of the sauce to the meat mixture. In a greased, rectangular baking dish layer the eggplant slices with the meat mixture, beginning and ending with eggplant. Add 3 well-beaten eggs to the hot bechamel sauce, blending well. Spoon this over the casserole and bake in a preheated 375-degree oven for about 45 minutes, or until golden.   Serves 8 to 10.

Moroccan Couscous

Eliezer Ben Yedhuda arrived in Palestine in 1881. Becoming aware of the need for a vernacular through which the Jews of Eastern European and those of Sephardic origins could communicate, he began efforts to make Hebrew the common tongue. There were great difficulties. Hebrew, for centuries, had been the "sacred" language, used only for prayer and some literary purposes. The needs of everyday life included the use of a modern vocabulary. Eliezer set about studying the original word roots and from them coined new words to broaden the language. For some time he was ridiculed for thinking that Jews would abandon their use of Yiddish or Ladino or Arabic and use the difficult, newly-revived ancient tongue. But Israel today is, in part, a tribute to his diligence and scholarship. Since 1948 Jews from a variety of areas, speaking many different languages, have been able to unite in a common effort through communication in Hebrew. Otherwise, the experience at the Tower of Babel might have been duplicated.

Ben Yehuda devoted himself to the concept of the Jewish homeland. He also enjoyed certain aspects of Middle East culture and cuisine. Among his favorite dishes were pilaf and couscous, of which he wrote.

1-1/2 lbs. stewing beef, cut into pieces	2 turnips, quartered
1-1/2 lbs. stewing lamb, cut into pieces	salt and pepper
	1/2 teaspoon saffron
1 chicken, cut into serving pieces	1/2 teaspoon ground ginger
flour	3/4 cup raisins
salt and pepper	4 zucchinis, thickly sliced
oil	3 tomatoes, peeled and chopped
3 onions, chopped	1/4 cup chopped parsley
1/2 cup chick peas, soaked overnight	2 tablespoons paprika
1/2 cup dried lima beans, soaked overnight	1 (10 oz.) package frozen string beans
4 carrots, thickly sliced	2 teaspoons hot pepper sauce
	2 cups couscous

Dredge lamb, beef and chicken in seasoned flour. Brown in the oil. Place, with oil, in a large saucepan. Add boiling water to cover. Add the onions, chick peas, lima beans, carrots, turnips, salt and pepper, saffron, and ginger. Bring to a boil, reduce heat and simmer for about an hour, or until meat is tender. Add the tomatoes, raisins, zucchini, parsley, paprika, and string beans. Cover and simmer until done.

Bring four cups of salted water to a boil. Add the couscous and cook until all the water has been absorbed. Add 3 tablespoons oil or margarine. Stir and cover. Let steam for 10 minutes.

Remove 2 cups of liquid from the stew. Add to it the hot sauce. Reserve. Serve stew over couscous. Pass hot sauce separately.

Serves 10 to 12.

Dolmeh Sit
(Persian Stuffed Apples)

The Rhadanites were an adventurous group of Jewish merchant travelers who owned their own ships and plied the seas from Western Europe to China in the ninth century. Their caravans also traversed deserts and mountains over two continents. In about 765, Charlemagne sent a mission to Baghdad to establish trade with Caliph Harun-al-Rashid. Beset by bandits and storms, only one of the mission survived, a Jew called Isaac. The Rhadanites were instrumental in bringing spices and fruits from distant places. They brought quinces and apples from Persia to the other populated areas.

8 large apples	1/2 cup raisins
1/3 cup yellow split peas	1/2 teaspoon ground coriander
1-1/2 cups water	1/2 teaspoon ginger
2 tablespoons oil	salt and pepper
1 onion, finely minced	2 tablespoons margarine
salt	1/2 cup lime juice
1 lb. ground lamb	1/2 cup water
1/2 cup nuts, chopped	1/3 cup sugar

Cook split peas in the water for 30 minutes or until done. Saute the onion in the oil. Add the meat and salt and stir until no pink is visible. Add the nuts, raisins, coriander, ginger, salt and pepper. Add the split peas. Stir.

Cut a thin slice off the top of the apples. Core and hollow them so that the sides are 1/2 inch thick and the bottom is 1 inch thick. Fill the apples with the meat mixture. Place in a shallow baking pan. Bake in a preheated 350-degree oven until about half done. In a saucepan, combine the margarine, lime juice, water, and sugar. Boil for about 1 minute. Baste the apples generously with this mixture. When apples are tender but still firm, remove from oven and serve with the sauce.

Serves 6 to 8.

Kadin Budu
(Turkish Ladies' Thighs)

The name of this dish was inspired by the pantaloon-clad Turkish women.

2 lbs. ground, lean lamb	1 tablespoon finely-chopped
1/2 cup parboiled rice	dill
4 eggs	3/4 teaspoon allspice
3 slices bread	salt and pepper
2 teaspoons oil	1 egg
1 onion, finely grated	matzo meal
1 tablespoon finely-chopped	salt
parsley	1/4 cup margarine

In a bowl, knead the lamb until smooth. Soak the bread in water and squeeze dry. Crumble into the meat. Add the rice and 4 eggs, oil, onion, parsley, dill, allspice, salt, and pepper. Knead to a smooth paste with hands rinsed in cold water. Mold into fat cigar shapes about three inches long. Arrange in a skillet with water about 1/2 inch deep. Cover and keep to a gentle simmer for about 20 minutes or until the meat is cooked. Drain and cool.

Beat the remaining egg. Dip the meat logs in the egg and roll in the salted matzo meal. Fry in the hot margarine. Remove when crisp and golden on all sides. This can be served plain or with tomato sauce.

Serves 8.

Lamb Roast With Grapes

Many Jews owned vineyards and olive groves in Rome in 1556 when Pope Paul IV issued his infamous bull, *Cum nimus absurdum,* which resulted in the Jews of the Papal State having to wear the yellow badge identifying them as Jews and being forced to live within the ghetto walls. Owners of groves, vineyards, homes, and businesses were forced to sell all of their belongings at token prices. The most prosperous and honored families were poverty-stricken virtually overnight. Some fled to other Italian states more friendly to the Jews, and began to build a new life.

A 4 lb. shoulder of lamb	2 tablespoons brown sugar
3 cloves garlic, minced	2 tablespoons tomato paste
2 teaspoons salt	1 cup dry red wine
1/4 teaspoon pepper	2 cups seedless grapes
1 teaspoon dry mustard	

Make a paste of the garlic, salt, pepper, mustard, sugar, and tomato paste. Rub it all over the meat. Put the meat in a shallow roasting pan and pour water in it to a depth of about an inch. Add a little water during the cooking to maintain that depth. Place in a preheated 350-degree oven for 2 to 3 hours or until tender. Skim the fat off the gravy. Put the gravy in a saucepan with the wine. Bring to a boil and remove from heat immediately. Add the grapes. Keep covered and warm. Pass separately with slices of the roast.   Serves 8 to 10.

Dali Mashi
(Stuffed Breast of Lamb)

Lamb is customarily identified with Pesach (Passover) because it is commanded (Exodus 12:3) that each family, unless it be too small, shall roast and eat a lamb. None of it could be used the next day. The blood was to be smeared on the two side posts and on the lintel so that the Angel of Death would pass over those houses, recognizing them as Jewish homes.

It is interesting that in Latin American, during the time of the functioning of the Inquisition, the Church issued Edicts of Faith, describing religious customs of Jews in order that the Christian population might thereby recognize those secretly practicing Judaism and report them to the Inquisition. Since most families could not possibly eat a whole sheep, they gave the unused portion to Christian neighbors. When so many families did this on the same night, the reason must have been obvious. Yet, there is not one known case in which Christian neighbors reported this to the Inquisition authorities.

2 whole breasts of lamb	1-1/2 cups rice
oil	1/2 pound ground beef
salt and pepper	3 cups boiling water
1 lb. orange marmalade	3 tablespoons finely-chopped
1/4 cup white creme de menthe	parsley
or 1 teaspoon mint extract	salt and pepper
and 1 teaspoon water	1 tablespoon grated orange rind
	1 cup coarsely chopped walnuts
Stuffing:	2 cups chopped prunes or
3 tablespoons oil	1 cup peeled, diced apples
2 onions, chopped	and 1 cup raisins

Have the butcher cut a pocket in the breasts. Combine the oil, salt, and pepper, and rub over the breasts.

Stuffing: Saute the onions in the oil. Add the rice and stir until the rice is transparent. Add the ground beef and stir until no pink is visible. Pour in the boiling water, add the parsley, salt and pepper. Cover and simmer for about 20 minutes or until the rice is tender. Cool. Add the orange rind, nuts, and prunes. Mix well. Stuff the breasts fairly firmly. Secure the ends with toothpicks or skewers to hold the stuffing. Roast in a preheated 450 degree oven for 20 minutes. Reduce the heat to 350 degrees and cook for 45 to 60 minutes, or until tender and browned. Pour off excess fat. In a saucepan melt the marmalade with the margarine. Add the creme de menthe. Stir. Spread over the tops of the lamb breasts and return to the oven for 5 or 10 minutes to glaze. Watch to prevent burning. Serves 8 to 10.

Giuvesti

During the Middle Ages, the husbanding of sheep took on great importance. Not only were the animals valued as meat but the milk and cheese which were produced in large quantities changed the eating habits over a wide geographical area. The wool and skins supplied clothing materials and without the parchment, which the skins also provided, much of history (recorded on parchment) might have been lost.

This Greek dish derives its name from the large, shallow, round casserole, giuvesti, in which it is traditionally cooked.

2 cloves, garlic, crushed
salt and pepper
2 tablespoons oil
2 tablespoons lemon juice
4 lb. shoulder of lamb
3 tablespoons margarine
1 (8 oz.) can of tomato sauce
1 teaspoon sugar

1 teaspoon dried oregano
1/2 onion, finely grated
3 tablespoons margarine
salt
1 cup tomato juice
2 cups boiling water
16 oz. broad noodles, broken into
     inch-long pieces

Combine garlic, salt, pepper, oil, and lemon juice. Rub over the lamb. Melt 3 tablespoons margarine in a paella pan or other shallow pan. In it put the meat and bake in a preheated 350-degree oven for 2 hours or until tender. In a large saucepan combine the tomato sauce, sugar, oregano, onion, margarine, salt, and tomato juice. Add the boiling water and bring mixture to a boil. Add the noodles. Cook, stirring frequently, for 8 minutes or until the noodles are almost cooked. There should be some liquid remaining. Arrange the noodles around the roast and add the liquid in which they were cooked. Return to the oven for about 40 minutes or until a light crust is formed.   Serves 8 to 10.

Veal

Veal

Bavarian Veal Shoulder

One of the greatest historic ironies exists in Berchtesgaden, Germany. Here Hitler had his luxurious home and established a hotel for his favored cohorts. Now the walls echo to Hebrew chants and prayers. Jewish chaplains serving with the United States Military Forces in Europe use the building for religious retreats, conferences, and services. Kosher meals are now served from the kitchen.

3 lbs. boned shoulder of veal	1 teaspoon salt
3 cloves garlic, minced	3 tablespoons margarine
2 teaspoons rosemary	3 tablespoons oil
1 teaspoon thyme	3/4 cup dry white wine
4 peppercorns, crushed	1/4 cup water

Combine garlic, rosemary, thyme, peppercorns, and salt. Rub into the inside surface of the meat. Roll the meat firmly and tie securely. In a Dutch oven heat the margarine and oil. Brown the meat on all sides, slowly. Cover and cook over medium heat for about 30 minutes. Add the wine and water. Cover and cook for about an hour, or until tender. For the last 30 minutes of cooking, place the lid so that it covers about 3/4 of the pot. There should be just enough liquid to spoon a little over each sliced serving.   Serves 6 to 8.

Veal Roast Barcelona

In a section of Barcelona which was the old Jewish Quarter, there is a main street called Calle de Call or La Call. Translated from Catalan, Call is a synonym for the Hebrew *kahal* or community. There are still evidences of that Jewish community—an old archway which was once part of a synagogue entrance; stones, inscribed in Hebrew, which are parts of buildings; and the tombstone of a martyred rabbi which is part of a house.

Incidentally, just off the Call, in one of the narrow streets, there is a

vegetarian restaurant where Jews who observe the dietary laws may
find full meals which they may eat.

4 lb. boneless veal roast	4 cloves garlic, crushed
2 tablespoons margarine	8 peppercorns, cracked
2 tablespoons olive oil	1/2 cup rum
1 bay leaf	2 cups white wine
1 (3 inch) cinnamon stick	salt and pepper
1 teaspoon marjoram	1 cup raisins
3 whole cloves	sliced oranges

In a Dutch oven brown the meat on all sides in the hot margarine and
olive oil. Add bay leaf, cinnamon, marjoram, cloves, garlic, and peppercorns. Stir and saute in the pan with the meat for 1 minute. Sprinkle
with salt and pepper. Add the rum and wine. Cover and cook at a simmer for 1-1/2 hours. Turn the lid of the pot askew to let some steam escape and cook for an additional 30 minutes or until tender. Add a few tablespoons of boiling water, if necessary. Strain sauce into a saucepan and
add the raisins. Heat to plump the raisins. Slice roast, placing a slice of
orange on each serving. Pour sauce over.   Serves 8 to 10.

Veal in Aspic

When Catherine of Medici came to France as the child bride of Henry
II, she and her entourage were accustomed to the cooking style, ingredients, and delicacies of the rich Florentine court. Her chefs introduced
and created a vogue for such dishes as iced cream, melons, artichokes,
and veal.

Upon the death of Henry, fighting broke out between the Calvinist
Huguenots and the Catholics, shifting attention away from the Jews.
This circumstance, together with the fact that there was an authority
vacuum in the Provence area, caused Jews to drift to the south. There
they established an important clothing industry.

12 thin slices of boneless veal	2 tablespoons lemon juice
1/2 cup oil	2 envelopes unflavored gelatine
2 cloves garlic, crushed	2 hard-boiled eggs
1/4 cup lemon juice	black olives
1/4 cup white wine	pimento strips
1/2 teaspoon prepared mustard	watercress
1/4 teaspoon nutmeg	
1/2 teaspoon sugar	*Dressing:*
salt	2/3 cup mayonnaise
oil	1 (4 oz.) can mushrooms
3-3/4 cups consomme	2 tablespoons chopped parsley
1/4 cup white wine	2 tablespoons white wine

Combine the 1/2 cup oil, garlic, lemon juice, wine, mustard, nutmeg and sugar, in a large flat pan. Put the veal slices in the marinade for an hour, turning twice. With paper towels, pat them dry and sprinkle with salt. Brown the slices in hot oil until lightly browned. Place the slices on paper towels to absorb excess oil.

Sprinkle the gelatine over 1/2 cup cold consomme to soften. Heat remaining consomme and add gelatine mixture. Stir to dissolve. Add the lemon juice and wine. Remove from heat.

In a flat, rectangular pan, pour consomme mixture to a depth of 1/4 inch. Refrigerate. When set to the consistency of unbeaten egg white, arrange slices of hard-boiled egg, slices of black olives, and pimento strips in a pleasing design. Refrigerate. When firm, but still a little sticky, spoon in consomme to an additional depth of 1/4 inch. Refrigerate. When partially set, arrange the veal slices. Refrigerate. When firm, spoon on the remaining gelatine consomme mixture. Refrigerate overnight. Turn out on a platter and garnish with watercress.

For the dressing, combine all the ingredients and whir in a blender for 2 seconds. Thin, if necessary with a teaspoon or two of the liquid from the canned mushrooms. Pass separately.

Vitello Tonnato

The word ghetto derives from its first use in Venice in 1516, when a walled section was designated as a place of required residence for Jews. The place so assigned was, originally, the site of a *gietto,* a foundry, and it was thus identified as a location. The concept was adopted from Spain where *Juderias* began in the twelfth century. Both the repressive idea and the word were given impetus and followed in other places. As business opportunity declined and crowding took place, the "ghettoes" came to imply not only a location but a substandard way of life. However, ghettoes were not necessarily slums and, in various places and times this type of Jewish quarter contained prosperous homes and beautiful public buildings. Always there were schools, synagogues, and other evidences of cultural priorities.

The old ghetto, the walled quarter, of Venice exists today. Those who live in it do so by choice. It surrounds a small picturesque plaza on which five synagogues front. They were built between the beginning of the fifteenth and the end of the sixteenth centuries. They are gems of architecture and ornamentation of their times. Also in the plaza is a well-kept home for the aged. In the same building there is a kosher restaurant.

A 4 lb. rolled veal roast
2 tablespoons olive oil
flour
salt and pepper
2 cloves garlic, crushed
a large carrot, diced
1 large celery stalk, chopped
2 bay leaves
4 sprigs parsley

1 onion studded with cloves
juice of 1 lemon
1 can tuna
1 small can anchovy filets,
  undrained
3 tablespoons capers
1 cup mayonnaise
1 cup white wine
2 cups boiling water

Dust the meat with the seasoned flour. In a Dutch oven, lightly brown the meat on all sides in the oil. Add the garlic, carrot, celery, bay leaves, parsley, and onion. Saute, stirring for a few minutes. Add the boiling water. Cover tightly and simmer for about 2 hours or until the veal is almost done. Add the wine, turn the cover askew and cook until tender. Remove meat and refrigerate. Strain the gravy and reserve.

In a blender puree the anchovies, tuna, and lemon juice. Add to the strained gravy. Add the mayonnaise and capers. Blend well. Refrigerate. When meat is thoroughly chilled, cut it into thin slices. Cover with a thin layer of the sauce. Pass the rest of the sauce separately.

Serves 8 to 10.

Stuffed Breast of Veal

According to the Koran, "Verily, on the favorites of God no fear shall come, nor shall they grieve." Such "favorites of God" were known as *welees.* They were humble in demeanor and poor of dress but were possessed of an extraordinary faith. They were known, as welees, only to each other. The *kutb,* also unrecognized by the world, had superintendence over them. Muslims believe that Elijah was the kutb of his time. They believe that the word Arab is the correct substitute for the word raven in First Kings 17:4,6. *"And I have commanded the ravens to feed thee,"* and *"the ravens brought him bread and flesh in the evening."* There are hermits today who, in parts of the desert, give themselves up to prayer and meditation. Fearing that these hermits may be among the unrecognized welees, their Arab co-religionists bring them bread and meat.

According to the statement of Abbaye in the Talmud, "The world must contain not fewer than thirty six (in Hebrew, *lamed vav*), righteous men who are vouchsafed the sight of the Divine Presence." The Talmud explains that while these are not the only righteous men, they are in a special category since they behold the Divine Presence with unique clarity.

There is a legend which holds that these humble men are not recognized or appreciated but because of their spirituality and virtue the world continues to exist. It is also said that, in times of crisis, they are revealed and bring salvation to the troubled people. They are called the Lamed Vavniks.

1 large breast of veal	salt and pepper
1 small challah or egg bread,	oil
sliced and toasted	garlic powder
1/2 cup oil	paprika
3 large onions, chopped	salt
top third of a bunch of celery,	3 large carrots, sliced
including leaves, chopped	2 onions, sliced
1/2 cup chopped parsley	2 large stalks of celery
1/2 cup chopped fresh dill	1 large sprig of fresh dill
1 (4 oz.) can mushrooms, chopped	4 sprigs parsley
2 eggs, beaten	

Have the butcher bone the breast of veal and cut a pocket in it. Cut away as much fat as possible.

In the 1/2 cup of oil saute the onions until transparent. Add the celery and heat through, stirring. Turn off the heat. Add the dill and parsley and cover the pan.

Soak the bread, a few slices at a time, in water. Squeeze almost dry and crumble into a large bowl. Add the sauteed onion mixture, the drained, chopped mushrooms, salt, and pepper. Mix. Add the beaten eggs and blend well.

Stuff the breast firmly but not too tightly. The stuffing will expand a little. Secure the opening with toothpicks or skewers. Smear a little oil all over the stuffed breast and sprinkle with salt, garlic powder and, generously, with paprika. Place in a shallow baking pan. Add 3 cups of water to the pan along with the sliced carrot, onions, celery, dill and parsley. Cover completely with foil to hold steam in. Place in a preheated 350-degree oven for about 1-1/2 to 2 hours, or until almost done. Remove foil and permit to brown and become very tender. Remove from oven and let rest for 20 minutes before slicing. Put the pan juices and the vegetables into a blender until pureed and smooth. Pour into a saucepan, correct seasoning, heat. Slice the stuffed breast. Pass the gravy separately.

Serves 8 to 10.

Perdices de Capelian
(Balearic Mock Partridges)

As in other parts of Spain, the Jews prospered in the Balearic Islands, especially Palma de Majorca, until they were forced to convert to Catholicism or leave Spanish lands. Many left, but some converted and remained. These people of Majorca were called Chuetas. Some say that the name originates with the word Chuya, one who eats pork, since they were now relieved of the Jewish dietary restrictions. There is an interesting similarity to the appelation "Marrano" (swine), used in other places for those who pretended to convert but who continued to practice Judaism secretly.

The Chuetas attend services in Montezion Church which was the original main synagogue of Palma.

12 very thin slices of veal	oil
12 very thin slices of pickled	1 teaspoon dried rosemary
beef tongue	1 teaspoon dried thyme
12 very thin slices of bologna	1 teaspoon dried basil
2 cups cooked rice	salt and pepper
1 teaspoon grated orange rind	3/4 cup white wine
flour	

Pound the veal slices to 1/8 inch thickness. On each slice place a slice of tongue and a slice of bologna. Over them place a rounded tablespoon of rice to which the grated rind has been added. Roll up, tucking in the ends to make a closed packet. Wind white thread around the rolls to hold securely. Roll in flour to cover. In a large skillet brown the rolls in the oil. Add the rosemary, thyme, basil, salt, pepper, and wine. Cover tightly and cook about 40 minutes. Add a little water if gravy becomes too thick. Remove thread and serve with gravy poured over.   Serves 6 to 8.

Roast Veal With Tehina

Sesame seeds and oil were used as foods in the Middle East from earliest times. Their high value is implied by the fact that in the Arabian Nights tales, when Ali Baba needed a magic formula for opening the robbers' den, he used the words, "Open, sesame!" Since then the expression has come into use to describe a wonderously effective way of achieving a desired result.

Tehina is a sauce made of puree of sesame seeds, chick peas, and spices. It is a staple of the Israeli diet. It is exported from Israel to the United States in small cans.

A 4 lb. veal roast
2 cloves garlic, crushed
1 teaspoon dried basil
salt and pepper
oil
4 large onions, cut into 1/2
  inch thick slices
4 tomatoes, peeled and coarsely
  chopped
1 bay leaf
salt
1 teaspoon hot pepper sauce
2 cups boiling water

4 large carrots, quartered
6 large potatoes, halved
3 small eggplants, quartered
8 small yellow squash,
  cut in half

Sauce:
1 (11 oz.) can tehina
juice of 1/2 lemon
1 clove garlic, minced
1 tablespoon finely-chopped
  fresh dill
1/2 cup water

Combine the garlic, basil, salt, and pepper, and rub all over the meat. In a large Dutch oven, brown the meat in the oil on all sides. Add the onions, tomatoes, bay leaf, and salt. Combine the hot pepper sauce and the boiling water and add to the meat. Place in a preheated 375 degree oven for 1 hour. Baste. Add carrots and potatoes. In 30 minutes add the eggplant and squash and bake about 30 minutes, or until all ingredients are tender. Slice roast and arrange on a platter surrounded by the vegetables.

Combine all the ingredients for the sauce and blend very well. Pass separately with the roast.   Serves 10 to 12.

Danish Veal and Pineapple

Apple was frequently used as a generic term for fruit in the fifteenth century. When Columbus first saw the Indians eating the small forerunner of our now luscious pineapples, the appearance of the fruit reminded him of a pine cone. Thus the fruit was called a pineapple. Its cultivation in Europe was difficult and acceptance was not immediate, but it ranks today as one of the fruit delicacies of the world, and is widely and variously used everywhere.

12 very thin veal slices
flour
1/2 lb. mushrooms, sliced
1/2 teaspoon dried thyme
1/2 teaspoon dried marjoram
2 tablespoons margarine
salt and pepper

1-1/2 cups non-dairy coffee
  lightener
1 tablespoon lemon juice
1 egg yolk, beaten
6 canned pineapple slices, cut
  in half, drained
1/4 cup sherry

Pour the sherry over the well drained pineapple slices. Reserve. Sprinkle the veal lightly with the flour to which has been added the salt and pepper. Brown in the margarine. Remove from pan and keep warm. Add a little more margarine, if necessary, and saute the mushrooms with the thyme and marjoram. Add the coffee lightener. Stir over low heat. Add a little of this mixture to the beaten egg yolk. Stir and return to pan mixture. Stir over low heat to thicken slightly. Correct seasoning.

Arrange veal slices on a platter. Pour gravy over. Place a half of a drained pineapple slice on each piece of veal.   Serves 6 to 8.

Barbecued Veal Ribs

The concept of a barbecue as a social eating occasion seems typical of the American culture. However, roasting meat or fish over an open fire is, obviously, the oldest method of cooking. The origin of the word, barbecue, itself stems from the Spanish word, *barbacoa,* now used as a synonym for the word, barbecue. The literal meaning of the Spanish word is "the wood lattice on which meat is cooked over an open fire." It is interesting to note that prior to the Spanish derivation, the Taino Indians (a now extinct segment of the Caribbean Arawaks), used a similar word for this method of cooking. Shipwrecked sailors or outlaws inhabiting the Caribbean islands, and finally making their way back to civilization, brought both the word and cooking method to more popular use.

A breast of veal	1/2 cup brown sugar
1 cup ketchup	1/4 cup vinegar
1 cup water	2 tablespoons Worchestershire
3 teaspoons salt	Sauce
1/2 teaspoon pepper	2 onions, finely chopped
2 teaspoons dry mustard	2 cloves garlic, finely minced

Have the butcher cut the ribs apart and crack the bones about halfway down. Also remove as much fat as possible. If this separates the meat from the bone too much, they can be tied together with string.

Brown the ribs in a large skillet. Combine all the other ingredients. Arrange the ribs in a large pan, in a single layer. Pour the sauce over them and cover to bake in a preheated 375-degree oven for 45 to 60 minutes. Uncover and bake for about an hour longer, or until very tender. Baste and turn the ribs frequently. Add a little more water, if necessary.

Skim off excess fat or make a day ahead of time and refrigerate. Remove solidified fat before reheating and serving.   Serves 8 to 10.

Veal with Almond Sauce

". . .And behold, the rod of Aaron for the house of Levi was budded, and put forth buds, and bloomed blossoms, and bore ripe almonds."

(Numbers 17:23)

12 very thin slices of veal	1 egg, beaten
1/4 cup oil	flour
juice of 1 lemon	1/2 cup toasted almonds
3 cloves garlic, crushed	1/4 cup sherry
2 tablespoons margarine	1-1/2 cups beef broth
2 tablespoons olive oil	salt and pepper

Place the pounded veal slices in a marinade made of the oil, lemon juice, and garlic. Leave for at least one hour, turning from time to time. Meanwhile, make a sauce by crushing the almonds to a paste in a mortar, with a little of the sherry. Or, whir in a blender, adding the sherry gradually. Gradually add the beef broth. Season with salt and pepper. Reserve.

Pat the veal slices dry with paper towels. Dust with flour. Dip in the beaten egg and again in flour. Heat the combined margarine and oil in a large skillet. Quickly brown the veal over moderately high heat. Pour the almond mixture over the meat. Bring to a boil, lower heat immediately, cover and simmer for 10 to 15 minutes, or until meat is tender. If sauce is too thick add a little beef broth. Correct seasoning. Serves 6 to 8.

Veal Marengo

Marengo was the name of the battle in which Napoleon defeated the Austrians in 1800. After the battle, Napoleon's chef, Dunand, sent some of the men to search the area for food suitable for Napoleon's dinner. They brought back an odd assortment of ingredients, which included chicken, garlic, tomatoes, eggs, and other items. Of all of these the master chef concocted a dish which pleased Napoleon. The dish is now made in several ways. Veal as well as chicken may be used, but the name Marengo remains.

Napoleon's policies toward the Jews of France and Germany were notable. In France he convened a Jewish Court which he called a Sanhedrin, after the high court and legislative body of Jerusalem which functioned prior to the destruction of the Second Temple in the year 70. The French "Sanhedrin's" function was not comparable to the authentic

Sanhedrin but it was the first time since Biblical days that any such
Jewish body was convened. In Germany, Napoleon's policies resulted in
greater emancipation than the Jews there had formerly known. When
surnames were being chosen, some people, in gratitude, selected the name
Schonteil, a German translation of Bonaparte.

3 lbs. boneless veal,
  cut into large cubes
flour
salt and pepper
4 tablespoons oil
2 onions, chopped
2 cloves garlic, crushed
1/2 teaspoon basil
1 (20 oz.) can tomatoes,
  drained and chopped

2 tablespoons tomato paste
1 cup white wine
1/2 cup non-dairy coffee
  lightener
1/2 cup beef broth
1/2 lb. sliced mushrooms
2 tablespoons margarine

Put the flour, salt, and pepper in a paper bag. Shake the veal pieces
in it. Brown them in the oil. Remove and keep warm.

In the same oil saute the onions and garlic. Add the basil, tomatoes,
tomato paste, wine, and broth. Stir and bring to a boil. Lower the heat
immediately and add the meat. Cover and simmer for about an hour or
until the veal is very tender. Saute the mushrooms in a little margarine
and add to the pan. Add the coffee lightener. Heat thoroughly.

Serves 6 to 8.

Poultry

Poultry

Chicken Breasts L'Orange

According to the Talmud, raising poultry in Jerusalem, or by priests anywhere, was forbidden because of the risk of polluting holy objects.

Stuffing:
3/4 cup fresh, white breadcrumbs
1/4 cup raisins
3 tablespoons sherry
6 tablespoons margarine
2 chicken livers, (grilled
  to conform with
  kashrut requirements)
1 small onion, chopped
1/2 cup walnuts, chopped
1/4 cup chopped celery
2 tablespoons chopped parsley
2 tablespoons grated orange rind

Chicken:
8 boned chicken breasts
2 tablespoons flour
1/4 teaspoon salt
1/2 teaspoon garlic powder
2 teaspoons paprika
1/2 teaspoon ground ginger
6 tablespoons margarine
3/4 cup orange juice
2 cups consomme
1/2 teaspoon cinnamon
2 celery stalks
salt and pepper
1-1/4 teaspoons cornstarch
2 tablespoons cold water
1/4 cup raisins
8 orange slices

Stuffing: Soak the raisins in the sherry for an hour. Saute the onions in margarine together with the chicken livers. Chop together finely. Add all the other stuffing ingredients. Mix well.

Fill the chicken breasts with the stuffing. Overlap the edges and fasten with toothpicks. Combine the flour, salt, garlic powder, paprika, and ginger. Roll the chicken breasts in the mixture. Melt the margarine in a large skillet. Brown the breasts on all sides. Add the orange juice, consomme, celery stalks, cinnamon, salt and pepper. Cover and simmer until the chicken is tender, about 30 to 45 minutes. Remove the celery stalks. Dissolve the cornstarch in the water. Add to the skillet, stirring. Add the orange slices and raisins. Cook 3 to 5 minutes. Serve the breasts garnished with the orange slices and covered with the sauce.

Serves 8.

Pollo con Keftes de Espinaca
(Chicken with Spinach Patties)

The mixed culture of the Salonika Jews is evidenced by the name of
this dish. All the words are Spanish except the word *keftes,* which is the
Greek word for patties. The origin of these Greek residents was Spain,
prior to 1492. Their language, values, and culinary style are a fascinat-
ing mixture of the two cultures.

A chicken, cut into serving pieces
3 tablespoons oil
1 large onion, chopped
1/2 teaspoon dried tarragon
1/2 lb. mushrooms, sliced
flour
salt and pepper
1/2 cup white wine

2 (10 oz.) packages frozen chopped spinach
1/2 cup chopped celery leaves
1/2 cup saltine cracker crumbs
3 eggs
oil
juice of 1 lemon
1 teaspoon sugar

Saute the onions, mushrooms and tarragon in the oil. Reserve.

Dredge the chicken pieces in the flour to which has been added the
salt and pepper. Brown in oil. Put the browned chicken in a large, flat
casserole. Add the mushroom mixture and the wine. Cover and place in
a preheated 400-degree oven for about an hour, or until tender.

In a large bowl put the very well drained spinach, the celery leaves,
cracker crumbs, and well beaten eggs. Mix to blend thoroughly. Drop by
large spoonfuls into hot oil. Brown lightly on both sides. Place the patties around the chicken in the casserole about 30 minutes before the
chicken is finished; at that point remove the cover from the casserole.
Just before serving, dissolve the sugar in the lemon juice and drizzle
over the chicken and spinach patties.   Serves 4 to 6.

Polish Turkey with Anchovies

Finely chopped or ground seasoned meat used as stuffing is now
known as forcemeat. However, it is more correctly termed farcemeat.
The word farce, originally, meant stuffing.

During the Middle Ages, travelling theatrical companies needed some-
thing to hold the attention of the audience between the acts. They often
put on comic, slapstick performances called farces (the French word
for stuffing), between the acts. Perhaps the corruption of the word resulted from the forcing necessary to stuff such things as sausage cas-
ings.

A young turkey
1 clove garlic, crushed
salt and pepper
1 teaspoon paprika
3 tablespoons margarine
1 onion, chopped
2 slices bread, soaked
1 small can anchovy filets

1 teaspoon grated lemon rind
1 teaspoon chopped dill
1 tablespoon chopped parsley
1 pimento, chopped
salt and pepper
1 lb. ground veal
3 cups water

Make a paste of the garlic, salt, pepper, and paprika. Rub the turkey with it, inside and outside. Soak the bread in water, squeeze almost dry and crumble into a large bowl. Saute the onion in the margarine. Add to the bread. Rinse and chop the anchovies and add. Add the lemon rind, dill, parsley, pimento, salt, and pepper. Add the veal. Mix very well to blend.

Without tearing, loosen the skin over the breast, thighs and legs. Push the stuffing between the skin and flesh. Put any left over stuffing in the cavity. Place the turkey in a roasting pan with 3 cups of water. Cover. Roast in a preheated 375-degree oven. When the bird is half finished, uncover and baste frequently until very tender and brown.

Lisboa Turkey

In Biblical times, fowl was considered food for the aged and feeble. As a "regular" food it was considered inferior to cattle, although those who could afford it consumed more poultry than did the poor. Perhaps that is where the idea originates that chicken and chicken soup are beneficial to the ill and infirm.

A young turkey
2 cloves garlic, crushed
1 teaspoon salt
1/2 teaspoon pepper
1 teaspoon paprika
1/2 teaspoon ginger
1/4 cup oil
1 onion, chopped
12 slices, white bread, toasted

3/4 lb. ground beef
1/4 teaspoon cinnamon
1/8 teaspoon mace
1/8 teaspoon nutmeg
salt and pepper
15 green olives, chopped
2 eggs, beaten
3 cups water

Make a paste of the garlic, salt, pepper, paprika, and ginger. Rub all over the turkey, inside and outside. Saute the onion in the oil. In a large bowl, put the toasted bread which has been soaked in water, squeezed almost dry and crumbled. Add the sauteed onion, the ground beef, cinnamon, mace, nutmeg, salt and pepper, olives, and well beaten eggs. Mix to blend, then beat until light and fluffy. Stuff the gullet and cavity of the turkey, not too firmly. Bake in a preheated 375-degree oven, covered. Remove the cover and baste frequently during the last half of the cooking period.

Chicken Liver Crepes

The mushroom was an important food in the Western Hemisphere in prehistoric times. Along with root vegetables such as the white and sweet potato, it made an important contribution to supporting life. In the nineteenth century, Charles Darwin wrote that the people of Tierra del Fuego, at the southern tip of South America, had a curious dietary predilection for mushrooms. They ate them raw and in great quantities. "With the exception of a few berries, chiefly of the dwarf arbutus, the natives eat no vegetable food beside this fungus," he wrote.

Crepes:
3 eggs
1-1/2 cups chicken broth
2 tablespoons oil
1-1/2 cups flour
1 teaspoon dried thyme
margarine

Filling:
2 lbs. chicken livers, (grilled
  to conform to kashrut
  requirements)
4 tablespoons margarine

1/4 cup finely chopped celery
  leaves
1 teaspoon margarine
1 onion, finely chopped
3/4 lb. mushrooms, sliced
salt and pepper
1 cup chicken broth
3/4 cup sherry
3 teaspoons flour
1/4 cup finely chopped parsley
1-1/2 cup breadcrumbs
1/2 cup margarine, melted

Crepes: Put all the crepe ingredients, except the margarine, into a blender. Whir until the batter is smooth and about the consistency of heavy cream. Heat a little margarine in a 6 inch frying pan. Pour 2 tablespoons (one large kitchen mixing-spoon full) into the pan. Lift it off the heat and very quickly rotate and tilt the pan so that the whole bottom is covered with the batter. Brown very lightly. Turn the crepe and cook on the other side for just a few seconds. Repeat the process until all the batter has been used. Use as little margarine as possible. Stack the crepes as they are made.

Filling: Saute the onion in the margarine. When transparent add the livers, cut into small pieces. Add the celery leaves and marjoram. Add the mushrooms, salt and pepper. Stir over moderate heat until everything is cooked through. Add the sherry and 1/2 cup of the broth. Cover and simmer for 10 minutes. Dissolve the flour in the remaining 1/2 cup of broth and add to the pan. Cook until the gravy is thickened.

Put about two tablespoons of filling down the middle of each crepe. Roll up and place seam side down in a generously greased baking dish. Combine breadcrumbs and margarine. Cover crepes with the breadcrumb-and-margarine mixture. Bake in a preheated 400-degree oven until lightly browned. Garnish with chopped parsley.

Makes 16 crepes.

Balkan Chicken and Rice

In the sixteenth century, Jews in Prague were almost entirely excluded from all trades and, specifically, forbidden to trade in spices, velvet, damask, silk, and ribbons. They were permitted to be butchers but not to belong to the guild. The butchers of the ghetto, however, formed their own guild. Their coat of arms was the lion of Judah, with the inscription *kasher*.

A large chicken, cut into serving pieces	2 tablespoons chopped dill salt and pepper
3 tablespoons margarine	1/2 cup white wine
2 stalks celery, finely chopped	1 cup rice
1 large onion, chopped	2-1/2 cups boiling chicken broth paprika

In a heavy, large skillet saute the onion and celery. Add the chicken pieces and brown lightly. Add the parsley and dill. Add salt and pepper, and wine. Cover tightly and cook until chicken is almost done. Pour the rice around the chicken. Add the boiling broth. Cover and cook over low heat until the rice is tender. Garnish with a light sprinkling of paprika.

Serves 4 to 6.

Cazuela Gaucho
(Argentine Chicken Stew)

A group of Jews left Russia in the late nineteenth century to form an agricultural colony in Argentina prior to Baron de Hirsh's colonization of that territory. Some of them became gauchos and followed a life style which centered around wild horsemanship and living on the pampas, as well as cultivating it. Stews such as this were made over camp fires in a clay pot called a cazuela, from which the dish takes its name.

A 5 to 6 lb. chicken	1/2 lb. green beans, cut
1/2 cup oil	1 lb. pumpkin or Hubbard squash,
1 clove garlic, minced	peeled, seeded, and cut into chunks
1 teaspoon paprika	1/2 cup barley
1 bay leaf	2 ears yellow corn, cooked and
3 large carrots, cut into chunks	cut into 1 inch pieces
8 whole, peeled potatoes	1 (10 oz.) package frozen peas
3 onions, cut in half	1/2 cup white wine
2 large parsnips, cut into chunks	1 egg, beaten
salt and pepper	boiling water

Heat the oil in a deep, large pot. Saute the garlic and paprika. Dredge the chicken pieces in seasoned flour and brown in the oil. Cover with boiling water. Turn down to a simmer. Keep at a simmer during the entire cooking time. After about an hour, add the carrots, potatoes, onions and parsnips, salt and pepper. Cook about 30 minutes, then add the pumpkin, barley, and green beans. After 15 minutes add the peas. When everything is almost ready, add the wine and cook for about 10 minutes. Beat the egg and to it add a little of the hot liquid. Stir vigorously. Return to the pot and stir. Correct seasoning. Serve in large soup bowls, sprinkled with chopped chives.   Serves 8.

Moroccan Chicken

This dish is a frequent Friday evening meal in Morocco.

3 tablespoons oil	salt and pepper
2 onions, chopped	1/2 cup water
3/4 teaspoon ground ginger	1/2 cup wine
3/4 teaspoon powdered saffron	8 hard-boiled eggs
1 teaspoon dried thyme	1/2 cup raisins
2 broilers, cut into serving pieces	1 cup toasted slivered almonds

In a large skillet saute the onions in the oil until transparent. Add the ginger, saffron, and thyme. Stir for 1 minute. Add the chicken pieces, salt, and pepper. Turn to coat all sides with the spices. Add water and wine. Cover tightly and cook over low heat for about 45 minutes or until the chicken is very tender. Add the raisins and whole hardboiled egg yolks and the whites, chopped, separately. Cook ten minutes longer. Garnish with the toasted, slivered almonds.   Serves 6 to 8.

Crimea Chicken in Egg Sauce

The Krimchaki Jews date their existence in the Crimea from the sixth century. Their customs vary in several aspects from the more widely followed procedures. Instead of using a *chuppah* (wedding canopy), they cover the bride and groom with a *tallit* (prayer shawl). The bridesmaid and the best man twirl chickens around the heads of the couple seven times. After killing the chickens, the bridegroom repeats the consecrating formula. This confirms the marriage.

5 dried mushrooms
3 tablespoons oil
1 chicken, cut into serving pieces
flour
salt and pepper
2 tablespoons flour

1 cup chicken broth
1/2 cup sherry
3 egg yolks, beaten
12 tiny pickled pearl onions
1 tablespoon chopped dill

Pour some boiling water over the mushrooms and let them soak for 30 minutes. Dry and chop them.

Dredge the chicken pieces in the seasoned flour. Brown in the oil. Place in a shallow baking pan and bake in a preheated 400-degree oven for 45 minutes to an hour, or until tender. In a saucepan dissolve the flour in the combined chicken broth and sherry. Stir over low heat until thickened. Add a little of this mixture to the beaten egg yolks, stir quickly. Return to the broth mixture and stir to a smooth sauce. Add the chopped mushrooms and onions. Pour over the chicken. Sprinkle with the chopped dill.

Serves 4 to 6.

Persian Chicken Polo

"And the Queen of Sheba came to Jerusalem with a very great train with camels that bore spices and very much gold and precious stones."

(1 Kings 10:3)

Polo is the Persian word for the more familiar pilaf.

1/2 lb. prunes
1/2 lb. dried pears
2 tablespoons oil
1 large onion, sliced
1/4 teaspoon turmeric
1/2 teaspoon coriander
1/2 teaspoon ground ginger
1 chicken, cut into serving
  pieces

salt and pepper
1 cup boiling water
1 teaspoon grated lemon rind
1/2 lb. burghul (cracked wheat)
1 clove garlic, minced
2 cups chicken broth
salt and pepper
3 tablespoons oil

Soak the prunes and pears in water to cover overnight.

Saute the onion in the oil. Add the turmeric, coriander, ginger. Stir for 1 minute. Add the chicken pieces. Saute lightly, turning to coat the chicken with the spices. Add salt and pepper and boiling water. Cover tightly and cook over low heat until the chicken is almost ready. Add the prunes and pears and enough of the water in which they were soaked to make 1-1/2 to 2 cups of liquid in the pan. Add the lemon rind and cook for another 30 minutes.

Lightly fry the burghul and garlic in the oil, stirring constantly. Add the chicken broth, salt, and pepper. Cover and cook over low heat until the broth has been absorbed and the burghul is fluffy, about 30 minutes. Serve chicken and fruit over the burghul.

Serves 6 to 8.

Armico

In Greece this dish is eaten on the evening before the Yom Kippur (Day of Atonement) fast begins.

2 tablespoons oil
1 bunch green onions,
  cut into 1/2 inch pieces
1 chicken, cut into serving
  pieces
1/2 cup chopped parsley
1 clove garlic, minced

3 large tomatoes, peeled
  and chopped
juice of 1 lemon
1 teaspoon sugar
salt and pepper
1/2 cup dry red wine

Saute the green onions, chicken, parsley, and garlic in the oil. Add the tomatoes, lemon juice, sugar, salt and pepper, and wine. Cover and cook over low heat until the chicken is tender.   Serves 4.

Gebratene Ente
(German Roast Duck)

In the late 1800s, Jewish groups, such as the Bilium, were formed to go to Palestine to found agricultural colonies and attempt to bring to reality a land flowing with milk and honey. The Chasidim, an ultra-orthodox sect, decried such movements. They believed that only when the Messiah came to lead them was it the Divine Will that they return to Zion. They were chided by some and gently made fun of by others for what seemed to be their vision of a ready-made Garden of Eden awaiting them in Palestine in some Messianic era.

A song was written describing such a place. It speaks of a garden where roast ducks fly through the air and wine flows without measure and where almonds grow on every stick.

A 5 lb. duck
salt
1 clove garlic
2 tablespoons margarine
1/2 orange
1 cup chicken broth

1/2 cup red wine
2 tablespoons brandy
1 cup currant jelly
grated rind of 1 orange
2 teaspoons water
1-1/2 teaspoons cornstarch

Salt duck inside and outside. Prick the skin all over with a fork. Rub skin and cavity with the half orange. Lightly brown the duck on all sides in the margarine in which the garlic has been sauteed. Place the duck and the chicken broth in a covered pan in a preheated 375-degree oven. Uncover after 45 minutes. Baste frequently. In a saucepan combine the wine, brandy, and currant jelly. Heat until the jelly is melted. When the duck is finished, drain the gravy into a bowl. Skim off the fat. Add the skimmed gravy to the wine mixture. Dissolve the cornstarch in the water and add to the saucepan. Stir over moderate heat until slightly thickened. Add the orange rind. Pour over the duck.   Serves 4 to 6.

Bukharan Chicken with Noodles

Titus thought that he destroyed the people of Israel by destroying the Temple in Jerusalem and carrying the holy objects to Rome. The only portion of the Temple left is the Western Wall (Kotel Hama'-aravi), formerly called the Wailing Wall. It is one of the most important sites in Jerusalem and is used, by a people very much alive, as a place of prayer. From the crannies of the wall grow caper plants which sometimes are used to symbolize the Jewish people. Both can survive despite being cut down, plucked out, or moved to alien environments.

A large chicken	2 tablespoons chopped dill
2 celery stalks	1/2 teaspoon saffron
1 onion, quartered	1 tablespoon capers
5 sprigs parsley	2 tomatoes, peeled, seeded,
1 carrot, quartered	chopped
salt and pepper	salt and pepper
2 tablespoons oil	1 lb. medium noodles
1 clove garlic, minced	1/4 cup margarine
2 large onions, chopped	1 teaspoon salt
2 green peppers, cut into	1/2 teaspoon dry mustard
strips	1/2 teaspoon garlic powder
4 large carrots, coarsely	1-1/2 cups chicken broth, heated
grated	1 cup non-dairy coffee
1/2 cup chopped celery leaves	lightener

Cook the chicken in water to cover, with the celery stalks, quartered onion, parsley, quartered carrot, salt, and pepper. Cook until very tender and falling off the bones. Cool and cut into neat pieces. Reserve the broth. Cook the noodles and set aside. Saute the remaining onions, garlic, and green peppers in the oil. Add the grated carrots, celery leaves, saffron, and dill. Stir for 2 minutes. Add the tomatoes, salt, pepper, and capers. Cover and cook for 10 minutes. Add the chicken pieces and stir.

In a flat casserole layer the noodles and chicken mixture, beginning and ending with noodles.

In a saucepan melt the margarine and add the flour combined with the mustard, garlic powder, and salt. Stir until foamy and lightly colored. Add the heated broth, all at once, and stir briskly with a wire whisk until smooth. Gradually add the coffee lightener. Stir, cooking over low heat until smooth and thickened. Add a little more broth, if necessary. Pour over the noodle casserole and bake in a preheated 400-degree oven for 20 minutes or until bubbling and golden.   Serves 6 to 8.

Walnut Fried Chicken

About 100 B.C.E., Wu Ti, the warrior emperor of China, conquered some lands to the south where lichi nuts, walnuts, and pomegranates grew. As a consequence, they were introduced into China and became a characteristic part of the Chinese cuisine.

This recipe is frequently made using slices of chicken breast rather than the American-style serving pieces. The Chinese custom of cooking things in small pieces and for short cooking times is said to have been the result of a scarcity of fuel. Much later, the Chinese Jews of K'aifeng-fu cooked duck in much the same way.

2 small fryers, cut into small pieces	1/2 cup matzo meal
	pinch coriander
1/2 cup cornstarch	1/8 teaspoon salt
2 teaspoons salt	1 cup oil
2 teaspoons sugar	
4 tablespoons dry sherry	*Sauce:*
3 egg whites	1-1/2 cups apricot preserves
2 cups very finely-chopped walnuts	1/2 cup hot mustard
	1/2 cup sherry

Mix together the cornstarch, salt and sugar. Add sherry and blend well. Stir, but do not beat, the egg whites. Add gradually to the cornstarch mixture. Blend well. Dip the chicken pieces into the cornstarch mixture and then into the combined nuts, matzo meal, coriander, and salt, coating well. Fry in the hot oil until golden and tender.

Make sauce by combining in a saucepan the apricot preserves, mustard, and wine. Blend well and warm. Serve as a dip for the chicken.

Serves 4 to 6.

Chicken Pilav

A pilav (variously spelled pilau, pilaf, and pilaw), came to the Middle East through Turkey from Persia. In both these countries and, subsequently in others, this dish consists of rice or rice with chicken, meat, or fruit. Whatever the other ingredients, pilav always is made with herbs, spices, or both.

Jews from Persia and Turkey consider pilav a regular part of their weekly menu.

2 small chickens, cut into serving pieces	3 sprigs fresh dill
salt and pepper	2 tablespoons tomato paste
1/2 teaspoon powdered garlic	1/2 teaspoon saffron
3 cups water	3 tablespoons oil
4 chicken bouillon cubes	1-1/2 cups rice
1 onion, quartered	1/2 cup almonds, toasted
1/2 cup chopped celery leaves	1/2 cup raisins

Sprinkle chicken pieces with salt, pepper and garlic powder. Heat oil in a large skillet and, over moderate heat, gently fry the chicken until golden. In a saucepan, bring the water to a boil and add the bouillon cubes. Add the onion, celery leaves, dill, tomato paste, and saffron. Simmer for fifteen minutes. Remove dill. In another pan saute the nuts and remove from the oil. To the oil add the rice and stir, browning. Put the rice in a baking pan. Pour the broth over and place the chicken on top. Sprinkle the raisins over the chicken. Cover and bake in a preheated 375-degree oven until chicken is tender, and liquid is almost entirely absorbed. Uncover, garnish with the almonds, and bake for 10 minutes longer.

Serves 8 to 10.

Chicken Enchiladas

Since earliest times, people all over the world wrapped one kind of food in another. In lieu of eating utensils, this was an efficient way to get some kinds of food to the mouth. As culinary skills developed, delicious dishes resulted from the technique of wrapping all sorts of foods in a variety of pancakes. Enchiladas is a Mexican version of this idea.

12 canned tortillas	*Sauce:*
3 tablespoons oil	2 tablespoons margarine
2 onions, chopped	2 tablespoons flour
2 large green peppers, chopped	1/2 teaspoon salt
6 tomatoes, peeled and chopped	1/2 teaspoon onion juice
1/2 teaspoon salt	1/8 teaspoon pepper
1/2 teaspoon garlic powder	1/2 cup chicken consomme
1/2 teaspoon hot pepper sauce	1/2 cup non-dairy coffee
12 green olives, coarsely chopped	lightener
2 cups cooked chicken, diced	

Keep the tortillas in the closed can until the filling has been made. Saute the onion and peppers in the oil. Remove half of the mixture to a bowl.

To the remaining onion and green peppers add the tomatoes, salt, garlic powder, and the hot pepper sauce. Simmer for 10 minutes. To the mixture in the bowl add the chicken and olives.

Sauce: Over low heat melt the margarine in a saucepan and add the flour, salt and pepper, stirring to a smooth paste. When frothy add the onion juice. Meanwhile, in another pan, bring the consomme and coffee lightener to a boil. Add this all at once to the flour mixture and mix briskly with a wire whisk. Stir continuously until smooth and thickened. Pour half of the sauce into the bowl containing the chicken mixture. Blend.

Remove the tortillas from the can. Heat a little oil in a small frying pan. Place each tortilla into the oil for not longer than 2 or 3 seconds on each side. Remove and fill immediately with a rounded tablespoon of the chicken mixture and roll up. Pour a little of the tomato mixture into a baking dish and into it place the rolled tortillas, close to each other. Pour the coffee lightener mixture over the tortillas in a random pattern. Pour the tomato mixture on the places not covered by the other sauce. Cover and bake in a preheated 375-degree oven for 20 minutes. Uncover and bake about ten minutes longer.   Serves 6.

Duck Belshazzar

In the fifth chapter of the Book of Daniel, the story is told of King Belshazzar who "made a great feast to a thousand of his lords." (Kings were lavish entertainers in those days. There is a record of a Persian king entertaining 15,000 men daily.) It was at Belshazzar's feast that the moving finger foretold the defeat of the Babylonians by writing on the wall, *"Menel mene, tekel upharsin."* At this feast duck sauced with mustard was served.

A 4 to 5 lb. duck	1 teaspoon salt
1/3 cup prepared mustard	1 clove garlic, minced
2/3 cup ketchup	3/4 cup dry red wine
1/3 cup brown sugar	

Quarter the duck, prick the skin, and broil for 10 minutes on each side. Turn the oven from Broil to Bake and set at 350 degrees. Roast the duck for 30 minutes. Remove the duck from the oven and brush with the sauce made by combining all the other ingredients. Bake, covered, for 20 minutes. Remove the cover and bake for 30 minutes longer. Brush again with the sauce and pour the remaining sauce over the duck. Continue roasting, uncovered until the duck is tender. Place the duck on a warmed platter. Skim the fat from the sauce and pour the skimmed sauce over the duck.   Serves 4 to 6.

Turkey Braziliana

Since ancient times, turmeric has been valued as a spice, but it was also used as a dye. Some sun-worshipping tribes declared it and its brilliant yellow color to be holy. A paint made of turmeric is used in India to decorate the faces of Hindu brides. Some women in India color their cheeks with a solution of turmeric. In some places in Asia, a piece of turmeric root is hung around the neck of babies to ward off evil.

The Israelites in their flight from Egypt took spices with them, among them were sweet cinnamon, myrrh, and sweet calmus, which is now thought to be turmeric.

A young turkey	1/2 lb. walnuts, chopped
2 tablespoons olive oil	2 cups tart apples,
3 cloves garlic, mashed	peeled and diced
1/2 teaspoon turmeric	1/2 lb. pitted prunes, chopped
1 teaspoon grated lemon rind	1/2 teaspoon dried thyme
1/4 cup oil	1/2 teaspoon dried marjoram
1 onion, chopped	3 tablespoons grated orange rind
10 slices white bread,	3 eggs, beaten
toasted	1/2 cup chicken broth
salt and pepper	3 cups water
1/4 teaspoon ground cloves	1 cup white wine
1/2 lb. Brazil nuts, chopped	

Make a paste of the olive oil, garlic, turmeric, and lemon rind. Rub the turkey all over, inside and outside. Saute the onion in the oil. Reserve. Soak the bread slices in water and squeeze almost dry. Crumble into a large bowl. Add the sauteed onion, salt and pepper, cloves, all the nuts, apples, prunes, thyme, marjoram, and orange rind. Mix well. Add the beaten eggs and the broth. Beat well to lighten the mixture. Stuff the turkey. Place in a pan with 3 cups of water and the wine. Cover and bake in a preheated 350 degree oven until half finished. Uncover and baste frequently until turkey is very tender.

Austrian Country-Style Chicken

In Eisenstadt, Austria, Sandor Wolf founded a museum in 1902, which is now named for him. Preserved in Wolf's house are many reminders of his religious observance. There is one room with a removable roof so that the room could be converted to a *succah*. Wolf was a wine dealer. Many of the houses in the old Jewish Quarter have stone jars carved above the doorways. The original Wolf wine cellars are still in existence and owned by the government. They run under the houses in Judengasse, (Jewish Street). The old ghetto gate was comprised of two pillars and a chain which closed the ghetto off from Friday evening to Saturday sundown. One of the pillars and the chain remain.

3 tablespoons margarine	flour
6 shallots, minced	salt and pepper
1/2 lb. mushrooms	2 tablespoons tomato paste
1/2 teaspoon dried marjoram	3/4 cup white wine
1 chicken, cut into serving pieces	2 tablespoons cognac

Saute the shallots, mushrooms, and marjoram in the margarine. Remove the mushroom mixture from the margarine. Add a little more margarine to the pan. Dredge the chicken pieces in the seasoned flour and brown on all sides in the margarine. Combine the tomato paste, wine and cognac and pour over the chicken. Add the mushroom mixture. Cook covered until the chicken is very tender.   Serves 4.

Fish

Fish

Cold Salmon Mold

The Talmud asks the question, "When may those who possess less than fifty shekels have the dish of vegetables and fish?" The answer is, "Every Friday night of the Sabbath."

Aspic:
1 teaspoon unflavored gelatine
1/3 cup white wine
1/3 cup lemon juice
1 egg, hard-boiled
1 green pepper
pimento strips

Salmon:
3 tablespoons lemon juice
1 envelope unflavored gelatine
2 (7 oz.) cans salmon, drained
1/2 cup celery, finely chopped
2 tablespoons onion, finely chopped
1/2 cup pimento stuffed olives, chopped
2 drops red food coloring
1/2 cup mayonnaise
1 cup sour cream

Aspic: Prepare a 5-cup mold by combining in a small bowl the wine and lemon juice in the aspic ingredients. Sprinkle the gelatine on top and let it stand for 5 minutes. Place the bowl in a pan of boiling water and stir to dissolve the gelatine. Pour the mixture into the mold and tilt the pan so that some of the mixture coats the sides about one inch up from the bottom. The mixture in the bottom should be at least 1/8 inch thick. Refrigerate until gelatine is sticky. Slice hard-boiled egg. Cut green pepper into thin rings and the pimento into strips. Arrange on the sticky gelatine in a pleasing design. Refrigerate until almost set.

Salmon: Combine the lemon juice and gelatine with 1/3 cup water in a small bowl. Let stand for 5 minutes. Place in a bowl of boiling water. Stir to dissolve gelatine. Put the drained salmon into a large bowl. Remove the skin and bones and flake with a fork. Add celery, onion and olives. Mix. Add the food coloring to the mayonnaise and blend. Add the gelatine mixture, mayonnaise, and sour cream to the salmon mixture. Spoon into the prepared mold. Refrigerate overnight. Turn out onto a chilled platter. Garnish with slices of cucumber, greens, and cherry tomatoes.

Russian Fish with Apples

The use of fruits in cooking has permeated the southwestern part of Russia from the Balkans. This unusual combination of flavors is zesty and pleasant.

3 lbs. sliced carp	2 cups firm cooking apples
1/2 cup chopped celery with leaves	1 tablespoon lemon juice
	1 teaspoon sugar
1 large onion, chopped	1 cup sour cream
2 bay leaves	4 tablespoons prepared
1 cup white wine	white horseradish
2 cups water	chopped parsley
salt and pepper	lemon slices

Combine the celery, onion, bay leaves, salt, and pepper in a pan with the wine and water. Bring to a boil. Place the fish in the pan and simmer until fish flakes easily. Peel the apples and cut into 1/2-inch dice. Cook in just enough water to cover. Add the sugar and lemon juice. Cook over low heat until apples are tender but still retain their shape. When slightly cooled, drain the apples and combine with the sour cream and horseradish. Remove fish from pan liquid and place on a platter. Cover with the sour cream mixture. Garnish with lemon slices and chopped parsley.

Serves 6 to 8.

Dutch Herring-and-Potato Casserole

Since the Dutch, in the fourteenth century, found a way to preserve herring by pickling in brine or salting, their fishing fleets grew to be the most formidable in Northern Europe. The Hanseatic League, the English, the French, and even the Spanish attacked their ships because of the inroads made on their respective economies by the herring fleets. But the Dutch guilds turned the catches into great profits for the Zeelanders. The black-sailed fishing boats still go out to snare the delectable herring.

Because herring was plentiful in Northern Europe, and methods of preserving it were known, it became a staple item of the Jews of Russia and Poland.

4 large herring filets	3 eggs, beaten
1-1/2 lbs. boiled potatoes	1/2 teaspoon pepper
1/4 cup scallions, chopped	1 tablespoon melted butter
1 tablespoon chopped dill	bread crumbs
2 cups milk	

Soak the herring filets overnight.

Generously butter a casserole. Cut boiled potatoes into slices not more than 1/4 inch thick. Place a layer of 1/3 of the potato slices in the casserole. Pat the filets with paper towels to absorb excess moisture and cut each filet into 2 or 3 pieces. Arrange 2 cut filets over the potatoes. Sprinkle with half of the scallions and half of the dill. Repeat the process, ending with a layer of potatoes. Combine the eggs with the milk and pepper. Pour carefully into the casserole. Cover the top with breadcrumbs. Drizzle the melted butter over. Bake in a preheated 375-degree oven for about 30 minutes or until browned.   Serves 4 to 6.

Broiled Fish Sophia

Emil Shekerdjinsky was a Jewish-Bulgarian war hero who died in the resistance efforts against the Germans. His memory is honored in Sofia by naming a Jewish Cultural Center for him. The building houses an exhibit of artifacts illustrating Jewish history in Bulgaria, a library, a lecture hall, meeting rooms for the Jewish Chorus and for the theatrical group, as well as a Jewish restaurant.

3 lbs. fish, whole or in thick slices	1/3 cup olive oil
1-1/2 teaspoons salt	1/2 cup breadcrumbs
1 tablespoon lemon juice	lemon wedges
1/4 cup white wine	chopped parsley

Rinse fish and dry well. Salt on all sides. Combine lemon juice, wine and olive oil. Marinate the fish in this liquid for an hour at room temperature. Broil, turning once and basting several times with the marinade. Serve on a warmed platter garnished with lemon wedges dipped in chopped parsley.   Serves 4.

Veracruzana

Vera Cruz, the City of the True Cross, was founded and named by Cortez when he landed there in 1519. He burned his ships in the harbor to make sure that no temptation to depart would divert his men from their mission to conquer the land. Among his *conquistadores* at least two were known to be Jews. One of them was the first Jew to be burned at the stake in the New World. He was Hernando Alonso, martyred on October 17, 1528.

Vera Cruz is a seafood center but among its fishes none is more appreciated than *huachinango,* red snapper, especially when prepared in this way.

2 lbs. thick red snapper filets
1/4 cup olive oil
1 large onion, chopped
1 large green pepper
1 (8 oz.) can tomato sauce

1/2 cup water
1/2 teaspoon salt
3/4 teaspoon hot pepper sauce
12 green olives

Saute the onion in the oil. Seed and cut the green pepper in 1/4 inch wide strips, add to the onion and stir for 2 or 3 minutes. Add the tomato sauce, water, salt, and hot pepper sauce. Simmer for 5 minutes. Generously butter a baking pan just large enough to hold the fish so that the sauce, when poured in, will cover the fish. Put a little sauce in the pan, then add the fish. Cover with the sauce. Add the olives. Bake in a preheated 375 degree oven for about 35 minutes or until fish flakes easily.

Serves 4 or 5.

Fruited Salmon Curry

Fresh, salted, and spiced fish were common among the Hebrews. A dish made of flaked fish was called *zachanah*. Fish was thought to be especially good for pregnant women.

1 medium onion, minced
1 small green pepper, cut
   into small pieces
1 clove garlic, minced
1 to 2 teaspoons curry powder
2 tablespoons butter
1/2 teaspoon salt
1/4 cup flour
1 (1 lb.) can salmon

liquid from the salmon and milk
   to make 1-1/2 cups
2 cups green grapes, melon
   balls, or slices of
   green gage plums,
   or any combination of
   them, sugared
1 teaspoon lime juice
4 cups cooked rice
1 cup slivered toasted almonds

Melt the butter in a saucepan and saute the onion, green pepper, garlic, and curry powder. Add the flour and salt and stir until the flour is blended into the mixture, about 2 minutes. Gradually add the combined salmon liquid and milk, stirring until the sauce is thickened and smooth. Simmer for 5 minutes, stirring. Add the sugared fruit to which the lime juice has been added. Add the flaked salmon. Stir gently over low heat until all ingredients are warmed through but not cooked. Serve on a bed of rice and garnish with the almonds.

Serves 4 to 6.

Tuna with Prunes and Apples

Fishing was one of the principal occupations of the ancient Hebrews. The town of Acre, or Acco, was one of the places where central fish markets were located. The proverb, "Carrying fish to Acre" is the equivalent of "Carrying coals to Newcastle." Among the fish mentioned in the Talmud are mackerel and tuna.

1 cup pitted prunes	3 tablespoons flour
1 cup diced apples	1 egg yolk, beaten
1 cup white wine	2 (7 oz.) cans tuna, drained
1 cup light cream	1 (4 oz.) can mushrooms

Peel and cut apples into 1/2 inch dice. Combine with prunes and wine in a saucepan. Cook over low heat until apples are barely cooked and still firm. Remove fruit from liquid and reserve. Combine egg yolk, cream, and flour. Blend into a smooth batter. Add to wine mixture in the saucepan. Stir and bring to a boil. Reduce heat and add the tuna, mushrooms, prunes, and apples. Heat through. Serve on a bed of rice.

Serves 4 to 6.

Dilled Salmon Balls

A number of Jewish fishermen came to Alaska with the Russian fishing fleets in the 1830s. In 1870, two Jewish partners obtained from the United States government a twenty-year contract giving them the exclusive fishing rights on the islands off the coast of Alaska. They established a steamship line between San Francisco and Alaska. This service enabled gold hunters to reach Alaska during the gold rush.

2 onions, finely chopped	3 egg whites
2 carrots, diced	3 egg yolks
2 stalks celery, chopped	salt and pepper
A (1 lb.) can salmon, drained	2 tablespoons finely-chopped dill
4 tablespoons matzo meal	2 cups sour cream
1/2 onion, grated	

Bring a quart of salted water to a boil. Add the chopped onions, carrots and celery. Remove the skin and bones from the drained salmon and flake with a fork. Add the grated onion, matzo meal, and three beaten egg yolks. Beat the egg whites until stiff and fold into the salmon mixture. Strain the vegetables out of the boiling water and reserve. To the gently boiling water add the salmon, formed into balls by handling as lightly as possible. Cook until fish balls are light and tender. Remove to a warm platter. Place in a blender the reserved vegetables and about 1/4 cup of water in which the salmon balls were cooked. Whir until smooth. Combine with the sour cream and chopped dill. Blend thoroughly. Pour over salmon balls. This may be served on rice or noodles.   Serves 4.

Fish Curry

Curry powder is a combination of spices which has been used since ancient times. The spices included in most commercial curry powder are cayenne pepper, turmeric, coriander, cumin, fennel and ginger. Many other spices may be added or substituted. There are hundreds of variations in the way that curry dishes are prepared. Some are highly spiced, as in Bombay and Madras. In other parts of India they tend to be more mild.

In India, curry powder is prepared daily by grinding or pounding the spices on a curry stone. The curry powder is always sauteed as part of the cooking process.

2 lbs. fish filets	1-1/4 teaspoons ground cumin
3 tablespoons oil	3 teaspoons powdered ginger
1 clove garlic, crushed	1/2 teaspoon cayenne pepper
1 onion, chopped	1/4 teaspoon allspice
1-1/2 teaspoons turmeric	1 cup canned tomatoes, mashed
4 teaspoons ground	salt
coriander	2 teaspoons lemon juice

Saute over low heat the onion, garlic, and all the spices. Stir for 2 minutes. Reserve half of the mixture. To the rest add the tomatoes and salt. Cook for several minutes until thickened. Cut the fish into serving size pieces and rub the reserved spice mixture into the flesh on all sides. Add the fish to the tomato mixture. Cover and cook over low heat about 15 minutes or until fish flakes easily with a fork. Add the lemon juice. Serve over rice.   Serves 4 or 5.

Pilsen Spiced Carp

In some Balkan countries prunes and raisins are added to this recipe. Although Czechoslavakia has no coastline, the Czechs eat a quantity of fish.

3 lbs. of carp	1 tablespoon vinegar
salt and pepper	beer
2 bay leaves	1 lemon, sliced
1 teaspoon ginger	2 egg yolks, beaten
1 teaspoon paprika	2 drops hot pepper sauce

Salt the carp and refrigerate overnight. Rinse and place in a large saucepan with salt, pepper, bay leaves, ginger, paprika, vinegar, and beer to cover. Simmer until fish is cooked through but firm. During the last ten minutes of cooking add the lemon slices. Remove fish to a warm platter. Strain the fish broth and return to the saucepan. Add a little of the hot broth to the beaten egg yolks and stir quickly. Return the egg mixture to the rest of the broth, stirring. Add the hot pepper sauce. Stir until thickened. Pour the sauce over the fish or serve separately.

Serves 4 to 6.

Scandinavian Herring Crepes

For untold millenia, herring has been used as food by man. In prehistoric caves along the coast of the North Sea, herring bones, together with other food remnants and artifacts, have been found. Herring was one of of the food staples for the Jews of Russia and Poland. Herring, prepared in an infinite variety of ways, is an important part of the diet of Scandinavians and people of Northern Europe.

This elegant dish can be prepared several hours ahead and baked just before serving.

Crepes:
3/4 cup milk
3/4 cup water
1-1/2 cups sifted flour
1/4 teaspoon salt
3 eggs
2-1/2 tablespoons melted butter
1 tablespoon finely chopped
  chives
1 teaspoon finely chopped
  tarragon leaves
1 teaspoon finely chopped
  parsley

Filling:
4 or 5 herring filets, cut
  into 1/2 inch dice
1/2 onion, finely chopped
2 tablespoons butter
1/4 cup finely chopped celery
  leaves
1/3 cup white wine
1/2 teaspoon cornstarch
1 teaspoon grated lemon rind
1-1/2cups sour cream

Crepes: Put the milk, water, flour, and salt into a blender. Blend at high speed for about 1 minute. Use a rubber spatula to push down any particles adhering to the container. Add eggs and butter. Blend again for 30 seconds. Add the chives, tarragon and parsley. Blend for 1 or 2 seconds. Cover and refrigerate for at least 3 hours.

Brush a 6-1/2 or 7 inch frying pan with oil. When hot, remove from the heat and pour in 1/4 cup of batter while quickly tilting the pan so that it is completely covered with a thin layer of batter. Pour any excess batter back into the container. Return the pan to the heat for about 1 minute. Lift the edges of the crepe with a spatula. If the underside is lightly colored, turn the crepe over. Do not tear or puncture. A highly effective way is to loosen the crepe around the edges, take a firm grip on the side of the crepe nearest you and, with your fingers, flip it over. Cook about 30 seconds on the second side. Stack the finished crepes. These may be made several hours in advance of filling them.

Filling: Saute the onion in the butter until just transparent. Add the celery leaves and stir for 1 minute. Add the wine in which the cornstarch has been dissolved. Cook until thickened slightly. Add the herring pieces and the lemon rind, to heat through. Remove from heat and stir in ½ cup sour cream.

Place 1/8 of the filling on each crepe. Roll up. Place in a buttered pan and cover with sour cream. Bake in a preheated 400 degree oven for 10 minutes. Sprinkle with chopped dill before serving. Makes about 8 crepes.

Negev Fish Filets

As the Hebrews wandered in the *negev* (desert), having a limited food supply they recalled their former more varied diet. *"Would that we were given flesh to eat! We remember the fish . . . the cucumbers and the melons and the leeks and the onions and the garlic. . ."*. (Numbers 11:4-7)

4 fairly thick white fish filets	1 teaspoon dried basil
1/4 cup oil	1/2 teaspoon salt
4 tablespoons white wine	4 scallions, chopped
1/4 cup lemon juice	1 cup tehina sauce
2 cloves garlic, crushed	1/2 cup slivered almonds

Combine the oil, wine, lemon juice, garlic, basil and salt in a non-metal pan. Place the fish in the marinade and cover with the chopped scallions. Cover lightly and marinate for several hours, turning several times. Remove fish from the marinade and place in a greased baking pan. Bake in a preheated 400 degree oven for 15 minutes or until almost done. Cover generously with the tehina sauce and slivered almonds. Bake 15 minutes longer or until fish flakes easily and the tehina is a pale gold.

Serve 4 to 6.

Trout with Orange

The Festival of the Chrysanthemums was celebrated annually in Japan. On this occasion the Emperor, members of the royal court, and other dignitaries spent time in the royal gardens admiring the lovely blossoms and writing poems commemorating their beauty. This was followed by a banquet at which was served wine, poured over chrysanthemum petals, and trout from the royal ponds.

There are fewer than one thousand Jews living in Japan today. There is said to be a number of Orientals living in Japan who have chosen to convert to Judaism, but most of the Jewish population is of American or European origin.

Currently teaching at the University of Miami, in the Department of Religion, is a Japanese rabbi. His wife and their sons have Hebrew names and profess Judaism. Another Japanese, Professor Kazuo Ueda, is a Yiddishist and has studied at Hebrew University in Jerusalem.

6 trout	2 small oranges, peeled
fine, dry breadcrumbs	and sliced
salt and pepper	1-1/2 tablespoons sherry
marjoram	2 teaspoons tarragon
6 tablespoons butter	chopped parsley

Combine the breadcrumbs, salt, pepper, and marjoram. Thoroughly coat the fish with the seasoned crumbs and fry gently in the butter, turning once. Place in a saucepan, the orange slices, their juices, and the sherry. Heat but do not boil. Transfer the trout to a warm platter. Loosen the crumbs in the pan. Add the tarragon. Add a little more butter, if necessary. Stir over moderate heat for a minute or two. Arrange the slices of orange down the length of each fish. Combine the orange liquid and the butter mixture and heat. Pour over the orange covered fish. Sprinkle lightly with chopped parsley.   Serves 6.

Fish Spetsiotiko
(Greek Fish Bake)

In Greece, the first purchase after marriage which a Sephardic husband makes is a fish. He goes to the market and brings home a fish to insure fertility and good fortune. The family and relatives join in feasting on his purchase on what is known as the Day of the Fish.

3 rather thick, white fish filets	6 cloves garlic, minced
3 tablespoons olive oil	1/2 cup water
3 large onions, sliced	1 teaspoon sugar
3 to 4 ripe tomatoes, peeled	salt and pepper
1/2 cup coarsely chopped black	3 hot boiled potatoes, diced
olives	juice of half a lemon
1 teaspoon dried oregano	

In a saucepan, saute the onion slices in the oil. Add the coarsely cut tomatoes, olives, oregano, garlic, water, sugar, salt, and pepper. Cover and cook over low heat for about 5 minutes to blend flavors. Arrange fish in a greased baking dish. Pour the sauce over and add the diced potatoes. Bake in a preheated 375 degree oven until fish flakes easily. When finished, squeeze the juice of half a lemon over the fish. Serve hot or cold.   Serves 6 to 8.

Mousse-Filled Sole with Grape Sauce

According to the Talmud, "A man who marries his daughter to a scholar is like one who mingles vine grapes with vine grapes, but he who marries his daughter to an ignorant man is like one who mingles vine grapes with berries of the thorn bush."

8 thin sole filets	*Sauce:*
2 tablespoons white wine	2 tablespoons butter
1 tablespoon lemon juice	2 tablespoons flour
salt and pepper	1/2 medium onion, grated
1 (1 lb.) can salmon	salt
1 tablespoon chopped dill	1/2 teaspoon nutmeg
2 tablespoons chopped scallions	1/2 cup light cream
3 eggs	1/2 cup white wine
1/2 cup heavy cream	2 egg yolks, beaten
1/2 teaspoon salt	1-1/2 tablespoons lemon juice
	1 lb. green, seedless grapes

Heavily butter a 5 or 6-cup ring mold. Wash and dry the filets and brush with a mixture of the wine and lemon juice. Sprinkle lightly with salt and pepper. Remove skin and bones from the salmon. Put the salmon, with its liquid, into a blender. Add the dill, scallions, eggs, cream, and salt. Blend at high speed until very smooth. Line the mold with the filets, dark side up. Place the middle of the filets at the bottom of the mold. Ends will overhang rims. Fill the lined mold with the salmon mixture. Cover the mousse by overlapping filet ends. Brush top generously with butter. Cover loosely with foil. Place the mold in a larger pan. Pour hot water into the larger pan to a depth of 1 to 1-1/2 inches. Bake in a preheated 375-degree oven for about 30 minutes. Do not overbake. Loosen around the edges with a spatula. Turn out on a warmed platter.

Sauce: Melt the butter in a saucepan. Add the flour and stir until foamy and lightly colored. Add the grated onion, salt and nutmeg. Stir. Combine the cream and wine. Add, stirring vigorously. Pour a little of the hot sauce into the beaten egg yolks. Stir and return to pan. Stir to thicken. Add the lemon juice and grapes and heat through. Pour a little over unmolded fish. Pass the rest separately.   Serves 6 to 8.

Salmon Filled Filet of Sole

One of the greatest demonstrations of Danish loyalty to and regard for their Jewish compatriots resulted in saving the Jewish population of Denmark during the Nazi invasion of 1943. At the beginning of the Rosh Hashanah holiday, Danish officials learned that the Germans planned to deport all Jews to the death camps of Czechoslavakia to be exterminated. The Underground informed Rabbi Marcus Melchior, who, from his pulpit, alerted the people to the imminent danger. The Jews fled immediately to the northern coast where people hid them in churches, attics, cellars, and the woods. The Resistance leaders organized the large fishing fleet in a dangerous enterprise. Despite the Danish need for fish in times of limited food supply, the fleet stopped all fishing activity and transported more than seven thousand Jews the thirty-mile distance across Ore Sound to Sweden in the ten-day period ending with Yom Kippur. The Jews returned in 1945 to find their businesses and homes awaiting them, all carefully maintained by the heroic Danes whose Christianity was more than verbal.

4 filets of sole	*Sauce:*
2 small slices fresh salmon	3 egg yolks, beaten
2 tablespoons butter	1/4 cup heavy cream
2 tablespoons shallots (or green onions), finely chopped	1/2 teaspoon cornstarch
	1 tablespoon water
3/4 cup white wine	salt and pepper
1/2 cup heavy cream	chopped dill
2 tablespoons lemon juice	

Cut pieces of salmon as long as the filets are wide, and about one inch thick. Place a piece at one end of each filet. Roll the filets up over the salmon and fasten with toothpicks. Pour the melted butter into a shallow baking pan. Add the filet rolls. Sprinkle with salt and the chopped shallots. Combine the wine and cream and spoon over the fish. Bake in a preheated 375 degree oven for 10 minutes or until fish is almost ready. Pour off liquid from pan and reserve.

Sauce: Beat the egg yolks with the cream. Continue beating while slowly adding the pan liquid. Add the cornstarch dissolved in the water. Stir. Pour over the filets. Return to the oven and bake for 10 to 12 minutes or until fish flakes easily with a fork.   Serves 4.

Uskumru Dolmasu
(Turkish Stuffed Mackerel)

Constantinople was conquered by the Turks in 1453. Later in the century, the sultans welcomed the Jews fleeing Spain. Throughout the Ottoman Empire, on both sides of the Bosphorus, new communities of Jews were established. Constantinople had a larger Jewish population than any city in Europe. Salonika also was a large center. Jews were granted all liberties, and soon international trade and commerce brought prosperity to the new Empire. Jews became doctors; interpreters;

craftsmen, bringing their knowledge of Spanish metal work; printers, establishing the first publishing houses in Turkey; and merchants.

Sultan Bajazet II said of King Ferdinand of Spain, "You are mistaken to call this king wise, for he has only ruined his country and enriched ours."

The influences of Turkish cookery remain strongly identified with much of the Sephardic cuisine.

A 4 lb. whole mackerel	1/2 cup fresh chervil, finely
3 tablespoons oil	chopped
1 cup finely chopped walnuts	1/2 cup parsley finely chopped
1/2 cup finely chopped	1/2 cup fine breadcrumbs
hazelnuts	2 eggs, beaten
1/2 cup seedless raisins	1 egg, beaten
salt and pepper	breadcrumbs
1/4 teaspoon each of allspice,	
nutmeg, cinnamon and cloves	

Remove the head and tail from the fish. Skin the mackerel so that the skin remains whole. Reserve the skin. Remove the flesh from the bones and cut into bite size pieces. Set aside. Saute onions in the oil. Add all the nuts, raisin, all the spices, the breadcrumbs, and fish. Stir until fiish is cooked. Cool. Add 2 eggs, chervil, and parsley. Stir and blend well. Stuff this filling into the fish skin and sew up the opening. Mackerel skin is quite strong and presents no problem if it is carefully done. Wipe the stuffed fish off with paper towels. Roll in the beaten egg and breadcrumbs. Fry in inch deep hot oil until cooked through and golden. Serve hot or cold.   Serves 6 to 8.

Madras Fried Fish

In India it was the custom, on dedicating a new home or moving to new quarters, for Jews to make a gift offering to the poor so that they could buy fish for the Sabbath.

4 fish filets	1/4 teaspoon chile powder
juice of 1 lemon	1 clove garlic, minced
1/4 cup oil	1/2 onion, finely chopped
1 teaspoon curry powder	four
	1 egg

Combine lemon juice, oil, curry powder, chile powder, garlic, and onion. Place the fish in this marinade for 1 hour, turning from time to time. Shake excess moisture off the filets and coat with flour. Strain the marinade and combine with the beaten egg and just enough flour to make a light batter. Dip the fish in the batter and fry in hot oil immediately until golden. Garnish with tomato slices and parsley.   Serves 4.

Fish With Eggplant

In Italy, basil is credited with having aphrodisiacal qualities. Women wear it as a means of attracting affection. Young rural swains stick a piece over their ears, and a pot of basil on a young lady's window sill is an invitation.

3 lbs. fish filets	leaves of 15 sprigs of parsley
1 large eggplant	3 garlic cloves
1/2 cup flour	1 teaspoon dried basil leaves
1/2 cup olive oil	1/2 cup white wine
1/2 cup butter, melted	1/3 cup grated Parmesan cheese
1/2 teaspoon salt	

Peel and cut eggplant into 1/2-inch thick slices. Salt and place in a collander to drain for 30 minutes. Rinse and dry well then cut into cubes. Fry lightly in the oil. Reserve. Dredge fish in flour. Oil an ovenproof serving dish and place the fish in the center. Add the eggplant around the fish. Combine in a mortar or bowl the oil remaining from frying the eggplant (add a little more, if necessary), the melted butter, salt, parsley, garlic, and basil. Mash and pound into a paste. (The blender may be used but with slightly different results). Spoon this mixture over the fish. Cover with buttered paper and bake in a preheated 375-degree oven for about 20 minutes or until fish flakes easily with a fork. Remove buttered paper and sprinkle with the Parmesan cheese. Bake about 10 minutes longer until cheese is melted and golden.   Serves 4 to 6.

Danish Salmon Roll

When the Nazis overran Denmark they imposed their usual anti-Jewish policies. Among many that were more repressive, was the order that all Jews had to wear the yellow star badge to identify them. King Christian X told the German leaders, "I can't, at the moment, prevent you from enforcing this, but you can't prevent me from wearing a badge, too." This he did until the defeat of the Germans.

2-1/4 cups sifted flour	2 hard-boiled eggs, coarsely
1 teaspoon salt	chopped
3/4 cup shortening	1/2 teaspoon chopped dill
5 tablespoons cold water	1-1/2 tablespoons butter
1 (1 lb.) can salmon	1-1/2 tablespoons flour
1/2 onion, finely grated	1/4 teaspoon salt
1 cup frozen peas, thawed	1 cup milk
	1 egg, beaten

Sift together the flour and salt into a bowl. With a pastry blender cut in the shortening until the mixture is the consistency of coarse sand. Sprinkle the water over and toss dough to form a ball. Refrigerate.

Discard the skin, bones and liquid from the salmon and flake with a fork. Add the onion, peas, chopped eggs, and dill. Toss lightly to blend. Melt the butter in a saucepan. Add the flour and stir until foamy and lightly colored. Add the salt and gradually add the milk, stirring to make a smooth sauce. Add sauce to salmon mixture. Mix gently to combine.

Roll out the dough to piecrust thickness in a rectangle having a width of 10 inches. On each long side of the rectangle cut strips (like fringe) which are 1 inch wide and 3 inches long. This leaves a 4 inch panel in the middle. On this panel place the salmon mixture, leaving 1 inch of unused space at each end. Turn up these ends. Cover the salmon with alternating strips from each side at a slight angle so that they cross in the center.

Brush with the beaten egg. Bake in a preheated 425 degree oven until brown and flaky, about 30 minutes.   Serves 8.

Fish a la Tripoli

When Jews were expelled from Spain in 1492, many had Italy or the Turkish Empire as their destinations. Unscrupulous sea captains, despite having been paid for the passage, frequently took their passengers to the northern coast of Africa where they were sold into slavery. Moorish slave markets existed in all the North African countries, but Tripoli was a large center for this activity. This continued even when, later, the Jews were forced to leave Portugal. King Manuel insisted that they leave on any departing ship, regardless of destination. Many went to North Africa. In the sixteenth century, some Jews owned and captained their own ships and manned them with Jewish crews. The infamous Barbary Coast pirates often captured these ships whose passengers and crews also were enslaved. Jews all over the world, including those in the distant New World colonies, raised funds to ransom as many of their coreligionists as possible. Ths fund raising was a continuous process for as long as the condition existed.

A 4 lb. solid fleshed fish	1 cup water
2 lbs. potatoes, peeled and sliced	6 anchovy filets
salt and pepper	6 strips pimento
melted butter	cooked carrots
3 chopped scallions	cooked broccoli
1 tablespoon chopped parsley	

In a generously buttered serving dish arrange sliced potatoes to cover the bottom. Sprinkle with salt and pepper. Add the scallions. Drizzle a little of the melted butter over potatoes. Place the whole fish on the potatoes, having first salted and peppered the cavity. Drizzle with butter.

There should be between 1 and 2 inches between the fish and the sides of the dish. Pour the water along the sides and cover with oiled paper. Bake in a preheated 375 degree oven for about 45 minutes or until fish flakes easily. Remove from the oven and pour a little more melted butter over the fish. Arrange the anchovy filets and 1/2 inch wide strips of pimento on the fish in a diagonal or cross hatch pattern. Sprinkle lightly with parsley. Arrange hot, cooked carrots on one side of the fish and hot cooked broccoli on the other. Cover and return to the oven for 5 minutes. Serve with Hollandaise sauce or a mixture of mayonnaise, prepared mustard, lemon juice, and a little wine. Warm slightly.   Serves 6 to 8.

Eggs, Cheese, Rice and Pasta

Eggs, Cheese, Rice and Pasta

Huevos Rancheros
(Mexican Ranch Style Eggs)

During the Inquisition period in Mexico, Simon Vaez was a leader of one of the secret Jewish groups. His hacienda, or ranch, was used for religious services. In order not to arouse the suspicion of the inquisitors or their informers, the Jews, who ostensibly professed Catholicism, arrived at his home in twos or threes and from different directions. Eggs were habitually eaten on the evening before Yom Kippur, as they were on all solemn occasions.

16 canned tortillas	1 (8 oz.) can tomato sauce
1/4 cup oil	1/2 cup vegetable bouillon
1 clove garlic	8 eggs
1/4 small onion, minced	salt
2 or 3 Jalapena chiles, minced	

Saute the onions and garlic in the oil. Discard the garlic. Add the tomato sauce, vegetable bouillon, chiles, and salt. Stir. Cover and cook for 15 minutes. In another frying pan, heat the tortillas in a little hot oil, about 3 seconds on each side. Quickly blot with paper towels and place four on each plate. Put two fried eggs on each plate and cover with the tomato mixture. This may be garnished with a little grated Swiss cheese. On the plate may also be added some *frijoles refritos* (refried beans). See page 163. Sliced avocado is also used as a garnish.   Serves 4.

Matzo Brie
(Egg Fried Matzo)

In the city of Carpentras, France, there is an old cellar in a synagogue courtyard. It still holds two wall ovens, large kneading blocks, a dough mixer, and a millstone. It was matzo bakery. One of the kneading blocks is inscribed with information of its origin, "Gad of Digne — a gift — 1652." According to a local story, one of the marble slabs was given to the bakery by the Pope to aid in the preparation of matzos.

Matzo is the unleavened bread used during Pesach. It is usually covered with good, fresh butter or cream cheese. A fine flour-like meal made from matzo is used in baking sponge cakes and other Pesach delicacies. The matzo itself is used in a variety of ways. One favorite breakfast or luncheon dish is the following *matzo brie*.

6 eggs	1 teaspoon vanilla
2/3 cup milk	8 matzos
1 teaspoon salt	butter
2 tablespoons sugar	

Beat together the eggs, milk, salt, sugar, and vanilla. Hold each matzo under hot running water for a few seconds. Break into a bowl and pour the egg mixture over. Mix well. The matzos should absorb much of the liquid. Heat some butter in a frying pan and add the matzo mixture. This may be fried, over low heat, without stirring, until one side is lightly browned or it may be stirred as with scrambled eggs. Cook until almost dry. Serve with sugar and cinnamon, honey, jam or cooked fruit.

Serves 6 to 8.

Pureed Onion Omelet

The word omelet derives from an old French form, *alemelle,* which meant a thin plate. The word described the egg dish which was thin, tender, and made with all sorts of imaginative additions.

6 or 7 large onions,	6 eggs
very finely chopped	salt
1/3 cup olive oil	

Heat the oil and add the onions. Stir over moderately high heat until the onions are coated with the oil. Cover tightly and turn the heat down. Do not stir for about 25 minutes. After that stir frequently to prevent sticking. After about an hour the onions will be dark and pureed. Beat three eggs with the salt. Stir half of the onion puree into the eggs and pour into the pan in which the onions were cooked. When the omelet is almost set, put a plate over it and invert the omelet onto the plate. Slip the omelet back into the pan to cook the other side briefly. Repeat with the remaining eggs and onions. Fold the omelet over in half. Garnish with watercress. Serve at once.   Serves 3 to 6.

Omelet Tarragona

In the cloister of the Cathedral of Tarragona, Spain, there is a seventh-century stone inscribed in both Latin and Hebrew to "Isadora, daughter of Jonathas and Axia." There is also a house nearby in which the stones surrounding one window are inscribed in Hebrew and are obviously two tombstones, one of Hayim ben Isaac and the other, Hananias ben Simeon, both from the year 1300. There was a sizable Jewish community in that city from the seventh century, as indicated by Jewish coins which were excavated and which now may be seen in the Archeological Museum. The Jewish Quarter had been in the part of the city now known as Plaza de las Monjas de la Ensenanza (The Plaza of the Teaching Nuns).

1/2 cup oil	6 potatoes, boiled and cubed
2 onions, coarsely chopped	6 eggs
1 teaspoon dried tarragon	salt and pepper

Saute the onions in the oil until they are limp. Add the cubed potatoes and fry until lightly colored. Beat the eggs with the salt and tarragon and pour over the potato mixture. Cook until almost set. Cover the pan with a plate and invert. Slip the omelet back into the pan to cook the other side. This may be served hot or cold as a luncheon dish or hors d'oeurve.   Serves 4 to 6.

Venetian Chanukah Souffle

In the Middle Ages, the Jews of Venice illuminated their homes during the week of Chanukah with lamps and torches set outside the doors and windows. Groups of Jews in gondolas, rowing through the canals of the Jewish Quarter, stopped to repeat the benediction and sing in a chorus before each illuminated house.

Pancakes are part of the Chanukah celebration. They take many forms, depending on the geographical area of the cook. In Eastern Europe the potato pancake was customary. In Israel the jelly doughnut is the "pancake," and in Italy this souffle is the Chanukah "pancake."

4 tablespoons butter	5 egg yolks
1/3 cup sugar	2 tablespoons grated
4-1/2 tablespoons flour	orange rind
1 cup milk	1/8 teaspoon salt
4 tablespoons orange liqueur	7 egg whites, beaten

Melt the butter in a saucepan and add the sugar. Stir until the sugar is melted. Dissolve the flour in the milk and add to the butter mixture. Add the liqueur, mixing continuously until thickened. Remove from heat and beat in the egg yolks, one at a time. Cool. Add orange rind. Add the salt to the egg whites and beat until very stiff. Fold into the yolk mixture. Pour into a 10 cup casserole and bake in a preheated 375 degree oven for about 45 minutes. Serve immediately.   Serves 4 to 6.

Curried Eggs

A curious mixture, called *mey'ah mubarakah,* used to be sold in Egypt only during the first ten days of the month of Moharram, in the Arabic calendar. This mixture contained coriander seeds, fennel seed, frankincense, and salt dyed to indigo blue, vermillion red, and saffron yellow. This concoction was kept all year and was used to throw into the fire when someone was ill or in danger. The smoke from the fire was directed toward the endangered person. This was thought to ward off evil spirits.

Salt has always been important in Jewish ritual. Sacrifices at the Temple always included salt. The piece of bread over which grace before meals is said is always salted first. In Ezra 4:14 is the passage, *"Now because we eat the salt of the palace . . . it is not meant for us to see the king's dishonor. . . ."* To eat the salt of a man or to eat the salt of the palace meant that the man or palace officials paid the worker "salt money" or a "salarium" or a "salary."

Salt was sprinkled on new mothers and on a child at the time of circumcision.

4 tablespoons butter	salt and pepper
1 large onion, chopped	8 hard-boiled eggs
1 clove garlic, finely minced	cooked rice
2 tablespoons curry powder	grated orange rind
4 tablespoons flour	chutney
2-2/3 cups milk, heated	finely-chopped parsley

Saute the onion in the butter until transparent. Add the garlic and curry powder and saute lightly. Add the flour and stir until foamy. Add the hot milk all at once and stir briskly with a wire whisk until thickened. Place the egg halves on a bed of rice. Pour the sauce over. Garnish with grated orange rind, chutney, and parsley.   Serves 6 to 8.

French Eggs

These eggs take their name from the fact that they are based on french toast.

6 eggs, beaten	1/2 teaspoon dried chervil
3/4 cup coffee cream	1 teaspoon finely-chopped
salt and pepper	parsley
6 slices white bread	salt and pepper
6 eggs	1/2 cup grated swiss cheese
3 tablespoons coffee cream	

Make French toast by combining 6 eggs, 3/4 cup coffee cream, salt, and pepper. Soak each slice of bread in the mixture and fry gently in the butter, browning both sides. Place in a flat, buttered baking pan. Lightly beat together the remaining 6 eggs, coffee cream, chervil, parsley, salt, and pepper. Scramble in butter. When about half finished, arrange on the toast pieces. Sprinkle with the cheese. Bake in a preheated 375-degree oven until the cheese is melted and the eggs are set.   Serves 6.

Huevos al Nido
(Eggs In A Nest)

Toledo holds much of interest for the Jewish historian. One of the less momentous evidences of Jewish life in that city is contained in the Provincial Museum where a wooden beam is inscribed in Hebrew with the date 980. There is also a stone of the eleventh century carrying the message, "Inn of the Esquina" (The Corner Inn). In Hebrew are added the words, "Food and rooms."

8 hard rolls	1/2 lb. Cheddar cheese, grated
1/2 cup milk	salt and pepper
4 tablespoons melted butter	4 egg whites, beaten
1 teaspoon dried tarragon,	1/2 cup olive oil
rubbed between the palms	1 clove garlic, halved
8 poached eggs	

Cut the top-third off each roll and scoop out most of the inside. Pour 1 tablespoon of milk and 1/2 tablespoon of the melted butter in each roll. Sprinkle in a pinch of the powdered tarragon. Put a poached egg in each roll. Sprinkle 1/4 cup cheese on each egg. Beat the egg whites with the salt and pepper until stiff. Make a mounded top of the meringue on each roll. Saute the garlic in the oil. Discard the garlic. Place the stuffed rolls in the hot oil and fry, spooning the oil over the egg whites, which will puff and brown slightly.

Cooked meat or salami may be substituted for the cheese, in which case omit the milk and substitute margarine for the butter, using a little more.   Serves 8.

Rice Omelet Oria

An interesting dedication took place in 1965 in the town of Oria, in the southern part of Italy. In front of the main gate of the city, still called Porta degli Ebrei (Gate of the Hebrews), a plaza was dedicated and named Piazza Shabatai Donnolo. In the middle of the plaza a small monument to Shabatai ben Abraham Donnolo was unveiled. He was a

Jew who lived in that town, as a member of the active Jewish community of the tenth century. He was a famous physician and wrote advanced tomes on medicine, the first Jew to do so in Europe. Among the things he advocated was restricted use of meat in the diet, substituting rice and vegetables.

5 tablespoons butter
4 red, but not completely
  ripe, tomatoes
3/4 cup matzo meal
1/2 teaspoon sugar
1/2 teaspoon salt
1/2 teaspoon pepper
1/2 teaspoon basil
2 green peppers, cut into
  strips

butter
1 large onion, coarsely chopped
8 eggs, beaten
2 tablespoons sherry
salt and pepper
3/4 cup cooked rice
chopped black olives

Cut the tomatoes in 1/2 inch thick slices. Combine the matzo meal sugar, salt, pepper, and basil. Coat the tomato slices with this mixture and fry in the butter. Reserve. In the same pan fry the strips of green pepper and the onion until limp. Beat the eggs, add the sherry, salt and pepper, and cooked rice. Stir. Pour into the hot pan containing the green pepper and onion. Cook until the eggs are set. Fold over and slide out on a warmed plate. Arrange tomato slices on top of the omelet. Garnish with chopped black olives. Serves 6 to 8.

Cheesed Apple Rings

Jonas Phillips opened a store in the wilds of Albany, New York, about 1759. He offered for sale "best Hyson green tea in pound cannisters, wines, brandies, raisins and nuts by the cask, Florence Oyl by the box, milk, fine cheese and butter, biscuits in casks" in exchange for "beaver and deer skins, small furs, etc." He married, fathered twenty-one children, went into bankruptcy as a result of British restrictions, became a *shochet* (ritual slaughterer) at a salary of £35 a year, served in the militia, became a successful merchant and respected citizen. (It is said that Washington attended the wedding of his daughter Zipporah to Mordecai M. Noah.) He was an active contributor of his time and money to Jewish interests and causes. He became the only outside person to address the Constitutional Convention. He pointed out the defective provision in the Pennsylvania constitution which required anyone holding public office to swear to the belief that the Old and New Testaments were both given by divine inspiration. He did not know that the decision had already been made to assure that no religious test shall ever be imposed as a qualification to any office or public trust in the United States.

4 large apples, cored, peeled, sliced	3/4 cup grated Cheddar cheese
sugar	1/2 cup coarsely chopped pecans

Cut the apples into slices about 1/2 inch thick. Lightly sprinkle with sugar. Place in the broiler about 6 inches from the heat and broil just long enough to make the slices tender. Do not permit them to get soft or lose their shape. Remove from the broiler, cover with the grated cheese, top with the nuts and return to the broiler. Remove when the cheese melts and begins to bubble.

This makes a nice accompaniment to broiled or fried fish. Serves 6 to 8.

Sirniki
(Cheese Pancakes)

Cottage cheese, also often called pot cheese, Dutch cheese or Schmier-kase, is one of the oldest forms of cheese. It is easily made in the home, where it was first produced and used, as indicated by its name. Another form of this curdled milk is called farm or farmer cheese, made originally, on the farms of France. In this form, the cheese is pressed under a weight to remove the whey. The result is a shaped cheese of slicing consistency.

3 cups cottage cheese	1/2 teaspoon baking powder
3 egg yolks	1/2 teaspoon salt
1 teaspoon vanilla extract	1/2 to 1 cup flour
1 teaspoon grated orange rind	1/2 cup raisins
3 tablespoons sugar	butter

Press the cottage cheese in a strainer to remove moisture. With an electric mixer combine the cheese, egg yolks, vanilla, orange rind, and sugar. Combine the baking powder, salt and flour. Add just enough to the egg mixture to cause it to hold its shape when dropped in a mound from a spoon. Add the raisins. Chill for an hour. Form pancakes about 1/2 inch thick and fry in butter until golden on both sides. Serve with sour cream, honey, cooked fruit, or a mixture of orange marmalade and sour cream.   Makes 15 to 20 pancakes.

Icebox Cheese Ring

At the end of the nineteenth century, Jews from Russia and Roumania were seeking means of leaving the oppressive living conditions and frequent persecutions of those countries. Jews in other parts of the world offered various kinds of help. Land was bought in Cyprus where some of the refugees were resettled and helped to establish agricultural colonies. Grapes and olives were planted, and cheese making was started. Unfortunately, these colonies failed. Recently there were about one-hundred-fifty Jewish families on Cyprus. On the site of one of the colonies, however, some Jews own and operate a large dairy farm and orange grove.

2 tablespoons unflavored
  gelatine
1/2 cup cold, clear vegetable
  broth
3 egg yolks
3/4 teaspoon curry powder

1/2 teaspoon salt
3 cups scalded milk
2 cups pot cheese, riced
1/2 cup pimento stuffed olives,
  chopped

Sprinkle gelatine over the broth. Beat the egg yolks with the salt and curry powder. Add a little of the hot milk to the egg mixture and cook over hot water, stirring until thickened. Gradually add the remaining milk. Add the cheese and blend well. Remove from the heat and stir in the dissolved gelatine mixture. Add the chopped olives. Pour into a 6 cup ring mold and refrigerate until set. Fill the center with fruit or vegetable salad. Serves 8 to 10.

French Fried Cheese Puffs

Jews in Strasbourg, France, suffered massacres during the Crusades and oppresions beginning in the twelfth century. For about four hundred years, ending with the French Revolution, Jews were not permitted in Strasbourg, except during certain hours, for stated purposes. The Jewish population in that city is now about thirteen thousand and supports a full complement of community organizations and institutions. It also has at least two kosher restaurants.

1/3 cup boiling water
1/2 cup butter
1 teaspoon dried thyme
1/2 teaspoon salt
1-1/4 cups sifted flour

4 eggs
3/4 cup grated Parmesan cheese
1/4 cup Cheddar cheese
oil for frying

Bring the water to a boil. Add the butter, salt, thyme. When butter is melted, remove from the heat and add the flour all at once, stirring quickly until blended. Return to heat and stir until mixture forms a ball. Remove from heat and add the eggs, one at a time, beating after each addition until completely blended. Add the cheeses and stir. Drop by the teaspoonful into deep, hot oil and fry until puffed and golden. These may be sprinkled with more grated Parmesan cheese while they are still hot.

Makes 4 to 5 dozen puffs.

Hungarian Cheese Balls

There is now one kosher restaurant in Budapest. It is the only public eating place in Hungary which is not state-controlled.

1/2 lb. pot cheese, riced	3 egg whites, beaten
3 egg yolks	1 cup fine, dry breadcrumbs
2 teaspoons chopped parsley	butter
salt and pepper	

To the cheese add the beaten egg yolks, parsley, salt and pepper. Blend thoroughly. Beat the egg whites until very stiff. Fold into the cheese mixture. Refrigerate for 30 minutes. Melt some butter in pan and add the breadcrumbs. Stir over low heat until golden. Reserve.

Form the cheese mixture into walnut-size balls and lower into gently boiling, salted water. Cook for about 10 minutes or until tender. Drain. Put the well drained cheese balls into the pan with the buttered breadcrumbs. Over low heat gently stir until the cheese balls are covered with the breadcrumb mixture. These dumplings are good with fish or vegetable dishes. Makes about 15 cheese balls.

Blintzes

Dishes made of dairy products, especially cheese, are part of the Shavuoth observance. Shavuoth is the Hebrew word for weeks. The festival marked the end of the weeks of the grain harvest in Palestine. It also marks the anniversary of the Giving of the Law on Mount Sinai. Confirmation of Jewish youth takes place in synagogues during this holiday.

Batter:	*Filling:*
2 eggs	3/4 cup cottage cheese
3/4 cup milk	2 egg yolks
1/4 cup water	1 teaspoon grated lemon rind
2 tablespoons salad oil	1/2 teaspoon vanilla extract
2/3 cup flour	2 tablespoons sugar
1/2 teaspoon salt	
butter for frying	

Batter: Beat eggs, milk, water, and oil together. Combine the flour and salt. Using a rotary beater, gradually add the flour to the egg mixture. Beat until smooth and the consistency of heavy cream. Melt about a teaspoonful of butter in a 6 or 7-inch frying pan. When it is hot, pour in the equivalent of 2 tablespoons of batter. (The usual large kitchen mixing-spoon holds about 2 tablespoons). Quickly tilt and rotate the pan to cover with the batter. Fry until lightly browned on one side. Cook only on one side. Repeat until all the batter has been used. Stack the crepes.

Filling: Combine all the ingredients for the filling and blend very well. Place about a tablespoon of filling on the cooked side of the crepe. Fold part of the crepe over the top. Fold in the sides and turn the filled blintz over so that the seam side is down. Place the blintzes in a large frying pan in which there is a generous amount of melted butter. Fry slowly, turning once, until golden on both sides. Serve with sour cream, berries or preserves.   Makes about 12 blintzes.

Boyo de Queso
(Cheese Filled Pastry)

The Jews of Greece serve these at teatime or on special occasions.

Filling:
1/4 lb. grated Parmesan cheese
1/4 lb. cream cheese
1/2 lb. cottage cheese
1/2 lb. Feta cheese
1 cup mashed potatoes
4 eggs
1/2 teaspoon salt

1/4 cup oil

Dough:
5 cups flour
1/2 teaspoon sugar
1/2 teaspoon salt
1/2 cup oil
1 cup cold water

Filling: Combine all the ingredients to make a smooth paste. Set aside.

Dough: Combine the flour, sugar, and salt. Combine the oil and water. Add 3 cups of the flour mixture to the water mixture. Stir until mixed then knead. Gradually knead in the remaining flour mixture. Cover with a tea towel and let rest for 15 minutes. Knead again for 8 to 10 minutes. Cut the dough into 12 equal pieces. On a lightly floured board, roll out each piece to approximately 10 x 20 inches. It should be paper thin.

Divide the filling into 12 equal portions. Place one portion of filling along the 10 inch side of the rolled out dough. Shape the filling so that it is about an inch in diameter and almost 10 inches long. Roll the filling firmly in the dough, turning the sides of the dough in. Repeat with each piece of dough. Place rolls about an inch apart on a greased cookied sheet. Bake in a preheated 350-degree oven for 1 hour, or until browned. Cut each roll in half to serve.   Makes 2 dozen 5 inch pieces.

Cheese Loaf

"And Jesse said unto David his son: 'Take now for thy brethren an ephah of this parched corn, and these ten loaves . . . and bring these ten cheeses unto the captain. . . . .'" (I Samuel 17:17) This errand to the camp of the Hebrews, who were engaged in a battle with the Philistines, resulted in David slaying Goliath.

1 cup cooked rice	salt and pepper
1 cup mashed potatoes	1/4 cup chopped canned tomatoes
1 tablespoon finely chopped	1/2 cup grated Cheddar cheese
onion	2 eggs, beaten

Combine all the ingredients. Mix very well. Pour into a well-greased loaf pan. Heat in a preheated 400-degree oven for 15 minutes. Cool. Refrigerate. Serve cold and sliced.

This is a good accompaniment to a luncheon salad.   Serves 8.

Kreplach

During Shavuoth and Simchat Torah (The Giving of the Law), *kreplach,* like blintzes and other cheese dishes, are eaten. There is a legend which says that when the Israelites returned from Mount Sinai, after Moses received the Ten Commandments, they found all their milk had curdled. Being weary and hungry, they ate it anyway. The eating of cheese, according to this story, commemorates that event.

Dough:	*Filling:*
2 cups sifted flour	1 lb. cottage cheese
1/4 teaspoon salt	2 egg yolks
2 eggs	1/2 teaspoon salt
2 tablespoons water	1/2 teaspoon grated lemon rind
	2 tablespoons sugar
	raisins (optional)

Dough: Combine the flour, salt, eggs, and water. Mix and knead on a floured board to a smooth dough. Roll out to 1/8-inch thickness. Cut into 2-inch squares.

Filling: Mix all the ingredients and blend well.

Place a spoonful of filling on each dough square and fold the dough over to make a triangle. Pinch the edges together. Drop into boiling, salted water. Remove when they rise to the top. Drain well. Top with melted butter and sour cream. Alternately, the kreplach can be fried after boiling. The dough squares may be filled with stewed fruit, as they are on Purim. They are then called *varenikes.* The dough, on other occasions, may be filled with cooked, chopped meat and served in chicken soup, in which case no cream or butter is used.   Serves 6 to 8.

Cheese Ramekins

Ramekin, or ramequin, originally indicated toasted or melted cheese. The recipe below is a variation of an eighteenth-century French Ramequin de Fromage. Other old ramekin recipes are similar to what we know today as Welsh rarebit. Now cheese ramekins are usually cheese filled tarts.

8 slices white bread, quartered	1-1/4 cups hot milk
8 slices Swiss or Cheddar cheese, 1/4 inch thick	1/2 cup wine
2 eggs, beaten	salt and pepper
	pinch nutmeg

Cut the bread slices into quarters, using half of them to line a generously greased, flat baking dish. Cover completely with cheese slices. Cover the cheese with the remaining pieces of bread.

Beat the eggs. Add a little of the hot milk, stirring. Add this egg mixture to the remaining hot milk which has been combined with the wine. Mix well. Add salt, pepper and nutmeg. Pour this over the bread and cheese. Let rest for 5 minutes. Place in a preheated 350-degree oven. Bake for about 20 minutes or until all the liquid has been absorbed and the top is golden.   Serves 6 to 8.

Tvoroinki
(Russian Cream Cheese Dumplings)

In Russia, for several centuries prior to the thirteenth, near what is now Astrakhan, lived a group of people called Khazars. For a long time they were unknown to the outside Jewish world, but in the tenth century, a traveller, Eldad ha-Dani, came upon them and found Jewish rites being observed. He thought that he had discovered the Lost Ten Tribes of Israel. However, only the *chaghan,* king, and those of the royal court and the nobles practiced Judaism. The story is told that Bulan, an early Khazar king, had a dream which resulted in his embracing Judaism. His court and nobles followed. From that time forward the ruling class was Jewish. During the Byzantine era, the Arabic writer, Al-Majdisi recorded, "The Khazari have honey and many sheep from which curdled milk is made into round pellets."

2 cups flour	2 tablespoons sour cream
1 tablespoon butter	salt and pepper
1/2 lb. cream cheese	paprika
3 eggs, beaten	finely-chopped parsley

Put one cup of the flour into a bowl. Add the butter and cheese. With a pastry cutter, cut the butter and cheese into the flour until very fine. Add the beaten eggs, sour cream, salt, and pepper. Blend thoroughly. Gradually add the remaining flour, making a smooth dough. Form balls the size of walnuts and drop into gently boiling water for about 15 minutes, or until they float to the top. Drain and serve with melted butter and sprinkled with paprika and chopped parsley.

Makes about 25 dumplings.

Tyropitta
(Greek Cheese Pie)

Phyllo is the Greek word for leaf. The dough so named is leaf thin and used in many layers. It can be bought in gourmet shops or Middle East grocery stores. This dish can also be made with a spinach filling. It is then called *spanakopitta.*

3/4 lb. Feta cheese	3 tablespoons butter
1/2 lb. cream cheese	3 tablespoons flour
1/2 lb. cottage cheese	1-1/3 cups milk
8 eggs	3/4 lb. (about 18 sheets)
1/8 teaspoon pepper	phyllo dough
1 teaspoon chopped dill	1/2 lb. butter, melted
2 tablespoons chopped parsley	

Crumble the Feta cheese into a bowl. Add the cream cheese and cottage cheese. Add the beaten eggs, pepper, dill, and parsley. Blend well. In a saucepan melt 3 tablespoons of butter, add the flour and stir to a smooth paste. Add milk gradually, stirring until thickened. Cool. Combine the milk and cheese mixtures. Mix well. Butter a 9x12 baking pan. Line the pan with a sheet of the dough. Brush with melted butter and add another sheet of dough. Butter and repeat the process until 9 sheets of dough have been used. (Keep the dough covered while preparing this dish. It dries out very quickly and becomes difficult to use). Pour the cheese mixture into the prepared pan. Cover with the remaining sheets, brushing each one with melted butter. Tuck in the edges of the dough around the pan. With a sharp, pointed knife, cut through the top sheets to mark off diamond shaped serving pieces. Brush top with remaining butter.

Bake in a preheated 350-degree oven for 30 to 40 minutes or until the pastry is flaky and golden. Serve warm. Serves 12.

Swiss Cheese Pie

This is one interesting variation of the *quiche*. The quiche originates in Alsace-Lorraine, which has dual French-German influences. Quiche is sometimes spelled *kiche*. Some say that the origin of both words is the German *kuchen*. Originally, quiches were made with bread dough but are now made with short dough or puff pastry.

Crust:
1-1/4 cups sifted flour
1/2 teaspoon salt
7 tablespoons shortening
3 tablespoons cold water

Filling:
3 tablespoons butter

4 large onions, chopped
1/2 lb. sliced mushrooms
salt and pepper
3 large potatoes, boiled
   and mashed
1/2 lb. Emmenthal cheese, grated
1/2 lb. Gruyere cheese, grated
2 eggs, beaten

Crust: Combine the flour and salt in a bowl. With a pastry cutter, cut in the shortening until it has the consistency of fine sand. Add the water and toss to form a dough which "cleans" the bowl. Push together into a ball. Roll out between two pieces of wax paper to line a 9-inch pie pan. Make a high, fluted rim.

Filling: Saute the onions and mushrooms in the butter. Add salt and pepper. Combine the mashed potatoes, the Emmenthal and Gruyere cheeses and the beaten eggs. Blend very well. Put half of the filling in the unbaked pie shell. Spread the mushroom mixture over the filling. Top with the rest of the filling. Bake in a preheated 425-degree oven for about 30 to 35 minutes or until nicely browned. This can be used either as hors d'oeuvre or a luncheon dish.   Serves 8 to 16.

Georgia Peach Cheese Puffs

Raphael J. Moses was elected to the first General Assembly of Georgia after the Civil War. He was a descendent of Dr. Samuel Nunez, physician to the King of Portugal. Nunez escaped from the Inquisition on an English boat and arrived in the new Georgia colony founded by Oglethorpe on the Savannah River in 1733. Moses practiced law in Columbus but experimented with fruit growing. He was the first person to ship peaches and plums by stagecoach to Savannah and then by steamer to New York. He was paid thirty dollars a basket and soon did more fruit shipping than law practicing. However, his prosperity ended with the war in which he served with distinction, achieving the rank of major. A fierce patriot, until his death at age eighty-three, his calling cards carried the words, "Major in the Army of the United States."

2 egg yolks	3/4 cup flour
1/4 cup water	1/2 cup finely diced fresh peaches
2 tablespoons sugar	or
1/2 teaspoon powdered ginger	well drained canned peaches
salt	2 egg whites
1 lb. cottage cheese	oil for frying

Thoroughly beat the egg yolks with the water, sugar, ginger and salt. Add the cottage cheese and flour, gradually, stirring until completely blended. Stir in the peaches. Beat the egg whites until stiff and fold into the cheese mixture. Heat the oil in a large frying pan and drop the cheese mixture into it by large spoonfuls. Fry until golden on both sides. Drain on absorbent paper. Sprinkle with sugar and cinnamon immediately.   Makes about 12 puffs.

Kashe Varnishkes
(Pasta with Buckwheat Groats)

Folksongs are the result of concerns of daily life. Many derive from the occupations of the impromptu troubadors. One such Yiddish folksong is the result of the concerns of a young lady in an East European *shtetl* (small town). She is making the dough for the *varnishkes*. She seems distraught when she asks, "Where can be found a board on which to roll the varnishkes? With flour, chicken fat, salt or pepper, where can be found a board?" She goes on to cry for a knife with which to cut the varnishkes and a pot in which to cook them. But the climax of her woes is expressed in the last verse when she asks, "Help! Where is to be found a young man to eat my varnishkes?"

1-1/2 cups coarse buckwheat groats	1/4 lb. margarine
1 egg, beaten	3 onions, chopped
2-1/2 cups boiling vegetable bouillon	8 oz. pasta bow knots
1 teaspoon salt	1 teaspoon salt
	1/2 teaspoon pepper

Combine the beaten egg and the groats, mixing well. Place over moderate heat and stir until groat kernels are separated and dry. Add the boiling vegetable bouillon and the salt. Cover and reduce heat. Cook for about 20 minutes or until groats are fluffy and dry.

In a large skillet, saute the onion in the margarine. Cook the pasta according to package directions. Drain well and add to the onions. Add the groats, salt and pepper. Mix lightly but thoroughly. Heat, if necessary.

Serves 6 to 8.

Kasha
(Buckwheat Groats)

Buckwheat is among the oldest of cultivated grains. Its short growing season and its hardiness have resulted in its widespread cultivation. It is a staple in the Balkan countries. *Kasha,* the cereal product, is closely identified with Russian cooking. It is used as a porridge, with noodle products, in *cholent,* as an accompaniment to meats and as a filling for *pirogin* (filled dough triangles). Buckwheat flour is used in *blini,* (Russian pancakes) and bread.

Without potatoes and kasha many Jews in Eastern Europe would not have been able to survive. There is a Yiddish expression to describe minimal earning or profit. "He will make enough to buy the water in which to cook kasha."

3 tablespoons margarine	1-1/2 cups coarse buckwheat groats
2 tablespoons finely minced parsley	1 egg, beaten
2 celery stalks, finely chopped	3 cups boiling vegetable bouillon
3 scallions, finely chopped	salt and pepper

In a large skillet saute in the margarine the parsley, celery and scallions. Reserve.

In another skillet, combine the beaten egg and the groats. Mix well. Over moderate heat, stir until the groats are separated and dry. Add to the sauteed mixture. Mix. Add the boiling bouillon, salt and pepper. Cook covered over moderate heat for about 20 minutes or until groats are fluffy and all the liquid has been absorbed. This makes a good accompaniment to meat or fish.   Serves 8.

Burghul Pilaf

Burghul is cracked wheat. During the paleolithic age, man's first cooking utensil was invented in order to crack the hard kernels of the wild grasses, progenitors of modern grains, to make them more digestible. Food, until that time, was held over or thrown into the fire to cook. There was no useful way to do this with the grass kernels, so stones were laid over the fire to heat. The kernels were placed on the stones and the husks cracked off the edible portion. Later it was discovered that they could be softened by soaking or boiling.

1/2 lb. margarine	2 cups burghul
1/3 cup pine nuts	2 cups beef broth
2 onions, finely chopped	1/2 teaspoon salt
1/2 lb. mushrooms, sliced	1/2 teaspoon dried mint leaves
1/2 cup celery, finely diced	

Melt 1/4 cup margarine in a skillet. Add the pine nuts and fry until slightly colored. Remove the nuts from the pan and reserve.

To the pan add the onions and mushrooms. Saute until soft. Add the celery and stir for 5 minutes. Add the burghul and continue to fry, stirring, for 10 minutes. Add the beef broth and salt. Mix well and cover. Simmer about 12 minutes or until all the liquid is absorbed. Rub the dried mint between the palms of the hands and sprinkle on top. Melt the remaining margarine and drizzle over the top.

Stretch a clean tea towel over the pan and replace the cover. Leave over lowest possible heat for about 30 minutes. Turn onto a warmed dish and sprinkle the toasted pine nuts on top.

This is a good accompaniment to fish, chicken or meat.

Serves 8 to 10.

Yemenite Burghul with Eggplant

In 1950 the Yemenites were brought to Israel by plane in Operation Magic Carpet. They had been isolated in Yemen for centuries. Their dress, use of Hebrew, customs and appearance were so unique that linguists and sociologists set about recording them. They are a delightful, industrious, artistic, and musical people. Much of the valued jewelry and embroidery in Israel is produced by them. They are also intensely religious, having relied on and guarded the religious forms which came down to them from their ancestors. There are several legends surrounding their origin. One states that while wandering in the desert, after having left Egypt, one group left the main body of people and went toward the south, remaining in what is now called Yemen. Another version, which has some acceptance, has it that the Queen of Sheba was so impressed with King Solomon's wisdom and success that she took back to her country some of Solomon's advisors, hoping to endow her realm with similar efficiency. The descendants of these advisors are said, according to this account, to be the Yemenites.

The Yemenites are a small, delicately structured people whose food tastes reflect this. They take whatever time is necessary to carefully prepare fresh food for each meal. Much of their diet consists of cereals and grains, which they are careful to balance with other ingredients.

2 eggplants	2-1/2 cups chicken consomme
salt	salt
1/2 lb. margarine	1/8 teaspoon cayenne
2 onions, coarsely chopped	flour
2 cloves garlic, minced	salt and pepper
1 lb. burghul	oil for frying

Peel and cut the eggplant into 1 inch cubes. Salt and place in a colander for 30 minutes.

Saute the onion and garlic in 4 tablespoons of the butter. Add the burghul and fry lightly. Add the consomme, salt, pepper, and cayenne. Cook, covered, over very low heat until liquid is absorbed and burghul is soft, about 30 minutes.

While the burghul is cooking, rinse and dry the eggplant cubes. Roll in the seasoned flour and fry in deep oil until golden.

Turn out the burghul onto a warmed plate and top with the eggplant cubes. Melt the remaining butter and drizzle over the top.

Serves 8 to 10.

Persian Burghul with Fruit

Since the holiday Shavuoth symbolized the marriage of God and the People of Israel, the Jews of Persia prepared for it as for a wedding. Grain and cereal dishes and dairy foods figured prominently on the menus. Fruits and sweet delicacies were also included. The men sat up all night reading from the Bible, particularly from the Book of Ruth. The women served coffee to help the men stay awake. A *ketuba* (marriage contract) was read, as it is at weddings.

1/2 lb. dried apricots	2 teaspoons dried rosemary
1/2 lb. raisins	1/2 teaspoon allspice
1/3 cup margarine	2 cups burghul
3 onions, chopped	3 cups boiling liquid
3 celery stalks, with leaves,	1/2 cup pistachio nuts, coarsely
chopped	chopped
1 tablespoon finely-chopped	
parsley	

Soak apricots and raisins in water to cover overnight. Drain. Reserve water.

In a large skillet saute the onions and celery in the margarine. Add the parsley, rosemary and allspice. Stir for 1 minute. Add the burghul and stir to coat the grains with the margarine and spice. Add the apricots and raisins. Stir. To the reserved soaking liquid add enough water to make 3 cups. Bring to a boil and add to the burghul mixture. Cover and simmer for about thirty minutes or until the liquid is absorbed and the burghul is soft. Garnish with the pistachio nuts.   Serves 8 to 10.

Mamaliga
(Yellow Cornmeal Slices)

Despite residence in one of the Iron Curtain countries, the Jewish population of Roumania fares somewhat better than the Jews of Russia. Jewish culture and religious life is permitted in some of its aspects. The distribution of *matzos* and kosher wine for Pesach is permitted.

This dish was added to the Jewish cuisine by those coming from Roumania where a ritual was made of cutting the cold *mamaliga* with a strong cotton thread.

1 cup yellow cornmeal	3 cups boiling water
1 cup cold water	3 tablespoons margarine
1 teaspoon salt	

Combine 1 cup of cold water with the cornmeal. Stir until smooth. Add salt to the boiling water. Very gradually add the cornmeal mixture to the boiling water. Stir constantly with a wooden spoon over very low heat. Keep the mixture smooth by stirring constantly until the mixture comes away from the sides of the pan when stirred. Add the margarine. Blend. Pour into a greased, flat pan. Smooth the top. Chill. Slice 1/2 inch thick.

At this point there are several choices in completing the preparation.
1. Fry the slices in butter and serve with jam or syrup.
2. Layer the slices in a greased pan, sprinkling grated cheese between the layers. Bake.
3. Pour tomato-meat sauce over the slices and bake. (Italian polenta).
4. Mix cheese, fried onions (or almost anything) into the hot mixture and serve, without chilling.   Serves 6.

Rice Casserole Vitoria

This dish is neither entirely French nor Spanish, coming as it does from the border area where these countries adjoin.

When the Jews were banished from Spain, the Jewish community of Vitoria, because of the fair treatment it had received, presented to the city its cemetery, Judemendi, Jewish Hill. The only condition imposed upon this town, close to the French border, was that "no plow shall ever furrow its soil." The condition was accepted and for more than four hundred years the cemetery was maintained. But there has not been a Jewish community in the immediate area since then. In 1953, the officials of Vitoria wanted to remove the disintegrating tombstones and turn the cemetery into a park but they would not do so without some kind of official Jewish permission. The nearest Jewish community was the one in Bayonne, France, just over the border. The officials sought and received the necessary permission. The place is today a lovely flowered and tree-shaded park. The city fathers erected a stone monument in the center indicating the history of the spot.

1/3 cup olive oil	1 can chick peas
1 onion, coarsely cut	salt and pepper
2 garlic cloves, minced	2 cups rice
1 bay leaf	5 cups chicken broth
1 teaspoon dried rosemary	4 eggs
2 chickens, cut into serving pieces	1 teaspoon chervil
2 lbs. boneless veal, cut into 2-inch pieces	

In a flat casserole or paella pan saute the onion and garlic in the oil. Add the bay leaf and rosemary. Stir. Add the chicken pieces and veal. Stir and brown lightly. Combine the liquid from the can of chick peas and 1 cup of water. Add to the chicken mixture. Add salt and pepper. Cover tightly and cook over very low heat until tender. Add 5 cups of chicken broth. Bring to a brisk boil. Add the rice and chick peas. Stir for a moment. Bring back to a boil. Lower heat and simmer, covered, until rice is tender. If the liquid is absorbed before the rice is tender add a little boiling water, but only enough to cook the rice. Beat the eggs with the dried chervil and carefully pour over the rice. Place immediately in a preheated 450-degree oven for a few minutes to form a golden crust.   Serves 8 to 10.

Jaffa Gate Saffron Rice

Saffron, the world's most expensive herb, is the stigma of a species of crocus. The Greek word for saffron is *krokus*. The stigmas are picked by hand, and almost one hundred thousand of them are required to make a pound. Saffron has been used through the ages as a dye, a cosmetic, a medicine, and an aromatic food ingredient.

Saffron, as well as other herbs and spices, are sold from the stalls inside the Jaffa Gate entrance to the old city of Jerusalem.

5 tablespoons butter	3/4 cup raisins, soaked in hot water and drained
2 teaspoons cumin seeds	1/2 cup whole almonds
1 teaspoon ground coriander	2 cups cooked rice
1/8 teaspoon saffron powder	salt and pepper

Lightly saute the cumin, coriander, saffron, raisins, and almonds in the butter. Add salt and pepper. Add the cooked rice and stir until each grain is buttered. Add 1 tablespoon water. Cover tightly and steam over low heat for 5 minutes. This is good with either meat or fish.

Serves 2 or 3.

Greek Fried Rice Balls

From its earliest appearance in India, the planting of rice spread to China, Egypt, and Greece. In medieval times, Spain traded rice and saffron for the wines of France and Gorgonzola cheese from Italy.

1 cup rice	1 onion, chopped
1 cup boiling water	1 teaspoon dried basil
2 cups scalded milk	oil for frying
1-1/2 teaspoons salt	2 tablespoons finely-chopped
1/4 cup butter	parsley
1/2 lb. mushrooms, sliced	

To the boiling water add the rice and cook over low heat until the rice has absorbed all the water. Add the scalded milk and salt. Cover and cook until the rice is quite soft. Lightly butter a flat pan and spread the rice in it to cool.

Saute the onion and mushrooms in the butter. Add the basil. Cover and remove from heat. Reserve.

Shape the cold rice into walnut-size balls and fry in deep oil until golden. Remove to a warmed dish and cover with the sauteed mixture. Garnish with the chopped parsley.

To use the rice balls for dessert, add 2 teaspoons of vanilla to the scalded milk. Omit the onion and mushrooms, basil and parsley. When fried sprinkle immediately with cinnamon and sugar, or serve jam or honey separately.

Serves 3 or 4.

Peruvian Fish-Rice Mold

The secret Jews in Latin America, from the sixteenth through the eighteenth century, were guilt-ridden about the way that they practiced their religion. Because of the persistent persecution by the Inquisition officials, the practice of Judaism had to be a strictly-guarded secret. Ostensibly, all the people were Catholic. Therefore, it was impossible to observe and fully practice traditional Judaism. In order to acknowledge recognition of their deficiencies and to make a symbolic sacrifice of repentance, the meals before religious holidays were restricted to eggs, vegetables, olives, and cereals.

24 pimento-stuffed olives
4 tablespoons butter
1 onion, chopped
1 clove garlic, minced
2 lbs. thick fish filet
flour
salt and pepper
1/2 cup white wine
1-1/2 cups tomato juice
1/2 teaspoon dried oregano
1/2 teaspoon dried basil

salt and pepper
1-1/2 cups cream
2 tablespoons butter
2 cups rice
4-1/4 cups vegetable bouillon
3/4 cup grated Swiss cheese
1/4 cup grated Parmesan cheese
2 tablespoons finely chopped
   parsley
1 tablespoon finely chopped
   dill

In a bowl, cover the olives with boiling water. After thirty minutes drain and set aside. In the 4 tablespoons of butter saute the onion and garlic. Cut the fish filets into 1-1/2 inch cubes. Dredge them in seasoned flour and saute quickly to brown. Dissolve 1 tablespoon of flour in the wine. Add to the fish. Add the tomato juice, oregano, olives, and basil. Add salt and pepper. Cover and simmer until fish is tender. Stir in the cream. Heat but do not boil.

In a flat casserole, brown the rice in 2 tablespoons butter. Bring bouillon to a boil and pour over the rice and stir. Quickly stir in the Parmesan and Swiss cheeses. Put the casserole into a preheated 400-degree oven for about 20 minutes, or until rice is tender and liquid has been absorbed. Pack the rice into a buttered 6 cup mold. In 10 minutes unmold it on a warmed plate. With a slotted spoon, put the fish mixture into the center of the molded rice. Spoon a little of the sauce over the fish and garnish with the parsley and dill. Pass the remaining sauce separately.   Serves 8.

Mejedrah
(Lentils and Rice)

Rice is the diet staple of over fifty percent of the world's population. It has been grown on every continent since neolithic times. For many people the idea of rice cultivation conjures up scenes of Orientals working in the marshy rice paddies. But rice also grows in normally irrigated soil at altitudes of over five thousand feet. Carolina rice is most popularly used in this country. The Italians and Spanish enjoy the Arborio variety. In Indian and Persian cookery, Basmati rice is preferred. In Mexico, Patna rice, originally from India, is sold. Each has distinctive size, shape and color. Their individual characteristics of starchiness, tenderness, or cooking time make each suitable for a particular cooking style.

4 large onions, sliced	1/2 lb. large, brown lentils
4 tablespoons olive oil	chicken or beef bouillon
1/2 cup pine nuts, almonds or pistachio nuts	1 cup rice

Heat the oil in a large pan. Fry the onion slices until lightly browned. Add the nuts and fry until golden. Remove onions and nuts from oil and reserve. Add the lentils to the oil in the pan. Add enough bouillon to cover. Simmer for 1 to 1-1/2 hours until lentils are soft but remain whole. Add the rice, and salt and pepper to taste. Add just enough hot bouillion to cover. Bring to a boil and immediately reduce heat to simmer. Cover and cook for 15 to 20 minutes or until rice is tender and the liquid has been absorbed. Serve hot, garnished with the fried onions and nuts.

Serves 6 to 8.

Arroz con Alcachofas
(Spanish Rice with Artichokes)

The Turks are credited with devising the method of cooking rice which includes sauteing as a first step. The results were so successful that the method spread to the Balkans and the Iberian Peninsula.

1/3 cup olive oil	2 tablespoons finely chopped dill
2 cups rice	1/2 teaspoon powdered saffron
2 small onions, finely chopped	3 pimentos, cut into strips
3 cloves garlic, minced	12 canned artichoke hearts
1 cup mushrooms, sliced	1/2 cup chopped peanuts
salt and pepper	1/2 cup black olives, well-
5 cups vegetable bouillon	drained, cut

Saute in the oil the rice, onions, garlic, and mushrooms, until the rice begins to color. Add salt and pepper. Bring the bouillon to a boil. Add to the rice mixture. Add the dill and saffron. Transfer to a flat casserole. Cover and bake in a preheated 375-degree oven for 35 minutes, or until rice is tender and liquid has almost been absorbed. Remove from oven and arrange the artichoke hearts and pimento strips on top. Cover and return to the oven for 10 minutes. Combine the chopped peanuts and the cut olives and sprinkle around the edges of the casserole.

Serves 6 to 8.

Spinach and Rice

In the Merced Market of Mexico City, the long line of chili stalls seem to hold hundreds of varieties of dried chilis. The colors are almost as numerous as the sizes and shapes. One wonders how so many chilis can be consumed since the majority are fiery enough for one of them to cause a digestive volcanic eruption in a whole family unaccustomed to them. However, chilis, skillfully used, add delightful savour and interest to many foods. The capsicums, or New World peppers, have added to the world's culinary repertoire since Columbus brought them to Europe from "the Indies."

6 tablespoons butter	2-1/4 cups milk, heated
2 onions, very thinly sliced	1-1/2 cups grated Swiss cheese
2 lbs. raw, chopped spinach	2 teaspoons celery seed
4-1/2 tablespoons butter	3 Jalapena chilis, finely chopped
4-1/2 tablespoons flour	2 cups cooked rice
salt	grated Cheddar cheese

Lightly brown the onion in the 6 tablespoons of butter. Add the chopped spinach to wilt. Stir. Reserve. In a saucepan melt the 4-1/2 tablespoons butter. Add the flour and salt. Stir until foamy and lightly colored. Add the hot milk all at once and stir briskly with a wire whisk. When thickened, add the celery seed, chopped chili, and grated cheese. Stir until the cheese is melted. Remove from heat. In a buttered baking pan, place a layer of cooked rice. Spoon on some cheese sauce. Layer on some of the spinach mixture and spoon on more of the sauce. Continue layering until all the ingredients have been used. A layer of rice should be on the top. Sprinkle on the grated Cheddar cheese. Bake in a preheated 375-degree oven for 30 minutes or until bubbling and slightly browned on top.   Serves 8.

Stuffed Vine Leaves

In Salonika, Sukkot was colorfully celebrated. The *succah,* the outdoor booth in which the family took meals, was decorated with ribbons, wreaths of flowers, and clusters of fruits. Windows and balconies of the houses were also decorated. In the synagogue the *Shamash* (beadle), walked among the congregants carrying a silver pitcher or urn into which he dipped his hand and sprinkled, on one and all, cologne. Food and flowers were exchanged as friends visited each others' succahs. One of the foods was stuffed vine leaves. Old Spanish songs, brought from Spain by the exiles in 1492 and handed down from one generation to another, were sung. Musical groups were spontaneously formed and, like troubadors, serenaded in the streets.

1 (16 oz.) jar vine leaves	2 cups water
3 tablespoons olive oil	2 tomatoes, peeled, chopped
1 onion, finely chopped	2 tablespoons chopped parsley
1 cup rice	2 tablespoons dried mint leaves
2/3 cup raisins	3 tablespoons olive oil
2/3 cup pine nuts	1/4 cup water
1/4 teaspoon cinnamon	1/4 teaspoon saffron
1/4 teaspoon allspice	2 teaspoons sugar
3 cloves garlic, minced	juice of 1 lemon

Carefully separate the vine leaves under running water. Place in a bowl and pour boiling water over them to cover. After soaking for 15 minutes, remove the leaves. Reserve.

Saute the onion in the oil until transparent, add the rice, raisins, nuts, cinnamon, allspice, garlic. Stir. When the rice looks transparent add 2 cups of water, the tomatoes, mint, and parsley. Cover and cook over low heat until the rice is tender and all the liquid has been absorbed.

On each leaf place about a tablespoon of the rice mixture. Turn the sides of the leaf in and fold the top down. Roll firmly toward the stem. When all the leaves have been filled, pack them tightly into a casserole in two layers.

Combine 3 tablespoons olive oil, 1/4 cup water, the saffron, lemon juice, and sugar. Pour over the rolls. Place any extra leaves on top. Weigh the stuffed leaves down with a heavy plate. Cover and bring to a boil. Reduce heat immediately and simmer for 1-1/2 hours. Add water 1/2 cup at a time as liquid is absorbed. Cool in the casserole. Arrange on a plate. Serve cold.

(Vine leaves may be bought in some gourmet shops and in Middle East grocery stores).

Ruota de Faraone
(Pharoah's Wheel)

This Italian dish is sometimes called the Wheel of Fate. The nuts and raisins are intended to represent the men and horses of Pharoah attempting to cross the Red Sea, in this case, tomato sauce.

1 lb. thin spaghetti	1 cup raisins
4 cups rich tomato sauce	1 cup broken walnut halves

Boil the spaghetti in salted water. Drain. Toss with nuts and raisins. Pour the sauce over the individual servings. Serves 4 to 6.

Kraut Fleckerl
(Austrian Noodles and Cabbage)

This dish was frequently the entire meal of poor farm families in Austria, but its savoury aroma and hearty good flavor took it to the finest tables. It was originally made with homemade one-inch squares of dough.

Many Jews, coming from the Austrian-Hungarian area, brought to America their own proportions of ingredients in the dish which some called *kraut pletzlach,* cabbage and dough squares.

1 medium cabbage	2 teaspoons sugar
1 tablespoon salt	3/4 teaspoon pepper
4 large onions	1 lb. broad noodles, broken
1/2 lb. margarine	into 1 to 2 inch lengths

Shred the cabbage as thinly as possible. Place in a bowl and sprinkle with the salt. Weigh down with a plate and let stand for 1-1/2 hours. Rinse, drain and squeeze out. Cut the onions in paper thin slices, then chop coarsely. Melt half of the margarine and add the onions and cabbage, sugar, and pepper. Cook over the lowest possible heat for at least an hour, stirring frequently, until the cabbage is brown. Add the remaining margarine as needed. Boil the noodles in salted water. When tender drain very well. Add to the cabbage mixture and stir. Serve hot with meat or fish.   Serves 6 to 8.

Tuna Lasagna

The Piazza Navona in Rome is now a gathering place for young people and tourists who enjoy its restaurants. During a two-hundred-year period, almost naked Jews were forced to race around the Corso Agonale, as it was called from the fifteenth through the seventeenth centuries, as part of the events of the carnival. Those who were stout, handicapped, or clumsy were especially chosen for the amusement of the jeering crowds, which used every opportunity to rain blows on the involuntary participants.

This activity is seen in sharp contrast to the heroic activities of the Italian population during World War II. The Italians, risking personal safety, hid, (frequently in churches, convents, and monasteries), fed and helped to transport to safety, many Italian Jews. German officials in Italy protested that the Italians weren't as enthusiastic or diligent as they should have been in enforcing anti-Jewish ordinances.

Tomato Sauce:
2 tablespoons olive oil
2 tablespoons butter
2 onions, chopped
1 garlic clove, minced
2 cups canned plum tomatoes,
   chopped
2 tablespoons tomato paste
1/2 teaspoon oregano

Filling:
1/2 cup olive oil

1/4 teaspoon dried basil
4 sprigs parsley
2 cloves garlic
1/2 cup pine nuts
3/4 cup Parmesan or Romano
   cheese, grated
1 cup cottage cheese
2 (7 oz.) cans tuna, drained
   and rinsed under hot water
8 oz. lasagna noodles
grated Parmesan cheese

Sauce: Combine the oil and butter and saute the onions and garlic. Add the tomatoes, tomato paste, and oregano. Mix, cover, and simmer for 30 minutes.

Filling: In a blender, combine the oil, basil, parsley, garlic, nuts, Parmesan and cottage cheeses. Add salt and pepper. Blend until smooth.

Cook lasagna noodles according to package directions. In a greased, flat baking dish, place 1/3 of the noodles. Cover with half of the cheese mixture and half of the rinsed, flaked tuna. Pour a little less than half of the tomato sauce over. Add a layer of noodles and repeat the process, ending with noodles. Pour the remaining sauce over the top and sprinkle generously with grated Parmesan cheese. Bake in a preheated 350-degree oven for 30 to 45 minutes or until bubbling and golden on top.

Serves 6.

Sour Cream Noodle Pudding

The story is told of Yankel, a poor Jew in Poland, who was called upon to do some repair work in the house of a Jewish merchant. A tantalizing cooking odor pervaded the house. The repairman could scarcely endure it. As he was leaving, he asked the merchant, "Tell me, Reb Chaim, what is cooking that smells so good?" Reb Chaim, closing his eyes and inhaling, replied, "A *lockshen kugel,* a noodle pudding. I like it so much that my wife makes one twice a week."

When Yankel arrived at his poor dwelling he told his wife about the heavenly fragrance of the merchant's kugel and asked her to make one. His wife said, "A kugel? How can I make a kugel when we have no eggs?"

"Then make it without eggs."

"But we don't have cream, either."

"So make it without cream."

"And we don't have noodles."

"Then do without noodles."
The wife cooked a porridge of *kasha* (buckwheat groats) and placed it before her husband saying, "Here is your lockshen kugel." Yankel tasted it and said, "The rich must be crazy! I don't see what's so good about lockshen kugel."

8 oz. medium noodles	1 teaspoon salt
1/2 lb. butter, melted	2 tablespoons brown sugar
1 pint sour cream	3/4 cup crushed cornflakes
3 eggs, beaten	

Cook the noodles according to package directions. In a large bowl beat together the butter, cream, eggs, and salt. Add the cooked noodles and blend thoroughly. Pour into a greased 7x12 inch baking pan. Refrigerate for several hours or overnight. Combine the sugar and cornflakes and sprinkle over the top. Bake in a preheated 375-degree oven for about an hour.   Serves 8 to 10.

Szilas
(Hungarian Potato Dumplings)

In 1240, the Jews were expecting the coming of the Messiah since that date closed the fifth millenium of the Jewish era. When the Tartars invaded Hungary at that time, this seemed to confirm the coming of the Messianic Era since it was foretold that such an era would be ushered in by the war of Gog and Magog. The wild Tartars and the oppressive Hungarian rulers of that century seemed to the Jews to symbolize Gog and Magog. However, the Messianic hope is still to be fulfilled, and the condition of the Hungarian Jews worsened under the added cruelty of the Tartars. Jewish residence in Hungary was sporadic through years of expulsion, recall, legal oppression and privilege, until contemporary times. Whatever else Jews gained or failed to gain in Hungary, their reputations as cooks is recognized throughout the world.

3 lbs. baking potatoes, boiled	1 tablespoon salt
1 egg, beaten	1 cup dry, fine breadcrumbs
1 egg yolk, beaten	1/2 cup melted butter
1 cup sifted flour	

Boil the potatoes in their jackets. Peel and put through a ricer, or mash, as soon as they are cool enough to handle. Add the beaten egg and egg yolk and mix well. Add the sifted flour and salt gradually to make a soft dough. (All the flour may not be needed). Knead the dough until it is smooth. Break off walnut size pieces of dough and roll them until they are about 3/4 inch in diameter. Cut off 1-1/2 inch lengths and drop them into a large pot of boiling, salted water, a few at a time. As soon as they come to the top remove them and drain.

Brown the crumbs in the butter. Roll the dumplings in the crumbs and serve hot.

These are sometimes served as a hot desert by stirring *lekvah* (prune butter) into them before serving.

The famous Hungarian plum dumplings can be made by rolling out the dough to about 1/2 inch thickness. Cut into 2 inch squares. Remove the stones from 15 Freestone purple plums and fill the cavities with cinnamon and sugar. Enclose each plum in a square of dough. Cook as above and roll in breadcrumbs.   Serves 6 to 8.

Vegetables

Vegetables

Carciofi alla Giudea
(Artichokes Jewish Style)

Just inside the old ghetto of Rome is Piperno's Restaurant, founded as a kosher restaurant a hundred years ago by Abraham Piperno. It was popularly called Father Abraham's. Father Abraham made a specialty of artichokes cooked in his own style which became known as *carciofi alla Giudea* (artichokes Jewish style). Although Piperno's is no longer kosher or owned by the Piperno family, they still serve carciofi alla Giudea.

6 artichokes	**2 cups oil**
juice of 1 lemon	**coarse salt**

Remove the tough outer leaves of the artichokes and cut the ends off the remaining leaves. Remove the choke but leave a short stem. Quickly wash the artichokes under running water and place in a bowl of water to which the lemon juice has been added. After 10 minutes remove and dry thoroughly with paper towels. Heat the oil in a deep fryer or saucepan. Fry one or two artichokes at a time until they are lightly browned all over. On a tray covered with several thicknesses of paper towels place the artichokes, stem up. They should drain completely. This can be done ahead of time. Before serving, reheat the oil. Impale the artichokes with a fork through the stem and suspend in the oil just long enough for the artichokes to expand and become crisp. Drain again on paper towels. Sprinkle with coarse salt.   Serves 6.

Eggplant and Tomato Sauce

The bay leaf used in cooking is, more accurately, the laurel leaf. It is a product of the laurel tree whose romantic history reaches back to Roman mythology.

Daphne was transformed into a laurel tree to escape the amourous advances of Apollo. This did not extinguish his love, however. He vowed that the tree would be a symbol of honor and fame. Apparently he succeeded in his goal for Caesar wore the laurel wreath, not only to help conceal his baldness, but also as a recognized crown. We speak of "winning one's laurels" and we acclaim the "poet laureate." A nineteenth century cook wrote this advice:

> "To win a laurel wreath for your brow.
> Put a laurel leaf in the stew pot now."

1 large eggplant	1 teaspoon dried oregano
1/4 cup olive oil	2 eggs, beaten
1 clove garlic, minced	1/4 cup milk
2 (8 oz.) cans tomato sauce	1 cup flour
2 bay leaves	salt and pepper
2 teaspoons sugar	1 cup grated Romano cheese
1/2 teaspoon salt	

Cut the eggplant into 1/2-inch thick slices. Place in a colander and sprinkle with salt. Leave to drain for 30 minutes.

In a saucepan, saute the garlic in the 1/4 cup olive oil. Add the tomato sauce, bay leaves, sugar, salt, and oregano. Simmer for 30 minutes.

Rinse the eggplant and dry with paper towels. Dip the slices in the combined beaten eggs and milk, then in the seasoned flour and fry in oil until golden. Pour a little of the tomato mixture into a flat shallow baking pan. Arrange the eggplant slices and put a spoonful of the tomato mixture on each slice and sprinkle with the grated cheese. Top with a second layer and repeat the process. Pour the tomato sauce over the top and end with the cheese. Bake in a preheated 400-degreee oven until heated through and the cheese is melted.   Serves 4 to 6.

Eggplant Casserole

In the early Arab world eggplant was known and cooked in combination with other vegetables and meat. In India, *brinjal* (eggplant), was among the ingredients of early *karis* (curries). In Judea, eggplant was combined with "parched corn," the generic term for toasted grains.

1 large eggplant	1 teaspoon pepper
1/2 cup oil	3/4 cup grated Cheddar cheese
1 garlic clove, minced	5 egg whites, beaten
2-1/2 teaspoons salt	5 egg yolks

Place the peeled and sliced eggplant in a colander and sprinkle with salt. Drain for 30 minutes. Rinse and pat the slices with paper towels to dry. Lightly brown the slices in the oil in which the garlic has been sauteed. Cool the eggplant and mash. Add the salt, pepper, and cheese.

Beat the egg whites until stiff. Add the yolks, one at a time, beating continuously. Fold into the eggplant mixture. Turn into a generously greased 9 or 10-inch casserole. Bake in a preheated 350-degree oven for about 40 minutes, or until puffed and lightly browned.   Serves 6 to 8.

Carrots with Green Grapes

"I found Israel like grapes in the wilderness."   (Hosea 9:10)

12 carrots, cut into shoestring
   pieces
2 teaspoons dried basil
1 teaspoon salt
1/2 cup margarine

1 teaspoon dried chervil
1/2 teaspoon ground ginger
2 tablespoons sugar
2 tablespoons lemon juice
3 cups seedless grapes

Cook carrots with the basil and salt added to the water. Melt the margarine. Add the chervil, ginger, sugar, and lemon juice. Stir over low heat for 5 minutes. Add the grapes and stir. Add the grape mixture to the well drained carrots. Serve hot.   Serves 8 to 10.

Crepes Florentine

Mushrooms have had a long and exotic role in history and literature. Robert Graves claims that they were the original ambrosia or food of the gods. Alice nibbled on a mushroom before her "hallucinogenic" adventures in Wonderland. The sudden and unpleasant demise of some Roman emperors have been traced to a mushroom feast. The Mexican Indians of Oaxaca once worshipped a mushroom god and still eat of the "magic" mushrooms which produce visions and religious ecstasy. Nonetheless, mushrooms play an ever increasingly popular role in the culinary arts of most countries of the world and add another dimension to many recipes, as they do to this one.

Crepes:
See page 96.
   (Chicken Liver Crepes)

1/2 cup grated Swiss cheese
3 cups Bechamel Sauce
1/2 cup grated Parmesan cheese

Filling:
3 tablespoons butter
1 clove garlic, finely minced
2 onions, finely chopped
1/4 lb. mushrooms, sliced
2 (10 oz.) packages frozen
   chopped spinach

Bechamel Sauce:
3 tablespoons butter
5 tablespoons flour
3 cups milk
salt and pepper
1/2 teaspoon nutmeg

Saute the garlic and onion in the butter until the onion is soft and transparent. Add the mushrooms and stir for 5 minutes. Add the thawed and well-drained spinach. Stir to combine with the onions and mushrooms. Cover and leave on low heat for a few minutes. Remove from heat and stir in the Swiss cheese. Make the Bechamel sauce by melting the butter over low heat and blending in the flour until the mixture is foamy and lightly colored. Heat the milk to scald. Add all at once to the butter mixture and stir briskly with a wire whisk. Stir continuously until the sauce thickens and comes to a boil. Add the salt, pepper and nutmeg.

Add one cup of the sauce to the spinach mixture. Stir to blend. Place 2 tablespoons of the filling on each crepe. Roll up and place, seam side down, in a buttered, flat baking pan. Pour the remaining sauce over the filled crepes and sprinkle with the Parmesan cheese. Bake in a preheated 375-degree oven for 15 to 20 minutes, or until heated through and lightly browned.   Makes 16 crepes.

Turlu
(Mixed Vegetable Casserole)

This is a Turkish recipe although variations are known throughout the Balkan and Near East area. It is called *ghivetch* in Roumania. The spelling changes to *guivetch* in Bulgaria. It takes its name from the earthenware pot in which it is cooked. In Greece, a similar pot is called *guivesti*.

1/2 cup olive oil
2 large onions, coarsely cut
1/2 eggplant, diced
3 potatoes, peeled and diced
1 celeriac, peeled and
   thinly sliced
2 carrots, scraped and sliced
6 scallions, cut into 2
   inch lengths
1/2 (10 oz.) package frozen
   lima beans, thawed

1/2 (10 oz.) package frozen
   green beans, thawed
1 green pepper, cut into
   strips
2 tomatoes, chopped
1/2 teaspoon thyme
1/2 teaspoon oregano
3 cloves garlic, minced
1 teaspoon sugar
salt and pepper

Put the oil in a flat baking dish and heat to boiling. Combine all the ingredients and add to the oil, stirring to coat. Cover tightly and place in a 375-degree oven. Bake for 30 minutes. Uncover and bake about 30 minutes more.   Serves 6 to 8.

Broccoli Italienne

Broccoli was introduced to France by Catherine de Medici when she arrived in 1533. Her Italian cooks and bakers prepared in the style of Venetian cookery the vegetables she introduced. That started what, later, developed into a Franco-Italian cuisine.

2 (10 oz.) packages frozen broccoli, thawed	2 hard-boiled eggs, coarsely chopped
1 bottle Italian salad dressing	12 black, pitted olives, sliced
4 pimentos, cut into strips	

Cook the broccoli according to package directions. Pour the salad dressing over the well drained broccoli. Heat. Garnish with the chopped egg and olives.   Serves 6 to 8.

Orange-Buttered Parsnips

In the sixteenth century, the Dutch sold parsnips, beets, carrots, and turnips in the town square. The English included few vegetables in their diet. Thus, an English traveller, upon seeing the vegetable stalls, commented that the Dutch dug and ate roots like swine.

Parsnips added appreciated flavor to the potato and other soups of the Jews of Middle Europe whose diet was limited by lack of availability of many foods and by economic deprivation.

3 lbs. parsnips	1/2 cup orange marmalade
1/2 teaspoon salt	1/3 cup water
3 tablespoons butter	1/4 teaspoon ground ginger

Scrape the parsnips and cook in salted water until just tender. Cool slightly and cut into pieces 3 inches long and about 1/4 inch thick. In a skillet melt the butter and add the marmalade and water. Mix and bring to a boil. Turn down the heat immediately and add the parsnips. Heat thoroughly, turning gently to coat on all sides.   Serves 6 to 8.

Frijoles Refritos
(Refried Beans)

Beans are a staple of the Mexican diet and are cooked in many ways, but this is probably the most popular. *Frijoles refritos* are spread on the delicious Mexican *bolillo,* hard roll, with thin slices of onion and tomato. It is eaten as a vegetable accompaniment to meat or fish or with eggs. Monterrey Jack cheese is sometimes cubed and combined with the beans in the pan. The melted cheese gives a distinctive flavor and texture.

A (1 lb.) can red kidney beans   1/2 teaspoon garlic powder
1 onion, diced   salt
4 tablespoons oil

Heat the oil and add the onion. Saute until soft. Add the drained kidney beans. Reserve liquid. Lower the heat and add the garlic powder and salt. Mash with a fork to a smooth consistency, adding liquid from the can gradually until enough has been added to prevent the beans from sticking to the pan. Don't use too much of the liquid. The bean mixture should not be soupy.   Serves 6.

Succotash Pudding

Succotash was a food frequently relied upon by the secret Jews of Brazil in the sixteenth and seventeenth centures. It was a popular food with the entire population so, when the secret Jews ate with Catholic friends or neighbors, they could profess a preference for this dish over the others served and thus avoid eating prohibited foods.

A (10 oz.) package frozen   1/4 teaspoon pepper
   lima beans, thawed   1 tablespoon sugar
A (10 oz.) package frozen   1/8 teaspoon nutmeg
   corn kernels, thawed   1/2 onion, finely chopped
3 eggs, beaten   1/2 green pepper, chopped
1/4 cup flour   3 tablespoons margarine
1 teaspoon salt   2 cups light cream

Combine corn, lima beans, and well-beaten eggs. Combine flour, salt, pepper, sugar, and nutmeg. Saute the onion and green pepper in the margarine. Add the flour mixture and stir to blend. Add the light cream and stir to blend. Add the vegetable mixture and stir. Pour into a greased casserole. Place the casserole in a pan containing hot water to a depth of one inch around the casserole. Bake in a preheated 325-degree oven for 1 hour or until a knife inserted in the middle comes out clean.

Serves 8.

Roasted Onions

A wall painting of ancient Egypt in the Oriental Division of the New York Public Library shows workers watering and weeding onion patches. This bulb was held in such high esteem that it was worshipped as a symbol of the gods.

4 large, yellow onions,   4 tablespoons butter
   unpeeled   1 teaspoon paprika

Trim, but do not peel, the onions. Cut a cross in the root end. Place the onions in a lightly-greased baking pan. Roast in a preheated 400-degree oven for about 1-1/2 hours, or until cooked but not limp. Peel. Pour the melted butter over and sprinkle with paprika.   Serves 4.

Stuffed Zucchini

The Romans brought parsley to Europe from Judea. Legend has it that the Roman gods fed parsley to their horses to assure swiftness and spirit. Parsley was also worn in wreaths and garlands to prevent inebriation at the orgies. In England it was so favored that pies were made of it and children, in answer to the question, "Where did I come from?" were told, "From the parsley patch."

4 large zucchini	2 tablespoons finely chopped
3 parsnips, cooked and mashed	parsley
3 carrots, cooked and mashed	1 cup cooked rice
3 tablespoons butter	1/4 cup cream
1 small onion, chopped	1 egg, well beaten
1 clove garlic, minced	1/2 cup grated Swiss cheese

Cut the zucchinis in half, lengthwise. Cook in salted, boiling water for about 5 minutes, or just until tender. Don't overcook. Rinse in cold water and drain to dry. This can be done ahead of time or the day before serving. Scoop out the seeds and pulp leaving a 1/2-inch thick shell. Chop the pulp in a bowl. Add the mashed carrots and parsnips. Mash and blend well. Add the parsley and cooked rice. Saute the onion and garlic in the butter and add to the carrot mixture. Combine the cream with the beaten egg and add to the vegetable mixture. Mix well. Stuff the well drained zucchini and sprinkle with the grated cheese. Place on a greased baking sheet and put into a preheated 400-degree oven for about 20 minutes, or until heated through and the cheese is melted.   Serves 6 to 8.

Zucchini with Walnuts

Dill is native to the Mediterranean area and grows wild in Israel. It appears in the earliest-known Roman cookbook, written in the first century. Its cultivation and use spread to all of Europe. William the Conqueror introduced it to England. In medieval times, dill was always one of the ingredients in potions used in witchcraft. In the American colonies it was called the "meetin' seed." Parents carried dill seeds to church to give to children who became restless and hungry during the sermons. Eating the seeds kept the children occupied and, temporarily, staved off hunger.

1/2 cup margarine
1/4 cup olive oil
2 lbs. zucchini, sliced
  1/2 inch thick
3/4 cup green onions
1/2 teaspoon salt

1/3 cup white wine
2 tablespoons lemon juice
2 tablespoons finely chopped
  dill
1-1/2 cup coarsely chopped
  walnuts

Combine the margarine and olive oil. Saute the onions and sliced zucchini. Add the salt. Add the wine and lemon juice. Add the dill and simmer for about 5 minutes or less. Add the nuts. Toss lightly. Serve hot.

Serves 8.

Tzimmes
(Carrot Casserole)

Among Jews of East European origin, *tzimmes* is traditionally served on Rosh Hashanah (New Year). The Yiddish word for carrots is *mehren,* which is also the word for "increase." Eating carrots symbolizes the wish that is expressed, "May our merits increase!"

2 lbs. carrots
1/3 cup margarine
2 tablespoons flour
1/2 teaspoon salt
1-1/3 cups chicken consomme
4 tablespoons brown sugar
1/4 cup honey

1 tablespoon lemon juice
1-1/2 teaspoons grated lemon rind
1 cup pitted prunes
1/2 cup dried apricots
1/2 teaspoon cinnamon
1/4 teaspoon ground cloves
1/4 teaspoon ground ginger

Cut the carrots into thin slices. In a large saucepan melt the margarine. Add the salt and carrot slices. Sprinkle with the flour and stir for 2 or 3 minutes. Add the consomme and bring to a boil. Remove from heat. Combine all the other ingredients and add to the carrot mixture. Stir. Pour into a casserole and cover. Bake in a preheated 375-degree oven for about an hour. Remove cover for last 15 minutes of baking. If necessary, spoon a few tablespoons of consomme over the top. Drizzle on a little honey before serving.   Serves 8 to 10.

Sweet Potato Bake

Yams were brought to the New World in the holds of slave ships. Blacks brought with them this food which was the mainstay of their diet. At first, planted and cultivated in the new environment by the slaves, yams were considered "slave food." However, the versatility, hardiness, and good flavor of the yam soon won wider popular use.

1-1/2 lbs. cooked sweet potatoes	1-1/2 cups orange juice
3/4 cup dark brown sugar	3 tablespoons sherry
1-1/2 tablespoons cornstarch	1 teaspoon grated orange rind
1/2 teaspoon salt	1/2 cup broken pecan halves

In a saucepan, combine the sugar, cornstarch, salt. Add the orange juice and blend to a smooth mixture. Cook, stirring, over low heat, until the mixture boils. Add the sherry, rind, and nuts. Arrange the potato halves in a greased, shallow baking dish. Pour the orange juice mixture over the potatoes and bake in a preheated 375-degree oven for about 30 minutes.   Serves 4 to 6.

South African Yams and Apples

The Dutch East India Company required that all its employees and settlers be Protestant. However, Jewish sailors did manage to get on these Dutch ships and are thought to be among the first Jewish settlers in South Africa. Some established shipping companies and fisheries. They cured, dried, and exported fish and brought back sugar and other commodities. The present Jewish population of the Union of South Africa is about one hundred twenty thousand.

6 large, cooked yams, cut into thick slices	1-1/2 cups brown sugar
	3/4 cup water
4 large apples, peeled, cored, and sliced	1/2 teaspoon salt
	4 tablespoons margarine

Combine the sugar, water, salt, and margarine and bring to a boil. Put the apple slices in a large sauce pan with 1/4 cup of water. Cover tightly. Over low heat permit the apples to wilt, but not cook. In a generously-greased shallow baking dish arrange a layer of the yams. Pour 1/4 cup hot water around them. Add a layer of apple slices. Spoon a little of the boiled syrup over the apples. Continue the layering process, ending with a layer of yams. Pour the remaining syrup over the top. Bake, covered, in a preheated 375-degree oven for 30 minutes, or until apples are tender. Remove cover and bake for an additional ten minutes. Spoon the syrup from the pan over the top.   Serves 6 to 8.

Tomatoes Au Gratin

The tomato, once considered an exotic fruit in Europe, inspired many romantic ideas which resulted in its being given such names as *pommes d'amour,* love apples, in France, and *paradieser,* fruit of paradise, in Austria. Originating in Mexico as a weed in the maize fields, tomatoes were brought to Europe by Columbus. The tomato was first known as the "golden apple," probably because its now characteristic red color was a later development.

6 ripe, but firm, tomatoes, sliced	1 teaspoon sugar
1-1/2 cups breadcrumbs	salt and pepper
1 teaspoon dried basil	1-1/2 cups grated Cheddar cheese
1 teaspoon chopped parsley	1/4 cup melted margarine

Add the basil and parsley to the breadcrumbs. Cut the tomatoes into 1/4 to 1/2-inch slices. Arrange one layer in a flat, greased baking dish. Sprinkle with sugar, salt, pepper, breadcrumb mixture, and cheese. Repeat process until all the tomatoes have been used. End with a layer of breadcrumbs. Drizzle the melted butter over the crumbs. Bake in a preheated 375-degree oven for about 45 minutes.   Serves 6 to 8.

Cabbage and Tomatoes Bratislavia

Shabetai Zvi, born in Smyrna in 1626, became fascinated with the Cabala and mysticism. His flamboyant and charismatic personality gathered a few admirers who respected his Talmudic and cabalistic knowledge. At age twenty-two he "revealed" himself as the Messiah, designated by God to overthrow opposing nations and restore the people of Israel to Jerusalem. He and his followers were banned from Smyrna. Shabetai Zvi wandered for many years, having a variety of adventures while attempting to carry out his "mission." At one point of banishment, the town of Bratislavia, in what is now Czechoslavakia, gave shelter to his followers. The false messiah converted to Islam. He died discredited and alone, in Albania, then part of the Ottoman Empire.

It is said that his followers, almost destitute, lived on cabbage, root vegetables, and cheese.

2 tablespoons margarine	salt and pepper
1 large onion, sliced	3/4 cup brown sugar
1 medium head cabbage, shredded into 1/4 inch wide strips	1/3 cup lemon juice
	1 cup boiling water
6 tomatoes, coarsely diced	

In a deep saucepan put the shredded cabbage, tomatoes, salt, pepper, sugar, lemon juice, and boiling water. Saute the onion in the margarine and add. Cover tightly and cook over low heat for about an hour until the cabbage is well cooked and all flavors have blended. Stir from time to time. This is even better when reheated the next day. Excellent with beef or veal.   Serves 6.

Acorn Squash

In the Talmud, Abaye is quoted as saying that if symbolic foods are valued, on Rosh Hashanah one should eat squash, fenugreek, beets, leeks, and dates, since they grow rapidly and are symbols of fertility and prosperity.

4 acorn squash	2 cups orange marmalade
1-1/2 teaspoons salt	1/2 cup white wine
1/4 cup margarine, melted	2 teaspoons ground ginger

Cut the squash in half and remove the seeds and membrane. Place squash, cut side up, in a baking pan. Sprinkle with salt. Place a little of the melted margarine in each cavity. Pour a little water in the pan. Cover tightly with foil. Place in a preheated 375-degree oven for 30 to 40 minutes, or until tender. Combine the marmalade, wine, and ginger, and heat. Spoon about 1/4 cup of the marmalade mixture over each squash half. Serve hot.   Serves 8.

Potato Latkes
(Potato Pancakes)

No food is more characteristic of the holiday of Chanuka among European Jews than is the potato *latke*. Pancakes are generally associated with this holiday but they take many different forms, depending upon the geographical area and culture.

1 onion, grated and drained	1 teaspoon salt
6 raw potatoes, grated	1/4 teaspoon pepper
2 tablespoons flour	2 eggs, well beaten
1/2 teaspoon baking powder	oil for frying
2 tablespoons cornstarch	

Combine the flour, baking powder, cornstarch, salt, and pepper. Beat the eggs in a large bowl. Grate the onion and add to the eggs. Quickly grate the potatoes, drain, and add to the egg mixture. Add the flour mixture. Mix well. Drop by the spoonful into the hot oil. Fry, turning once, until brown and crisp. Serve with applesauce, sour cream, or plain to accompany a meat dish.   Serves 6.

Potato and Tomato Casserole

Well-known among Polish Jews was a Yiddish chant-like song which was also used by children as an accompaniment to games such as rope jumping. It points up the limited number of foods available to the oppressed and poverty-stricken people.

"Sunday spuds, Monday spuds,
Tuesday and Wednesday — spuds!
Thursday and Friday, again spuds!
And on the Sabbath, as a novelty — potato pudding.
Sunday — spuds again!"

1/2 cup butter	5 eggs, beaten
4 green onions, coarsely chopped	1/2 teaspoon dried basil
4 large potatoes, peeled and sliced	1/2 cup light cream
4 firm tomatoes, sliced	salt
salt and pepper	

In a large skillet saute the green onions in the butter. Remove the onions and reserve. Slice the potatoes 1/4 inch thick. Rinse and dry thoroughly. Fry in the remaining butter until lightly colored and tender. Sprinkle the onions over the potatoes. Arrange the tomato slices on top. Partially cover and simmer for 30 minutes. Combine the beaten eggs and cream. Add the salt and basil. Pour the egg mixture over the contents of the skillet. Cook over low heat about 10 minutes or until eggs are set.   Serves 6 to 8.

Potato Casserole

The history of the Jews in Russia is characterized by relentless poverty and mindless pogroms (unprovoked massacres of the populations of whole towns). Forced army service was for such long periods and under such difficult conditions that young men chopped off their trigger fingers to avoid conscription. Jewish survival probably can be attributed to the sustaining influences of the religion, which centered on study and family life; industriousness; and to an unquenchable sense of humor.

One of the old Yiddish folksongs is called "Vie Trinkt der Keyser Tey?" (How Does the Czar Drink Tea?) An old man is talking to his friend and says that when he drinks tea, he is lucky to find hot water, while he thinks about tea and lemon. And the potatoes he eats have been pushed into the coals. He eats them charred; skin and all, while he recalls that butter exists somewhere. When he wants to sleep, he rolls up his coat in a corner of the synagogue and hopes that the draft won't be too cold or the floor too hard. "But," he says, "the Czar! With his resplendent wealth, in what luxury he must drink tea, eat potatoes, and sleep!"

His equally impoverished friend creates the most lavish procedures he can conjure up to describe how the Czar does these things. He says that the Czar has many soldiers to attend him and when he wants tea the soldiers place a funnel of sugar in the Czar's mouth. One soldier pours hot tea through it while another energetically squeezes lemon into it. That's how the Czar drinks tea! And when the Czar wants potatoes, the soldiers erect a wall of butter. The Czar stands on one side and the soldiers and the hot potatoes are on the other side. The soldiers shoot the potatoes through the wall of butter right into the Czar's open mouth. That's how the Czar eats potatoes! And when the Czar wants to sleep, the soldiers fill up an entire building with eiderdown. They then swing the Czar back and forth and hurl him onto the feathers. And all night long a whole regiment of soldiers marches around the building shouting, "Quiet! the Czar is sleeping!"

7 potatoes, peeled	1 teaspoon pepper
1/4 cup butter	3 teaspoons salt
1-3/4 cups grated Swiss cheese	3/4 cup heavy cream

In a buttered casserole, arrange a layer of thinly sliced potatoes. Dot with butter, sprinkle with pepper, and salt, and with cheese. Add another layer of potatoes and repeat the process until all ingredients have been used. End with a layer of cheese. Pour the cream over all. Place in a preheated 325-degree oven for about an hour, or until the potatoes are tender and the cheese is melted. Serve hot.   Serves 6 to 8.

Salads and Accompaniments

Salads and Accompaniments

Tappuah
(Glazed Apples)

The origins of the apple are lost in the misty eons of time but its early appearance is noted as the succulent catalyst of temptation to the first man and woman. The word apple is derived from the Hebrew word for fruit, *tappuah*. Frequent Biblical references are made to the apple tree and to the fruit which was valued for its fragrance, sweetness, and restorative powers. In the Songs of Solomon, a lover is described: *"As the appletree among the trees of wood, so is my beloved among the sons."*

Apples, dipped in honey, are eaten on the eve of Rosh Hashanah (New Year) while the following words are spoken, "May it be Thy will, O Lord, that the year just begun be as good and sweet a year" as this food.

3 firm red apples,	1/8 teaspoon salt
sliced 1/2 inch thick	1/4 teaspoon ground ginger
3/4 cup sugar	1/4 teaspoon ground cloves
1 cup water	1/8 teaspoon red food coloring

In a large skillet combine the sugar, water, salt, ginger, cloves, and food coloring. Bring to a boil. Add the slices of cored, unpeeled apples. Turn heat down to moderate. Cook, turning once, for about 20 minutes or until the slices are transparent. Do not overcook. The slices should be tender but firm. With a broad spatula, carefully transfer them to a flat platter. Pour any clear pan liquid over the slices. Serve at room temperature.

This is a good accompaniment to poultry dishes or chops.

Serves 6 to 8.

Beet Cups

Beets, especially in the form of preserves, are frequently eaten on
Rosh Hashanah because a play on the Hebrew words, "May our sins
depart," equals the Hebrew word for beet.

6 medium beets, cooked and peeled	1 medium onion, finely diced
3/4 cup of water in which	1 teaspoon salt
beets were cooked	pepper
1/4 cup cider vinegar	mayonnaise
2 tablespoons sugar	3 hard-boiled eggs
1/2 teaspoon salt	chopped parsley
4 whole cloves	lettuce leaves
3 medium boiled potatoes,	
coarsely chopped	

With a sharp spoon hollow the beets to form cups. Combine beet water, vinegar, sugar, salt, and cloves. Bring to a boil and simmer for 10
minutes. Remove from heat. Put the beet cups into the mixture. Cover
and cool. Refrigerate overnight.

Combine potato, onion, salt, and pepper. Add enough mayonnaise to
bind the mixture together. Add the eggs and mix lightly.

Drain the beet cups very well. Fill with the potato mixture, place on
lettuce leaves and garnish with chopped parsley.   Serves 6.

Bayonne Avocado-Tuna Molds

According to some authorities, the salad dressing called mayonnaise
was invented in the French city of Bayonne where it was called *bayon-
naise*. The initial letter was somehow changed in usage and the word
became mayonnaise.

The Association des Etudes Juives was founded in Bayonne in 1894. This
was a group dedicated to the scientific study of Judaism.

Aspic:	2 (7 oz.) cans water-packed tuna
2 envelopes unflavored gelatine	1 cup diced celery
1/2 cup cold water	1/2 cup finely-diced onion
3 cups clear vegetable broth	2 ripe avocados
2 tablespoons dry sherry	mayonnaise
lemon juice	pimentos
	3 hard-boiled eggs
	lettuce

Aspic: Soften the gelatine in the cold water. Stir and heat to dissolve.
Add the broth, lemon juice, and sherry. Refrigerate briefly to get it to
the syrupy stage.

Drain and flake the tuna. Add the celery and onion and just enough
mayonnaise to bind the mixture together.

Peel and cut the avocados in half, horizontally. Remove the seeds and cut to make eight rings. Sprinkle with the lemon juice. On a serving platter arrange the avocado slices. On each slice mound some of the tuna mixture. Top with a piece of pimento cut into a diamond shape. Carefully spoon a thin coating of the aspic over the mounded tuna and avocado. Refrigerate. When the aspic is almost firm on the mounds, spoon more on. Continue until the mounds are completely glazed and covered with the aspic. Garnish the platter with lettuce, wedges of hard-boiled egg, and pimento.   Serves 8.

Nut, Olive, and Green Bean Salad

"I went down into the garden of nuts,
To look at the green plants of the valley. . . ."
(Song of Songs 6:11)

1-1/2 lbs. cooked green beans
1-1/3 cups herbed cheese
  salad dressing
1-1/2 cups pitted, sliced
  black olives
1 cup broken pieces of
  walnuts or pecans

Herbed-Cheese Salad Dressing:
3/4 cup olive oil
2 tablespoons wine vinegar

3 tablespoons lemon juice
1/4 cup chopped chives
1/4 teaspoon sugar
2 teaspoons salt
1/2 teaspoon pepper
1-1/2 teaspoons dried basil leaves
1-1/2 teaspoons dried
  tarragon leaves
1/2 teaspoon minced garlic
4 oz. Blue cheese, crumbled

Drain and cool the cooked green beans. Combine in a tightly-lidded jar all the salad dressing ingredients. Shake well. Combine in a bowl the beans and sliced olives. Add the salad dressing and toss lightly. Just before serving toss again and sprinkle with the nuts.   Serves 6 to 8.

Herring Salad

A woman was shopping for herring. She asked the storekeeper the price of *matjes* herring. When told that the herrings were a dollar each, she was indignant.

"A dollar! Mr. Braun, who has the store across the street sells them for seventy five cents!"

"Why don't you buy from him at that price?"

"He happens to be out of them just now."

"Oh. Well, when I'm out of them I sell them for even less."

lettuce
4 pickled herring filets,
   diced
4 medium beets, boiled,
   peeled and diced
4 medium potatoes, boiled,
   peeled and diced

1-1/2 cups sour cream
1 teaspoon salt
1-1/2 teaspoons sugar
4 tablespoons white vinegar
4 hard-boiled eggs, in wedges
3 small onions, cut into very
   thin slices

On a platter arrange crips lettuce leaves. In a bowl combine the herring pieces, beets, and potatoes. Combine the sour cream, salt, sugar, and vinegar. Blend well. Pour this mixture over the herring mixture and toss. Mound the salad on the lettuce leaves and garnish with the onion slices and wedges of hard-boiled eggs.   Serves 4 to 6.

Salata Meshwiya

Hard-boiled eggs have always had a symbolic place in the diet of Jews. They are a food symbolizing mourning and hope. Eggs are eaten after a funeral and when commemorating such events as the destruction of the Temple in Jerusalem. In Latin America, under the dominance of the Inquisition, fried eggs were eaten during periods of mourning or included in meals prior to fast days. The egg shape and its function as the origin of life signifies faith in the continuous existence of the Jewish people.

4 firm, ripe tomatoes
3 medium green peppers
4 scallions, sliced
1 (7 oz.) can tuna, drained
2 large stalks celery, sliced
4 hard-boiled eggs, coarsely
   chopped

1 cup black olives, halved

Dressing:
3 tablespoons lemon juice
1/2 cup olive oil
salt and pepper
pinch chili powder (optional)

Plunge the tomatoes into boiling water for a few seconds and peel. Cut them in half and scoop out the seeds and flesh. Discard. Cut the remaining portions into 1/2 inch pieces. Under the broiler or over a burner, quickly grill the peppers until the skins are blistered on all sides. Peel, seed, and cut into strips. Cut the scallions, including the green part, into 1/4 inch pieces. Drain and break the tuna into small chunks. Add the sliced celery. Combine all in a bowl and toss. Add the hard-boiled eggs and olives. Mix lightly. Chill. Just before serving, combine all the salad dressing ingredients and pour over the salad. Toss lightly. Mound on a serving platter and garnish with chopped parsley and onion rings.

Serves 4 to 6.

Munkazina
(Orange-Onion Salad)

Official British attitudes toward Israel have fluctuated with varying political breezes but actual breezes waft the fragrance of Israeli orange blossoms from the garden of the famous 10 Downing Street house. Sir Frances Rundall, British Ambassador to Israel, brought the trees when he returned to England in 1959. He had them planted near the window of the office of the Under-Secretary of State.

4 large oranges	2/3 cup coarsely chopped
2 sweet onions	black olives
2 cups boiling water	1/2 cup coarsely chopped
3 tablespoons salad oil	green olives
salt and pepper	shredded lettuce

Pour the boiling water over the whole olives. Drain when the water has cooled. Chop.

Remove the skin and white pith from the oranges and slice. Cut the onions in paper thin slices. Stack orange and onion slices in alternating layers. A slice of orange should be on top. Place on a bed of finely shredded lettuce. Dribble a little oil over the salad. Sprinkle with salt and pepper. Scatter chopped olives over all. Serves 4 to 6.

Sherried Cranberry-Apple Relish

Until the eighteenth century, the cranberry was known as the fenberry. It was also called by that name in the American colonies. The Dutch name for the same fruit was *kranbeere*. It was they who brought the name to the New World. The anglicized spelling turned it into cranberry. The cranberry is also grown in Russia.

1 lb. fresh cranberries	2 tablespoons finely chopped
3 medium apples	crystalized ginger
1/2 cup broken walnut halves	1-1/2 cups sugar
1/2 cup thinly sliced celery	2 teaspoons grated lemon rind
	3 tablespoons sherry

Wash and drain the cranberries. Peel the apples and cut into wedges. Put the apples and cranberries through a foodchopper using a medium blade. Add all the other ingredients to the chopped apples and cranberries. Mix well to blend. Refrigerate, covered, overnight.

Makes about 4 cups.

Canned Cranberry Chutney

The fruiting season of a fig tree lasts for several months. The Midrash says that the people of Israel are like a fig tree, some "ripening" before others. The first to "ripen" was Abraham, followed by other patriarchs, and then the other people.

3 cups whole canned cranberry	1/4 teaspoon ground ginger
sauce	1/4 teaspoon cinnamon
3/4 cup raisins, chopped	1/4 teaspoon allspice
1/4 lb. Smyrna figs, chopped	1/8 teaspoon ground cloves
1/2 lb. dates, chopped	1/8 teaspoon salt
1 cup apples, peeled, diced	1/2 cup vinegar
1/2 cup sugar	

Combine all the ingredients in a saucepan. Cook slowly for 20 minutes. Pack into sterilized jars. Makes about 1½ quarts.

Cranberry-Wine Mold

Rishon le-Zion is a village founded in Israel in the late nineteenth century as an agricultural colony. Poor soil and constant marauding by Arab neighbors caused the settlers great difficulty. However, Baron Edmond de Rothschild came to their assistance by sending stock vines for wine grapes, equipment for wine making, and experts to oversee the operation. Today Rishon le-Zion (The First in Zion) is the home of the famous Carmel wine distillery, which exports its excellent wines to most parts of the world.

A (3 oz.) package	1 (1 lb.) can whole
orange gelatine	cranberry sauce
1/4 teaspoon salt	1/2 cup coarsely chopped nuts
1 cup boiling water	1/2 cup diced celery
1/2 cup sweet red wine	1 cup peeled, diced apples

Dissolve the gelatine and salt in boiling water. Cut the cranberry sauce into teaspoon size pieces and stir into the hot gelatine mixture until melted. Add the wine. Chill until slightly thickened. Fold in the nuts, celery and apples. Pour into a 6 cup mold and chill until firm. Unmold and garnish with orange slices. Serves 8 to 10.

Mexican Bean Salad

"And it came to pass when David was come to Nahanaim that Shobi . . . brought . . . wheat and barley and meal and parched corn and beans . . . for David and for the people who were with him to eat . . ."
(II Samuel 17:28)

2 tablespoons oil	2 (15 oz.) cans kidney beans, drained
1/2 cup diced onion	4 tablespoons oil
2 cloves garlic, minced	1/4 cup tarragon vinegar
1/2 teaspoon chili powder	1/2 teaspoon salt
2 tomatoes, chopped	onion rings

In the 2 tablespoons of oil lightly saute the onion, garlic, and chili powder. Remove from heat and add the chopped tomato. Mix. Add the drained beans. Mix well. Chill.

Combine the remaining oil, vinegar, and salt. Add to the bean mixture and toss. Garnish with onion rings.   Serves 6 to 8.

Sauteed Bananas

In the Hindu religion there is a legend which relates that it was the banana, rather than the apple, which was the forbidden fruit. The Garden of Eden, according to this tale, was on the Island of Ceylon. Adam and Eve covered their nakedness, not with fig leaves but with banana fronds. Two banana species which grow in India are called Adam's Fig Tree, and Paradise Banana.

6 firm, ripe bananas	3/4 teaspoon ground ginger
1/2 cup orange liqueur	1/8 teaspoon salt
2 eggs, beaten	1/2 cup margarine
3/4 cup fine, dry breadcrumbs	

Peel bananas and cut in half lengthwise and then in half crosswise. Place in a shallow dish in one layer. Pour the liqueur over them and turn the pieces to be sure that all sides are moistened. Marinate for 30 minutes.

Beat eggs well and add 2 teaspoons of the liqueur in which the bananas have been marinating.

Add salt and ginger to the breadcrumbs. Dip the bananas into the beaten eggs and into the breadcrumbs, coating on all sides. Saute in margarine. Serve hot with any of the remaining pan liquid poured over them.

Good as an accompaniment to poultry or chops.   Serves 6 to 8.

Banana Roquefort Salad

The Sumerian diet included lettuce, which they cultivated. The Egyptians also ate a form of greens resembling lettuce.

6 large, ripe bananas	1/2 cup chopped nuts
juice of 1/2 a lemon	1/2 cup finely chopped nuts
1/4 lb. Roquefort cheese	1/2 cup mayonnaise
2 tablespoons butter	juice of 1/2 a lemon
1 tablespoon Worchestershire	2 teaspoons sugar
Sauce	lettuce

Peel and slice bananas lengthwise. Sprinkle with lemon juice. Mash the cheese with the softened butter. Add the Worchestershire Sauce. Mix to a smooth paste. Add 1/2 cup of the nuts. Mix. Make sandwiches of the banana halves and the cheese mixture. These may be left whole, cut in half crosswise or cut into 1 inch segments. Roll in finely chopped nuts. nuts.

Add the lemon juice to the mayonnaise. Add the sugar. Mix. Place the banana sandwiches on crisp lettuce leaves and pass the mayonnaise mixture separately.   Serves 6 to 8.

Salat Chatsilim
(Eggplant Salad)

The Egyptians believed that onions, as well as radishes and garlic, contributed to muscular strength, so they added large quantities of these foods to the diet of the Jewish slaves who were engaged in building the pyramids. Herodotus recorded that an inscription on the Great Pyramid of Cheops indicated that sixteen hundred talents of silver were spent on these foods for the slaves.

1 large eggplant	1-1/2 teaspoons salt
1-1/2 tablespoons oil	1/4 teaspoon pepper
2 tablespoons lemon juice	1/2 teaspoon sugar
2 cloves garlic, minced	lettuce
1 small onion, chopped	

Broil the eggplant, turning from time to time until soft. Cool until it can be handled. Peel and chop with a wooden spoon. Drain off any liquid. Add all the other ingredients and mix well. Serve in lettuce leaf cups, garnished with chopped tomato and parsley. Salat Chatsilim is the Hebrew name for this frequently served salad.

Greek variation: Garnish with black olives and pepper rings and sliced Feta cheese.   Serves 4 to 6.

Ensalada de Pappas
(Spanish Potato Salad)

The potato, a native of the Andean regions of South America, was first introduced into Europe as an ornamental plant. It was brought to Spain in 1540 and cultivated as a food in Galicia. Its use spread all over Europe and became a mainstay in the diet of several national and ethnic groups—especially the Jews of the *shtetls* (small villages) of Eastern Europe.

7 medium potatoes
6 anchovy filets
1/2 cup diced celery
1/4 cup olive oil
5 tablespoons lemon juice

1 clove garlic, finely minced
salt and pepper
2 tomatoes, sliced
1 green pepper, cut into rings
paprika

Boil the potatoes in their skins in salted water. When cool enough to handle, peel and slice. Drain the anchovy filets and cut into small pieces. Combine the potatoes, celery, anchovy pieces.

Combine the oil with the lemon juice, finely minced garlic, and salt and pepper. Gently toss the potato mixture with the oil mixture. Place salad on a platter and garnish with the tomato slices and pepper rings. Sprinkle a little paprika on top. Serves 8.

Prophecy Fruit Salad

"And by the river upon the bank thereof on this side and on that side, shall grow every tree for food, whose leaf shall not wither, neither shall the fruit thereof fail; it shall bring forth new fruit every month, because the waters thereof issue out of the sanctuary; and the fruit thereof shall be for food, and the leaf thereof shall not wither."

(Ezekiel 47:12)

2 cups canned pineapple
chunks, drained
1 cup green, seedless
grapes, halved
1 cup canned mandarin
orange sections, drained
2 cups canned dark, sweet
red cherries, drained
1 cup canned pear halves
drained and cut into chunks
1 cup pecans, coarsely
chopped

1/2 lb. cream cheese
4 tablespoons honey
1/4 cup orange liqueur
5 tablespoons coffee cream
2/3 cup mayonnaise
5 tablespoons lime juice
2 teaspoons grated lime rind
1/4 teaspoon salt
2 cups heavy cream, sweetened
and whipped
lettuce

Combine all the drained fruits. Add the nuts. Mix together the cream cheese, honey, liqueur, coffee cream, mayonnaise, lime juice, rind, and salt. Fold in the whipped cream. Fold the cream mixture into the fruit mixture. When well blended pour into a 12x16 inch pan or a 12-cup mold. Cover with foil and freeze overnight. Unmold and serve on lettuce leaves. Serves about 16.

Curried Mixed Fruit

The Hebrew Synagogue in Brighton, England, is a small but extraordinary building. Among the beautiful carvings, stained glass windows, and other ornamentation, are golden clusters of fruits representing all the varieties mentioned in the Bible.

1 cup canned apricot halves, drained	2 tablespoons margarine
1 cup canned purple plums, drained	3 to 5 teaspoons curry powder
1 cup canned peach halves, drained	2-1/2 cups mixed fruit juice
1 cup canned sliced apples, drained	1/2 cup lemon juice
1 cup canned pineapple chunks, drained	5 teaspoons cornstarch

Drain all the fruits very well and place in a shallow container. Reserve 2-1/2 cups of combined fruit juices. Add the lemon juice. Saute the curry powder in the margarine. Dissolve the cornstarch in the fruit juice mixture and add gradually to the sauteed curry powder, stirring. Cook, continuing to stir, over moderate heat until liquid is clear. Pour over the drained fruits. Cover and let stand at room temperature for 2 hours. Mix occasionally.

This is a good accompaniment to meat, poultry or fish.   Serves 8.

Minted Cucumber Salad

The street vendors of the ancient city of Ur, in Chaldea, sold cooked fish, cooked beans, leeks, and cucumbers to pedestrians, who ate them as they walked. The city of Ur was the birthplace of Abraham of the Bible, who, forsaking his idol-worshipping family, beheld the concept of one God. He is considered the father of the Jewish people.

2 large cucumbers, scored and thinly sliced	1-1/2 cups yogurt
salt	3 cloves garlic, finely chopped
	4 tablespoons fresh mint, chopped

Score the cucumbers by running a fork down the length of each cucumber on all sides. Slice thinly and place in a shallow bowl. Sprinkle lightly with salt. Place a weighted plate on the cucumbers. After 30 minutes rinse under cold water and squeeze gently by the handful.

Mash the garlic with a little salt. Add the yogurt, a little at a time, blending thoroughly. Add the mint. Mix. Fold in the cucumber slices. Refrigerate for an hour. Mix again. Garnish with a little more chopped mint.   Serves 4.

Red, White, and Green Salad

The cauliflower, though of Oriental origin, was known in Italy in the sixteenth century. Later, in France, Madame du Barry was so fond of the vegetable that chefs, seeking her favor, competed to concoct cauliflower recipes to please her.

2 cups raw cauliflower
2 cups green beans
1 (7 oz.) can of pimentos
1 cup dry, fine breadcrumbs

Dressing:
2/3 olive oil
3-1/2 tablespoon wine vinegar

1 teaspoon salt
1/8 teaspoon pepper
1/2 teaspoon sugar
1 clove garlic
1/2 teaspoon paprika
1/4 teaspoon oregano
1/4 cup finely chopped
   parsley
lettuce

Separate cauliflower into flowerets. Place in a bowl and cover with boiling water. Let stand until the water cools. Drain.

Cook the beans in salted water until just tender but still crisp. Drain well. Cut drained pimentos into strips 3/4 inch wide.

Make the salad dressing by combining all the ingredients in a blender and whirring for 2 seconds. Combine the cauliflower, beans, and pimentos. Toss lightly with some of the salad dressing. Reserve a little for topping.

Serve on a bed of lettuce. Sprinkle generously with the combined breadcrumbs and chopped parsley. Dribble a little salad dressing on top. Garnish with hard-boiled egg wedges.   Serves 4 or 5.

Pineapple-Grape Slaw

"And Moses sent them to spy out the land of Canaan. . . . And they came unto the valley of Eschol, and cut down from thence a branch with one cluster of grapes, and they bore it upon a pole between two; they took also of the pomegranates, and of the figs. . . . And they told him and said:' We came unto the land, whither thou sent us, and surely it floweth with milk and honey; and this is the fruit of it.'"

(Numbers 13:17)

3 cups finely shredded cabbage
2 cups canned crushed
   pineapple, drained
1-1/2 cups seedless grapes, halved
1 cup yogurt

4 tablespoons honey
1/2 teaspoon ground anise
1/2 teaspoon salt
Boston lettuce

Mix together the cabbage, crushed pineapple, and grapes. Combine the yogurt, honey, anise, and salt. Pour over the cabbage mixture and toss to combine thoroughly. Serve on lettuce leaves.   Serves 8 to 10.

Breads

Breads

Challah

The *challah,* a white bread, has been used to celebrate the Sabbath and holidays for centuries. The shape in which it is made varies with the customs of Jews in different geographical areas and with the holidays. Traditionally, in most of Europe, and in the United States today, the Sabbath loaf is formed as a large braid topped by a smaller one, and sprinkled with poppy seeds to represent manna. For Rosh Hashanah, the shape is always a round, snail-like form to indicate hope for a full uninterrupted year. In some places, a knob, shaped like a bird's head, is placed on the top, symbolizing the phrase in Isaiah 31:5. *"As birds hovering, so will the Lord of Hosts protect Israel."* In other places, a ladder is made of thin strips of dough and placed over the bread to symbolize prayers ascending to heaven. Some Europeans, for Succoth, make spiral bread with a hand at the end. It is said by some that the judgment decreed by God on Yom Kippur becomes a written verdict (kvitel) on the seventh day of Succoth and the hand of bread is extended to receive it.

5 cups flour (approximately)	1/8 teaspoon saffron
6 tablespoons sugar	2 tablespoons brandy
1-1/2 teaspoons salt	1 cup very warm water
1 package dry yeast	3 eggs plus 1 egg white
1/2 cup softened margarine	1 egg yolk plus 1 teaspoon water

Combine 1-1/2 cups of the flour, the sugar, salt, yeast, and margarine. Dissolve the saffron in the very warm water to which the brandy has been added. Add to the yeast mixture. Beat thoroughly. Add the 3 eggs and egg white and 1/2 cup flour. Beat vigorously. Gradually add the remaining flour to make a soft dough. Turn out on a lightly floured board and knead for at least 10 minutes to make a smooth, elastic dough. Place in an oiled bowl, turning to grease dough on all sides. Cover with plastic wrap and let rise in a warm place, free of drafts, for about an hour, or until a dent is left when a finger is pressed a half inch into the dough. Stir down and, on a floured board, divide into 3 parts. Combine two of the pieces so that one piece is 2/3 of the total. Divide this piece into thirds. Roll each of these thirds into a rope about 16 inches long. Braid the three pieces together. Place on a greased baking sheet. Divide the remaining dough into thirds and roll each piece into a rope about 13 inches long. Braid them together and place on top of the larger braid and attach the braids together at the ends. Let rise again for about an hour. Brush with the beaten egg yolk and water. Bake in a preheated 400-degree oven for about 25 minutes or until the loaf is brown and sounds hollow when tapped on the bottom.

This makes one large or two small challahs.

Krentenkranzbrod
(Currant Crown Bread)

In the War of 1812, an American Jewish naval captain was captured by the British and incarcerated in Dartmoor Prison. One day, a Jewish baker who sold bread to the prisoners pressed a loaf into the captain's hand even though he protested that he couldn't pay for it. Upon breaking open the bread, he found a newspaper clipping announcing the American victory at New Orleans. This reactivated the American's determination to escape, in which he succeeded. On this return home he regained his position in the navy and went on to a long and distinguished career in the service of his country.

2 packages dry yeast	2 tablespoons crystallized
2 cups warm milk	ginger, chopped
1-1/4 cups butter	1 egg yolk
2/3 cup sugar	1 egg white
4 eggs	candied cherry halves
6-1/4 cups flour	walnut halves
1-1/2 teaspoons salt	
3/4 cup currants (or raisins)	*Icing:*
1/2 cup candied cherries,	1-1/2 cups confectioner's sugar
cut in half	2-1/4 tablespoons cream
1/2 cup walnuts, coarsely chopped	1 teaspoon almond extract

Dissolve the yeast in the warm milk. Cover and set aside. Cream the butter until light and add the sugar and cream until fluffy. Add the 4 eggs, one at a time, beating after each addition, until light. Sift together the flour and salt. Add the currants, cherries, nuts and ginger. Mix. To the egg mixture add, alternately, the flour mixture and the yeast mixture. Knead well. Place in a greased bowl and turn dough so that all sides are greased. Cover with plastic wrap and let rise in a warm place, free from drafts, for about an hour or until a dent is left when a finger is pressed about 1/2 inch into the dough. Stir down and divide the dough into thirds, reserving about 1-1/2 cups of the dough. Roll each third into a rope about 15 inches long. Secure the three together at one end and braid them closely. Secure the other end. Bring the ends together to form a circle and place the loaf in a round pan. Use the reserved dough to make walnut size balls with a raisin or two pressed into the centers. Let the braid and dough balls rise separately for about two hours. Brush the braid with the egg yolk beaten with a teaspoonful of water. Lift the balls with a spatula and place on the braids at intervals, to form a crown. Brush the balls with egg yolk. Bake in a preheated 375-degree oven for about 40 minutes. Remove from the oven. Place the candied cherry halves and walnut halves on the crown, as jewels, by brushing them with slightly beaten egg white and attaching them to the braid. Combine the icing ingredients and drizzle over the entire crown.

Viennese Streizel

"Of the first of your dough ye shall set apart a cake for a gift. . . .
Of the first of your dough ye shall give unto the Lord a portion for a
gift throughout your generations."   (Numbers 15:20)

2-1/2 to 3 cups sifted flour	1/4 cup candied cherries, chopped
1 teaspoon salt	1 tablespoon candied orange peel,
1/4 cup sugar	chopped
1 package dry yeast	1 egg white, slightly beaten
3/4 cup milk	
3 tablespoons soft butter	*Glaze:*
1 teaspoon vanilla extract	1 cup confectioner's sugar, sifted
1 egg, room temperature	2 teaspoons milk
2 teaspoons grated lemon rind	1 teaspoon almond extract
1/2 cup seedless raisins	

In a large bowl, combine 3/4 cup of flour, the sugar, salt, and dry yeast. Combine the milk and butter and place over low heat until the milk is very warm. The butter need not be entirely melted. Gradually add to the yeast mixture, beating, vigorously. Add the vanilla. Beat at medium speed of an electric mixer until smooth, about 3 minutes. By hand, gradually blend in enough flour to make a soft dough. Turn out on a lightly floured board. Knead until dough is smooth and elastic, about 10 minutes. Place dough in a warmed, greased bowl, turning dough to grease all sides. Cover with plastic wrap and let rise in a warm place, free of drafts, for about an hour, or until a dent remains when a finger is pressed about 1/2 inch into the dough. Turn out on a lightly floured board. Spread dough out and sprinkle it with the rind and fruits. Roll up and knead very well. Cut the dough in half. Cut one half into four equal parts. Roll each of these parts into a rope about 14 inches long. On a greased cookie sheet, pinch one end of the ropes securely together. Braid them and pinch the other ends together. Cut the other half of the dough into 5 equal parts. Braid 3 of them together, pinching the ends securely. Make a depression in the first braid, down its length and paint it generously with the slightly beaten egg white. Place the smaller braid in the depression, setting it firmly. Make a depression in the second braid and paint it with egg white. Make two ropes of the remaining two pieces of dough and twist them around each other. Set them firmly in the depression on the second braid. Let rise in a warm, draft free place for about an hour. Test again by indenting. Cover the whole loaf with the remaining egg white, to which a very little bit of water has been added. Bake in a preheated 350-degree oven from 30 to 45 minutes. When cool drizzle with the glaze, made by combining all the glaze ingredients.

Saffron Coffee Cake

A bas relief on the Arch of Titus in Rome, shows Jewish captives carrying the spoils taken by Titus from the Temple in Jerusalem. They are carrying silver trumpets; the large Menorah (seven-branched candlestick); and the golden showbread table, used for holding the twelve loaves of bread offered on the Sabbath by the priests in the Temple as a sacrifice to God.

4 cups sifted flour (approximately)	1/2 teaspoon ground saffron
1 package dry yeast	2 tablespoons brandy
1 cup sugar	1 egg
1/4 teaspoon salt	1 egg yolk, beaten
1/2 cup butter, softened	1/2 cup hazelnuts, coarsely chopped
1 cup milk	1 cup thick raspberry preserves
1/4 cup water	1 teaspoon sherry

In a large bowl, mix one cup flour, the yeast, sugar, salt. Combine the butter, milk and water in a saucepan. Place over low heat until very warm. The butter need not be entirely melted. Add the brandy in which the saffron has been dissolved. Gradually add to the yeast mixture, beating for 3 minutes at medium speed of an electric mixer. Add the egg and 1 cup of flour, beating at high speed for 3 minutes. Gradually add flour until a soft dough has been formed. Turn out onto a floured board and knead for 10 minutes until the dough is smooth and elastic. Place in a greased bowl, turning dough to grease all sides.

Cover with plastic wrap and let rise in a warm place, free of drafts, for about 1-1/2 hours or until a dent is left when a finger is pressed about 1/2 inch into the dough. Stir down and turn onto a lightly floured board and knead for a minute or two. Divide dough in half. Cut each half into 4 parts. Roll each part into a rope about 12 inches long. Braid 4 together to make a loaf. Let rise for 20 minutes. Brush with the beaten egg yolk and sprinkle with the nuts. Mix the raspberry preserves with the sherry. Use 1/3 cup to fill crevices in the braid. Repeat process to form a second loaf. Bake in a preheated 350-degree oven for 25 minutes, or until golden. Add the remaining raspberry preserves to the crevices.   Makes 2 loaves.

Sabbath Coffee Cake

"Also we made ordinances for us, to charge ourselves yearly with the third part of a shekel for the services of the house of our God; for the showbread . . . for the sabbaths."   (Nehemiah 10:33)

3 cups sifted flour	*Topping and Filling:*
2 teaspoons baking powder	1 cup walnuts, chopped
1 teaspoon baking soda	1/2 cup coconut, chopped
1 cup margarine	1/2 cup raisins
1-1/2 cups sugar	1 teaspoon cinnamon
5 eggs	1 teaspoon grated orange rind
1 cup orange juice	3/4 cup sugar
2 teaspoons almond	1/2 cup orange juice
extract	1/4 cup sugar

Sift together the flour, baking powder and baking soda. Cream the margarine and sugar until very light and fluffy. Add the eggs, one at a time, beating continuously. Combine the orange juice and almond extract. Add to the egg mixture, alternately, the flour mixture and the orange juice. Mix to a smooth batter. Pour half of the batter into a greased 9x12 inch baking pan. Add a little less than half of the combined walnuts, coconut, cinnamon, rind, sugar and all of the raisins. Pour the remaining batter over. Sprinkle the rest of the filling over the top. Bake in a preheated 350-degree oven for about 40 minutes. While still hot, prick the entire surface deeply with a long fork. Dissolve the remaining sugar in the orange juice and spoon over the hot cake so that the juice is absorbed into the cake.   Serves 12 to 15.

Apricot Coffee Cake

The first western coffee house is thought to have been opened in Oxford, England, in 1650. Coffee houses soon became centers of discussion and gossip. Various breads and cakes were offered to entice customers and encourage coffee consumption.

3 cups sifted flour
4 teaspoons baking powder
1 cup sugar
1 teaspoon salt
5 eggs
1/4 cup light cream
1-1/2 teaspoons almond extract
1/2 cup butter, melted

Lattice Topping:
1/2 cup reserved dough
1/2 cup almond paste
3 to 4 tablespoons flour

Filling:
2/3 cup very soft butter
1/2 cup sugar
1 (1 lb.) jar apricot preserves
1 teaspoon lemon juice
1 cup almonds, coarsely chopped

Sift together the flour, baking powder, and sugar. In a large bowl, beat the eggs, add the cream and almond extract. Gradually add the flour mixture and melted butter. Blend just until the ingredients are combined. Do not beat or overmix. Reserve 1/2 cup of dough. Spread batter evenly in a well buttered 9x12 inch baking pan.

Combine the soft butter, sugar, apricot preserves, and lemon juice. Mix until blended. Spread evenly over the entire top of the batter. Sprinkle with the chopped almonds.

Combine the reserved dough with the almond paste and 2 or 3 tablespoons of flour, to make a stiff, but not dry, dough. Shape into ropes the thickness of a pencil and long enough to cover the filling in a diagonal lattice pattern. Bake in a preheated 375-degree oven for about 30 minutes.   Makes 12 to 15 servings.

Date Nut Muffins

"For the Lord thy God bringeth theee into a good land, a land of brooks of water, of fountains and depths, springing forth in valleys and hills; a land of wheat and barley, and vines and fig trees and pomegranates; a land of olive trees and honey; a land where thou shalt eat bread without scarceness. . . ."   (Deuteronomy 8:7)

1 cup sifted flour
1/2 teaspoon salt
2 teaspoons baking powder
1 teaspoon baking soda
1/2 cup nuts, coarsely chopped
3/4 cup dates, chopped

1 egg, beaten
1/3 cup salad oil
1/3 cup sugar
1/2 cup orange juice
1/2 cup milk

Sift together the flour, salt, baking powder and baking soda. Add the nuts and dates. Beat together the egg, oil, and sugar. Add the milk and orange juice. Stir into the flour mixture. Grease 12 muffin cups. Fill the cups 2/3 full. Bake in a preheated 400-degree oven for about 25 minutes.

Cheese Muffins

In early Roman times, square loaves of bread were made which included the ingredients oil, anise, wine, and cheese. These breads were called dice. Jews in Greece made square loaves of bread which they cut into thick slices and smeared with oil and cheese and then toasted. Sometimes they poured milk over them as a breakfast or lunch dish.

2 cups flour	1/4 lb. grated Cheddar cheese
4 teaspoons baking powder	1 egg, beaten
1/2 teaspoon salt	1/2 cup tomato juice
1 tablespoon sugar	1/2 cup milk
1 teaspoon dried basil	2 tablespoons butter, melted

Sift together the flour, baking powder, salt, sugar, and basil. Add the cheese. Beat the egg and add the tomato juice and milk. Add gradually to the flour mixture. Beat until smooth. Add the melted butter. Blend. Generously grease 12 two inch muffin cups. Fill about half full. Bake in a preheated 400-degree oven for about 20 minutes.

Rice Muffins

"Thy shoots are a park of pomegranates,
With precious fruits;
Henna with spikenard plants,
Spikenard and saffron, calamus and cinnamon,
With all trees of frankincense;
Myrrh and aloes, with all the chief spices.
Thou art a fountain of gardens,
A well of living water,
And flowing steams from Lebanon."

(The Song of Songs 4:14)

1 cup sifted flour	2 teaspoons butter, melted
3/4 teaspoon baking powder	2 egg yolks, beaten
1/4 cup sugar	grated rind of 1/2 lemon
1 teaspoon cinnamon	2 egg whites, beaten
1 cup cooked rice	1/4 teaspoon salt
1/2 cup warm milk	

Sift together the flour, baking powder, sugar, and cinnamon.

Combine the cooked rice and milk. Stir to eliminate lumps. Add melted butter and beaten egg yolks. Stir. Gradually add the flour mixture and lemon rind. Beat to a smooth batter. Add the salt to the egg whites and beat until stiff. Fold into the batter. Grease 12 muffin cups and fill 2/3 full of batter. Bake in a preheated 400-degree oven for about 15 minutes.

Pita
(Middle East Bread)

This bread is eaten in all Middle East countries. In Greece, children have a game to which they sing a ditty describing the activities in preparation for the Sabbath:

> "Today is Friday
> We have hot pitas.
> Mama is using her ladle
> And Papa is using his teeth."

5-1/2 cups flour (approximately)	2 packages dry yeast
2 teaspoons sugar	2 cups very warm water
2 teaspoons salt	

Combine 1-1/2 cups of the flour with the sugar, salt, and yeast in a large bowl. Gradually add the very warm water. Beat into a smooth batter. Add, gradually, another cup of flour, beating vigorously. Continue adding flour and beating to make a soft dough. Turn out on a floured board and knead for 10 to 12 minutes until smooth and elastic. Place in a greased bowl and turn to grease all sides of the dough. Cover with plastic wrap and let rise in a warm, draft free place for an hour or until a dent is left when a finger is pressed about 1/2 inch into the dough. Stir down and divide the dough into 8 equal pieces. On a floured board, roll each piece out into a 1/4 inch thick circle. Cover and let rise for 30 minutes. Bake on the lowest rack of a preheated 475-degree oven for about 10 minutes, or until puffy. The *pitas* should be only very lightly colored.

These will be hollow and can be opened like pockets and filled with various meats, relishes, *felafel* or salads.

Armenian Thin Bread

Armenia is one of the fifteen republics of the Soviet Union. Located in the Caucasus Mountains, its culture is identified with those of the Near East, and its cuisine includes such typical Eastern foods as "flat bread" or "thin bread."

The Caucasian Jews claimed to be descendants of the Lost Ten Tribes taken captive by Nebuchadnezzar. After the Persians took over the area in 366, the Jews adopted the Persian language called, "Parsee" or "Tat." However, they actually used a vernacular composed of Parsee, ancient Hebrew, and additions from local tribes, which they wrote in square Hebrew characters.

1 cup very warm water	2 teaspoons sugar
1 package dry yeast	2 teaspoons salt
1/4 cup oil	1 egg, beaten
3-1/2 cups flour (approximately)	1 cup toasted sesame seeds

Pour the very warm water into a bowl. Sprinkle the yeast over it and mix to dissolve. Add the oil, 1-1/2 cups of the flour, the sugar, and salt. Beat until the batter is smooth. Gradually add the remaining flour, beating, until a stiff dough is formed. Turn out on a lightly floured board and knead vigorously for 10 to 12 minutes until dough is smooth and elastic. Place in an oiled bowl and turn dough to grease all sides. Cover with plastic wrap and let rise in a warm, draft free place for about an hour, or until a dent is left when a finger is pressed about 1/2 inch into the dough. Stir down and divide into 4 equal pieces. On a floured board, roll out each piece as thinly as possible, then stretch the dough and roll again to achieve a circle of paper thinness. Place on ungreased baking sheets. Brush with the beaten egg and sprinkle with the sesame seeds. Bake in a preheated 375-degree oven for about 15 minutes, or until lightly browned and crisp. Remove to cool on a rack.   Makes 4 thin breads.

Orange Tea Scones

The word "scone" comes from the Dutch word, *schoon,* meaning "fine." White bread or tea bread was called *schoonbrod,* fine bread. White bread remained a delicacy until recent times and is still used in various forms as an adjunct to religious observances.

2 cups sifted flour	2 teaspoons water
1/4 cup sugar	1 egg, beaten
1/2 teaspoon salt	1/4 cup milk
2 teaspoons baking powder	3/4 cup sour cream
1 teaspoon baking soda	grated rind of 1 orange
4 tablespoons butter	1 egg, beaten

Sift together the flour, sugar, salt, baking powder, and baking soda. With a pastry blender cut the butter into the flour mixture until it has the consistency of coarse sand. Beat the egg with the water and add to the flour mixture. Combine the sour cream, milk, and orange rind and add to the batter. Mix well to blend. Turn out on a lightly floured board and knead lightly for about 5 minutes. Divide the dough in half. Form each half into a ball. Pat each ball of dough out on a greased cookie sheet to form a circle 1/2 inch thick. Cut each circle into 8 wedges and separate them so that there is space between the wedges. Glaze them with the slightly beaten egg. Bake in a preheated 425-degree oven for 12 to 15 minutes. Makes 16 scones.

Bohemian Buns

Rolls and buns, usually made of white flour, were beyond the economic means of most East European Jews. Sacrifices were made to buy white flour for the Sabbath *challah* (braided white bread). The yearning for the luxury of fresh, white bread is evidenced by the repitition of this theme in song and story. In some songs about a promised land appear such lines as, "On all the trees will grow rolls and buns."

The famous Yiddish writer Peretz wrote the story of Bontshe, the Silent, who suffered in silence a lifetime of frustrating and cruel occurrences. He was finally released from his suffering and arrived in heaven. The angels were so moved by his life of pain and by his virtue that they told him to choose anything in heaven or earth as his reward. Unbelieving that such fortune could befall him, he pondered his answer. Finally, trembling and deeply grateful, he asked if it would be possible for him to have a warm roll—with butter!

4 cups flour (approximately)
2/3 cup sugar
1-1/2 teaspoons salt
2 packages dry yeast
1 cup milk
1/4 cup water
1/2 cup butter
1 egg, beaten
2 teaspoons grated orange rind

Filling:
1 cup sugar
1 teaspoon cinnamon
1/2 cup chopped nuts
1/2 cup raisins

Glaze:
melted butter
honey

In a large bowl, combine 1-1/2 cups flour, the sugar, salt, yeast. In a saucepan, combine the milk, water, and butter. Heat to very warm. Gradually add to the yeast mixture and beat with an electric mixer for 2 or 3 minutes, at medium speed. Add the egg and 1/2 cup of flour and the grated rind. Beat at high speed until the batter is smooth, about 2 minutes. Gradually add enough flour to make a very stiff batter. Cover with plastic wrap in a warm, draft free place and let rise for an hour, or until a dent is left when a finger is pressed 1/2 inch into the dough.

Combine all the filling ingredients.

Turn dough out onto a floured board. Knead lightly and divide in half. Roll each half out into a rectangle 7x18 inches. Cut each piece into 18 one inch strips. Make a deep groove in each strip and fill with the filling. Pinch the dough together over the filling. On a greased baking sheet, make snail shapes of the filled strips. Cover and let rise for an hour. Brush with a little melted butter. Bake in a preheated 400-degree oven for about 20 minutes. Combine a little melted butter and honey and brush the tops of the hot buns.   Makes 36 buns.

Chelsea Buns

The Church of Saint Jacob stands in Rothenburg, Germany. Among its many other decorations are some old stained glass windows. These depict the Children of Israel in the desert. Manna is falling from heaven. The manna takes the form of buns, rolls, and pretzels!

1 package dry yeast	1 egg, beaten
4 tablespoons sugar	1/4 cup chopped candied fruits
1/2 cup warm milk	1/4 cup raisins
2-1/2 cups sifted flour	melted butter
1/2 teaspoon salt	1/2 cup raspberry jam
1/4 cup butter	

Dissolve the yeast in the combined milk and sugar. With a pastry blender, or 2 knives, cut the butter into the combined flour and salt until it has the consistency of coarse sand. To the flour mixture add the yeast mixture. Beat to combine thoroughly. Add the beaten egg. Beat until a smooth dough is formed. Turn out onto a floured board and knead until smooth and elastic. Place in a greased bowl and turn dough to grease all sides. Cover with plastic wrap and leave in a warm, draft-free place for about 45 minutes, or until a dent is left when a finger is pressed into the dough 1/2 inch. Roll out to a 12 inch square. Brush with melted butter. Sprinkle with fruits and raisins. Roll up as for jelly roll. Cut into slices 1-1/4 to 1-1/2 inches thick. Arrange the slices, touching each other, cut side up, in a greased baking pan. Let rest for about 15 minutes. Bake in a preheated 400-degree oven for about 20 minutes or until lightly browned. Melt the raspberry jam and brush the hot buns lightly.

Makes about 18 buns.

Georgia Corn Bread

The first white, male child born in the colony of Georgia was Isaac
Minis, born in 1734. Jews have lived in the South since earliest colonial
times and became identified with the mores of the majority culture.
Cooking habits were accepted and adapted to conform with religious
regulations.

2 cups sifted flour	1 cup sugar
4-1/2 teaspoons baking powder	2 cups yellow corn meal
2 teaspoons salt	4 eggs
pinch nutmeg	2-1/4 cups milk, warmed
1 cup butter, softened	2 tablespoons cream

Sift together the flour, baking powder, salt, and nutmeg.

Cream the butter and gradually add the sugar, beating until light and
fluffy. Add 1/2 cup of the cornmeal, combining thoroughly. Add eggs,
one at a time, beating after each addition. Combine the remaining cornmeal with the flour mixture and blend. Combine milk and cream. Alternately, add the flour mixture and the milk to the egg mixture. Beat. Pour
into a well greased 10x10 inch baking pan. Bake in a preheated 350-de-
gree oven for about 50 minutes, or until an inserted toothpick comes out
clean.

Cut into 2 or 3 inch squares to serve.

Jaffa Orange Bread

A combination of factors in Russia during the last half of the nineteenth century caused waves of emigration of Jews from that country.
Many came to the fabled America, but many others, wary of further
oppression and labor in a land of strangers, were inspired to form
groups in order to return to Zion (Palestine), the traditional homeland.
There, they felt, they could develop the land, and labor and reap in a
place of their own.

One of the songs popularized by this sentiment was called, "The Song
of the Bread." The harvesters of the wheat sang, "See, the bread will
come out well. We will never go back (to Russia). Let our children know
that every bite of the bread is from our own fields."

2-1/4 cups sifted flour	1/2 cup chopped candied orange peel
1 cup sugar	1 egg, beaten
2 teaspoons baking powder	2 tablespoons grated orange rind
1/2 teaspoon baking soda	1/2 cup sherry
1/2 teaspoon salt	1/2 cup orange juice
1 cup coarsely chopped pecans	2 tablespoons margarine, melted

Sift together the flour, sugar, baking powder, baking soda, salt. Add the nuts and candied peel. Combine the beaten egg, orange rind, sherry, orange juice and melted margarine. Stir into the flour mixture until well combined. Pour into a well-greased 9 x 5 inch loaf pan. Bake in a preheated 350-degree oven for about an hour.

Wheat and Oat Bread

"Take thou also unto thee wheat and barley and beans and lentils and millet and put them in one vessel, and make the bread thereof . . . and thou shalt eat thereof."   (Ezekiel 4:9)

2 cups sifted flour	1 cup raisins
2-3/4 teaspoons baking powder	1 cup coarsely chopped nuts
1/2 teaspoon baking soda	1 cup rolled oats
1 teaspoon salt	1-1/4 cups buttermilk
1/4 cup sugar	2 tablespoons butter, melted
1/4 teaspoon nutmeg	1/4 cup honey

Sift together the flour, baking powder, baking soda, salt, sugar, and nutmeg. Add the nuts and raisins. Add the oats. Combine well. Combine the buttermilk, butter and honey. Add to the flour mixture and mix thoroughly. Pour into a very well greased 9 x 5 inch loaf pan and bake in a preheated 425-degree oven for about 25 minutes.

Hushpuppies

One popular story concerning the name of this recipe describes the dogs barking for their share of the newly caught, frying fish. Someone fried a little of the breading in the sizzling fat and threw it to the dogs with the command, "Hush, puppy!" But more than puppies liked it so it became a regular accompaniment to fried fish.

This southern speciality is said to have originated with fishing enthusiasts of South Carolina. Regardless of origin, this is a variation of the Jewish *chremslach*.

The first synagogue in Charleston, South Carolina, Bet Elohim, was established in 1750 with Isaac da Costa as the rabbi.

2 cups white cornmeal	1 cup milk
2 teaspoons baking powder	1/2 cup onion, finely chopped
1 teaspoon salt	1 green pepper, finely chopped
1/8 teaspoon pepper	oil for frying
2 eggs, beaten	

Sift together the cornmeal, baking powder, salt, and pepper. Beat the eggs and add the milk. Combine with the cornmeal mixture. Mix well.

Add the onion and pepper. Stir. Drop into deep, hot oil from the side of a spoon, making finger length cigar shapes. Fry until golden. These can also be fried in the oil in which the fish has been fried.   Serves 6 to 8.

Soft Pretzels

When the Jewish immigrants arrived in New York early in the twentieth century, they came, primarily, from rural villages. They had been prohitibed from working in urban areas so their skills were minimal. Heads of families learned new skills in America and found employment. At first, their earnings were meager. Children were sent to school to acquire an education in order to lay a basis for careers which had been closed to their parents. But because there is always a demand for food, the women frequently found themselves participants—indeed sometimes the principal participant—in supporting the family. They often served meals, on a regular basis, to men whose wives had not yet left Europe. They baked bread and sold it in the neighborhood. They pickled herrings and cucumbers to sell. And they baked pretzels. These they sold from huge baskets on street corners all over the city. Many people developed a taste for this snack. Even in the subways, men, women or children might come through the cars selling pretzels while other men, women and children bought and ate them with gusto.

1-1/2 cups warm water
1 package dry yeast
1 tablespoon sugar
5 cups sifted flour
2-1/2 teaspoons salt

6 cups water
6 teaspoons bicarbonate of
  soda
1 beaten egg
coarse salt

Dissolve the yeast in 1/2 cup of the warm water. Add the remaining water and sugar. Cover and set aside for an hour.

Sift together the four and salt. Put the yeast mixture into a large bowl. Gradually add the flour to make a stiff dough. Turn out onto a lightly floured board and knead for 10 to 12 minutes until dough is smooth and elastic. Put the dough into a greased bowl, turning to grease all sides of dough. Cover with a piece of plastic wrap and let rise in a warm, draft-free place for 45 to 60 minutes, or until a dent is left when a finger is pressed 1/2 inch into the dough. Roll dough on a board into sticks 3/4 inch in diameter and about 16 inches long. Twist each into a pretzel shape. Combine the 6 cups of water with the bicarbonate of soda and bring to a boil. Drop 3 or 4 pretzels into the water at a time. When they float to the top, cook for another minute or two, then very carefully remove with a slotted spoon or spatula. Drain. Place the boiled pretzels on a greased baking sheet. Glaze with the beaten egg and sprinkle with coarse salt. Bake in a preheated 450-degree oven for about 15 minutes or until golden.   Makes about 12 pretzels.

Zum-Zum Squares

Sesame seeds and oil were used in Greece as early as 3000 *B.C.E.* The use and popularity of sesame seeds in baking, confections and oil has grown in recent years. In Israel, sesame seeds are called zum-zum. Sweet zum-zum cookies are sometimes used to break the Yom Kippur fast. The seeds symbolize prosperity and fruitfulness.

2 cups sifted flour	1/3 cup water
3/4 teaspoon baking powder	1 egg, beaten
1/2 cup sesame seeds	4 teaspoons oil
2 teaspoons salt	

Combine the flour, baking powder, sesame seeds, and salt. Combine the water, egg, and oil. Add the egg mixture to the flour mixture. Mix thoroughly. Turn out onto a lightly floured board and roll out to 1/8 inch thickness. Cut into 2 inch squares. Bake on lightly greased cookie sheets in a preheated 375-degree oven for 8 to 10 minutes or until lightly colored and crisp. These are good salad or soup accompaniments.

Bagels

There are many "authentic" stories concerning the origin of the bagel. One of them centers on an event which seems to have had culinary consequences as important as the historical ones. The use of coffee in the Western world and the creation of various pastries are said to have been by-products of the saving of Vienna from Turkish attack in 1683 by the King of Poland, John Sobiesky. Some attribute the creation of the bagel to this same rescue operation.

Having driven off the Islamic hordes, Sobiesky rode into the city where the relieved and grateful townspeople hung on to his stirrups as they cheered him. Bakers made sweet bread in the almost circular shapes of stirrups to commemorate the occasion and called them *beugels,* the German word for stirrups. Jews leaving Austria, took with them the taste for beugels and the recipe for making them. The spelling and recipe changed in accordance with the language and taste in each country where they were made.

Another story has it that a square roll, with a hole in the center, was popular among the Essenes, a Jewish sect which kept records in the second century *B.C.E.* The roll was called a *legab.* Archeologists, finding records in which it was mentioned, translated it backwards as "bagel" before realizing that Hebrew is written right to left!

Another version refers to Abigail's flight across the Negev to avoid King David's romantic overtures. Before leaving, her servants loaded camels and asses with many lumps of dough which they strung on sticks. They planned to bake them into pancake shapes on heated stones, as they needed them. However, the blazing desert sun baked the dough in their sacks. All that had to be done was remove them from the sticks. They were found to be very good and were named Abigails, later called "bigails", then "bagels."

Still another tale has its genesis in Egypt where, it is said, that a High Priest, called Bhagelrameses, ordered baked for him doughnut-like pastries. His fondness for them was so great that they were buried with him to sustain him on the journey to the afterlife. They were subsequently named "bhagels" in his honor. Some were found by archeologists in his tomb, but despite fabulous offers from museums which want to purchase examples of them, the archeologists refuse to sell these priceless relics.

2 packages dry yeast	4 cups sifted flour
4 tablespoons sugar	1 teaspoon salt
3 tablespoons oil	1 egg
1 cup warm water	1 egg yolk

Mix the yeast, sugar, and oil together. Add the warm water and dissolve the yeast.

Sift together the flour and salt in a bowl. Make a well in the center and add the yeast mixture and the egg. Gradually, work in the flour until a dough has formed. Turn out onto a floured board and knead until very smooth and elastic. Place in a greased bowl, turning to grease all sides. Cover with plastic wrap and let rise in a warm, draft free place for about 45 minutes. Knead again, briefly. Cut the dough into 4 equal pieces. Cut each fourth into 5 or 6 pieces. Roll each piece into 8 inch lengths. Form into doughnut shapes, overlapping the ends slightly and pinching together. Cover and let rise on the board for about 10 minutes, or until they begin to swell. Carefully remove to a greased and floured baking sheet and place under the broiler in a preheated 400-degree oven for 3 to 5 minutes. No longer! Remove and drop into a large pot containing rapidly boiling water. Cook for about 20 minutes, or until bagels rise to the top. Drain and replace on the baking sheets. Brush with the beaten egg yolk and bake in a preheated 400-degree oven about 15 minutes, or until brown and crisp.   Makes about 2 dozen.

Pies

Pies

Irish Coffee Pie

There are several legends concerning the origins of coffee as a beverage. One of these concerns a Muslim *ulama* (religious teacher). Scyadly, whose memory is still honored in Muslim countries. It is told that he was guilt-ridden and plagued by feelings of unworthiness because he couldn't stay awake long enough to complete his prayers. Because of his sincerity, Mohammed appeared to him and directed him to seek help from a certain herdsman who reported strange antics of his goats. The herdsman said that whenever the goats ate of a particular bush they seemed never to sleep but spent the night playing and jumping from rock to rock.

The priest found the herdsman and picked some of the red berries from the bush and from them made a strong and fragrant brew. Having drunk it, he was able to complete his prayers and even remain alert all through the night. For awhile he told nobody of the wonder berry, but his dervishes, noticing the difference in his behavior, asked him the reason for the change. He told them of Mohammed's help in directing him to the miracle bush. Soon all were drinking coffee and proclaiming it a special divine gift to the faithful.

The custom of drinking coffee during prayers soon spread to mosques all through the Middle East. It is drunk with added reverence before the tomb of the Prophet in the Holy Temple in Mecca.

The custom of adding special flavoring or perfume to coffee is not uncommon. Many Sephardic Jews drink spiced coffee. In Holland those of Spanish or Portugese extraction flavor it with cinnamon. In Syria cardamom is used and in Yemen, ginger. In Egypt pieces of ambergris are stuck to the bottom of the coffee cup and reused with each pouring of the brew.

Crust:	2 egg yolks
1 cup sifted flour	3/4 cup sugar
1/2 teaspoon salt	1/4 cup Irish whiskey
6 tablespoons shortening	1 cup heavy cream
2 tablespoons cold water	2 egg whites

Filling:	Topping:
2 envelopes unflavored	1/2 cup heavy cream
gelatine	2 tablespoons confectioners'
1/4 cup water	sugar
1-1/4 cups hot, very strong coffee	1/2 teaspoon vanilla extract

Crust: Combine the salt and flour. Cut in the shortening with a pastry blender until the mixture has the consistency of coarse sand. Add the water and toss lightly to form a dough. Push it together into a ball and refrigerate for 30 minutes. Roll out between pieces of wax paper to fit an 8 inch pie pan. Fit the dough into the pan and flute the edges. Over the dough place a piece of greased foil and fill with dried beans, or place another pie pan on the foil. Bake in a preheated 450-degree oven for 6 minutes. Remove the foil and beans or the upper pan and continue baking for about 7 minutes or until the crust is golden. Cool completely before filling.

Filling: Sprinkle the gelatine over the water in a medium bowl. Let it stand for 5 minutes then add the hot coffee and stir to dissolve the gelatine. In a small bowl, beat the egg yolks until very thick and almost white. Gradually add 1/2 cup of the sugar, continuing to beat. Add the egg yolk mixture and the whiskey to the gelatine mixture. Mix well and refrigerate until it has the consistency of unbeaten egg white. Beat the egg whites until soft peaks form. Gradually add the remaining sugar, beating until stiff. Beat the cream just until stiff. Fold into the gelatine mixture, then fold the egg whites into the mixture. Blend well but do not beat. Turn into the baked pastry shell. Refrigerate for at least 2 hours. Decorate with the topping of cream whipped with the sugar and vanilla.

Serves 6 or 7.

Apricot Cream Pie

One of the new commercial crops of Israel is that of apricots. It may soon equal the export of its excellent melons. Israeli citrus is already being exported to countries from Japan to the United States.

Pie Shell:
1-1/3 cups graham cracker crumbs
1/3 cup brown sugar
1/2 teaspoon cinnamon
1/3 cup butter, melted

Filling:
1 teaspoon unflavored gelatine
1 (3 oz.) package vanilla pudding
1-1/2 cups milk
2 egg yolks

1/3 cup heavy cream, whipped
1/2 teaspoon almond extract
1 large can apricot halves

Meringue:
2/3 cups white corn syrup
2 egg whites
1/4 teaspoon cream of tartar
1/2 teaspoon salt
1/2 teaspoon vanilla extract
toasted flaked coconut

Pie shell: Combine all the ingredients until crumbly. Press into a 9 inch pie pan. Refrigerate until well chilled.

Filling: Place the apricot halves into a sieve to drain.

Add the gelatine to the dry vanilla pudding mix then prepare according to package directions, using 1-1/2 cups milk to which 2 beaten egg yolks have been added. Cool. Fold in the whipped cream and almond extract.

Reserve about 8 apricot halves for the top of the pie. Slice the remaining halves, about 3 slices to each half. Arrange the sliced apricots in the bottom of the cooled pie shell. Spoon in the cooled filling. Decorate the top by placing the reserved apricot halves around the pie about 1 inch from the edge.

Meringue: Make the meringue by boiling the corn syrup for 3 or 4 minutes. Beat the egg whites until foamy. Add the cream of tartar and salt. Continue beating until the whites are stiff but not dry. Continue beating while pouring the hot syrup in a very thin stream, very slowly, into the beaten egg whites. Continue beating until the whites stand in stiff peaks. Pile the meringue inside the ring of apricots halves. Sprinkle with toasted coconut. Serves 8.

Dutch Apple Pie

Judah Halevi, the Jewish poet of the eleventh century, wrote,
> *"Lovely apple, noble work of God*
> *To delight the sense of taste and smell;*
> *In thy green and ruddy hue I can view*
> *The faces of the lover and his gazelle."*

The apple was the allegorical reference to the Scriptures and to feminine beauty.

Crust:
2-1/2 cups sifted flour
1 teaspoon salt
3/4 cup shortening
1/3 cup cold water

Filling:
6 cups peeled, sliced apples
1 cup light brown sugar
1/2 teaspoon ground ginger
1/2 teaspoon cinnamon
3/4 teaspoon nutmeg
1/8 teaspoon salt
1/2 cup heavy cream

Crust: Sift together the flour and salt. With a pastry blender, cut in the shortening until mixture has the consistency of coarse sand. Add the water and toss to form a dough that "cleans" the bowl. Form into a ball. Divide in half. Roll out one half, between pieces of wax paper, to a diameter of 11 inches. Roll out the other half to a rectangle 11 inches long. Cut the rectangle into strips 3/4 inch wide. Place the round of dough into a 9 inch pie pan. Put in the peeled, sliced apples. Sprinkle on the sugar, ginger, cinnamon, nutmeg, salt and cream. Use the strips to weave an entirely closed lattice. Turn the overhang of dough up and press into a high, fluted rim. Brush the top with milk. Place in a preheated 450-degree oven for 10 minutes. Reduce the heat to 375 and bake for 30 to 40 minutes.   Serves 8.

Apple Tart

"A word fitly spoken
Is like apples of gold in settings of silver."
(Proverbs 25:11)

Crust:
1-2/3 cups sifted flour
1/3 cup finely ground almonds
1/4 cup sugar
1/2 teaspoon salt
2/3 cup shortening
1 egg yolk, beaten
ice water

Filling:
4 lbs. apples

1 teaspoon lemon juice
3 tablespoons sugar
1/2 cup apricot preserves
1/4 cup cognac
2/3 cup sugar
3 tablespoons butter
grated rind of 1 orange

Glaze:
1/2 cup apricot preserves
a teaspoon cognac

Crust: Combine the flour, ground almonds, sugar, and salt. With a pastry blender cut in the shortening to the consistency of coarse sand. Add the beaten egg yolk and mix. Add ice water, one tablespoon at a time to make a dough which "cleans" the sides of the bowl. Gently form into a ball and chill for 1 hour. Roll out between pieces of wax paper to fit a 10 inch tart or flan pan. Bake in a preheated 375-degree oven for 10 minutes or until lightly colored.

Filling: Peel, core and cut 3 cups of apples into slices 1/8 inch thick. Put the apples in a bowl and sprinkle with the lemon juice and 3 tablespoons of sugar. Peel, core and cut the remaining apples into pieces. Place in a saucepan with the apricot preserves, cognac, sugar, butter, and rind. Cover and cook over low heat for about 25 minutes or until thick enough to mound. Beat to a smooth consistency. Cool to lukewarm and carefully spoon into the baked pie shell. Arrange the apple slices in an overlapping ring around the edge of the pie. Arrange the remaining slices to cover the entire surface. Bake in a preheated 375-degree oven for about 30 minutes or until the apple slices are slightly browned around the edges.

Heat and strain the apricot preserves. Add the cognac and stir. Spoon over the entire top of the tart to glaze.   Serves 10.

Apple Blossom Tart

"Keep my commandments and live,
And my teachings as the Apple of thine eye."
(Proverbs 7:2)

Crust:
2 cups flour
1/4 teaspoon salt
2 teaspoons baking powder
1/3 cup margarine, melted
1 cup sugar
2 eggs, beaten
1 teaspoon vanilla
  extract

Filling:
6 to 8 apples, peeled and cut
  into wedges

Topping:
1/2 cup margarine
1 cup sugar
1/2 teaspoon nutmeg
1/2 teaspoon ginger
2 eggs, beaten

Crust: Sift together the flour, salt and baking powder. Gradually add the melted margarine to the sugar, beating. Add the beaten eggs and vanilla and mix thoroughly. Add the flour mixture and mix well. Pat into a 9 inch springform pan to cover the bottom and halfway up the sides.

Stand the apple wedges on end in the prepared pan, pressing them down lightly. They will look like the petals of an open flower. Bake in a preheated 350-degree oven for an hour.

Topping: Cream the remaining margarine with the sugar to which the nutmeg and ginger have been added. Add the beaten eggs and mix well. When the apple torte is removed from the oven, pour the topping over the apples and return to the oven for 12 minutes.   Serves 10 to 12.

Strawberry Pie Venezia

Although this recipe is of American origin, Abrahams, in his nine-teenth-century publication, "Jewish Life in the Middle Ages", speaks of festival meals in Venice at which pies of fruit and cream were served. Maimonides, the Jewish philospher-physician of the twelfth century, did not recommend eating uncooked fruits or berries.

Crust:	*Filling:*
4 egg whites	4 egg yolks
1/4 teaspoon cream of tartar	3 tablespoons lemon juice
1-1/2 cups sugar	1 tablespoon grated lemon rind
3 tablespoons shredded coconut	1/8 teaspoon salt
	2 cups heavy cream, whipped
	2 cups sugared strawberries

Crust: Beat the egg whites until foamy. Add the cream of tartar. Beat just until stiff. Gradually add one cup of the sugar, beating continuously, until the whites stand in stiff peaks. Spread the meringue in a well greased 9 inch pie pan. The meringue should not extend above the rim. Sprinkle the meringue rim with the coconut. Bake in a preheated 275-degree oven for 1 hour or until it is pale gold and crisp. Toast the remaining shredded coconut in the oven at the same time.

Filling: Beat the egg yolks slightly, over hot water. Stir in the remaining sugar, lemon juice rind, and salt. Stir until thick. When cool, fold into 1 cup of the whipped cream. Slowly pour the filling into the cooled meringue shell. Smooth the top. Refrigerate for at least 12 hours. Arrange the strawberries in the center of the pie. Garnish with big spoonsful of whipped cream. Sprinkle with toasted coconut.   Serves 8 to 10.

French Strawberry Tart

In our country a tart is usually a small, open-faced fruit pie intended for an individual serving. The larger size pastry is, to us, a pie. In France, the flan is a one-crust pastry with a custard, fruit, or savoury filling. These are usually baked in round pans having straight sides which are fluted. The word "flan" is used interchangeably with the word "tart." The pastry takes its name from the pan in which it is baked. The word "flan," in metallurgy, is a metal disc.

Even in the sixth century, the flan must have been a special treat since the poet Fortunatus in 569 sang of the virtues of Saint Rategondus by describing how he did penance. He made flans but forced himself to forego the filling. He ate only the crust which he made of coarse wheat.

Crust:
2 cups sifted flour
1/8 teaspoon baking powder
4 to 5 tablespoons sugar
1/2 cup shortening
1 egg, beaten
2 teaspoons water
1/2 teaspoon vanilla extract

Filling:
1 teaspoon unflavored gelatine
1 (3 oz.) package vanilla pudding
1-1/2 cups milk
1 egg yolk
2 tablespoons Kirsch or
    orange liqueur
1 pint ripe strawberries

Glaze:
1 cup red currant jelly
2 tablespoons cognac
2 tablespoons sugar

Crust: Sift together the flour, baking powder and sugar. Add the shortening and rub into the flour mixture with the fingertips until the mixture is very fine grained. Beat the egg with the water and vanilla. Add to the flour mixture. Knead the mixture into a ball. Turn out onto a board. Pinch off egg-size pieces of dough and smear each quickly with the heel of the hand. The dough will be sticky. Scrape off the board and form all the dough into a ball. Refrigerate for several hours or overnight. When cold, press into a 10-inch flan or tart pan, preferably with a removable bottom. Work quickly. Line the dough filled pan with greased foil and put enough dried beans on the foil to hold the dough close to the pan. Place in a preheated 375-degree oven for 6 minutes. Carefully remove the foil and beans and prick the crust all over. Bake about 10 minutes more and cool on a rack. Remove crust from the baking pan to a plate.

Filling: Add the gelatine to the dry pudding mix. Prepare the pudding according to label directions using 1-1/2 cups milk to which the beaten egg yolk has been added. Cool. Add Kirsch or liqueur. Mix well. Refrigerate until cold but not set. Pour into the prepared pastry shell. Arrange the washed and hulled strawberries on the top.

Glaze: Melt the currant jelly. Add the sugar and cognac and stir until the sugar is dissolved. Cool to luke warm. Spoon over the strawberries and entire surface of the tart. Refrigerate.   Serves 10 to 12.

Walnut Pie

The Midrash compares the people of Israel to a heap of walnuts. If one walnut is taken from the heap each of the others is affected. There is also a comparison of the Jewish people to a walnut which, if it falls into the mud, can be cleaned without the heart of the nut being affected.

Jews, too can be cleansed of sins on Yom Kippur because they have been only externally soiled through succumbing to human fraility while their hearts remain, basically, unsullied.

Crust:
1 cup plus 2 tablespoons sifted flour
1/2 teaspoon salt
1/2 cup shortening
2 tablespoons plus 1 teaspoon
   water

Filling:
1/2 cup butter or margarine

1/2 cup sugar
1 cup dark corn syrup
3 eggs, beaten
2 teaspoons brandy
1 teaspoon vanilla extract
1 cup broken walnuts
1 cup walnut halves
1 cup heavy cream, whipped

Crust: Sift salt and flour together. With a pastry blender, cut the shortening into the flour mixture until it has the consistency of coarse sand. Add the water and toss lightly to form a dough which "cleans" the bowl when pushed into a ball. Roll out between pieces of wax paper to fit a 9 inch pie pan. Make a fluted edge. Prick all over and bake in a preheated 375-oven for 10 minutes so that it is partially baked. Remove from oven and keep warm.

Filling: Cream the butter until light. Add the sugar and cream until fluffy. Gradually stir in the corn syrup and well beaten eggs, brandy, vanilla, and the cup of broken nuts. Pour carefully into the partially baked pie shell. Arrange walnut halves on top. Bake in a preheated 350-degree oven for about 45 minutes. Cool and garnish with the sweetened,whipped cream.   Serves 8 to 10.

Pomeroon Mousse Pie

A letter from Abraham Beekman, the Commander at Essequibo (Dutch Guiana), addressed to the West India Company, under the date March 31, 1684, reads as follows:

"The Jew Salomon de la Roche having died some eight or nine months ago, the trade in vanilla has come to an end, since no one here knows how to prepare it so as to develop the proper aroma and keep it from spoiling. I have not heard of any this whole year. Little is found here; the most of it is to be had in Pomeroon and Barima (coastal towns of the Guianas), whither this Jew frequently traveled, and he used sometimes to make me a present of a little. In navigating along the river, too, I have sometimes seen some on the trees and picked it with my own hands, and it was prepared by the Jew, although I was never before acquainted with the virtues and value of this fruit, which grows wild after the fashion of the banana. I have, indeed, sometimes used it in chocolate. The Jew has without my knowledge secretly sent a deal home; however, I shall do my best to obtain for the Company, in Pomeroon or elsewhere, as much as feasible, but I am afraid that it will spoil, since I do not know how to prepare it."

Crust:	*Filling:*
1 cup sifted flour	6 oz. semi-sweet chocolate pieces
grated rind of 1 orange	1 egg
2 tablespoons ground almonds	2 egg yolks
1/4 cup oil	2 teaspoons vanilla extract
2 tablespoons orange juice	2 egg whites
	1-1/4 cups heavy cream, whipped
	shaved bitter chocolate

Crust: Combine the flour, rind, and ground almonds. Combine the orange juice and oil and beat until frothy. Add to the flour mixture. Blend well. Roll out on well floured wax paper to fit a 9-inch pie pan. Flute the edges and prick all over. Place in a preheated 400-degree oven for 10 minutes or until lightly browned. Cool on a rack.

Filling: Melt the chocolate pieces in a double boiler over simmering water. Remove from heat and beat in, one at a time, the egg and the two egg yolks. Beat the whites until stiff but not dry. Whip 1 cup of the cream and fold into the chocolate mixture. Fold in the egg whites. Spoon into the baked pie shell. Chill. Sweeten and whip the remaining cream and use as a garnish on top of the pie.   Serves 8.

Zephyr Lime Pie

The word zephyr comes from the Greek word *zephyros,* meaning soft, gentle west wind. That describes the quality of this delectable, fluffy dessert. If feelings of guilt accompany enjoyment of the calories, it may help to remember that the lime juice contributes to health. It was part of the regular prescribed diet of British sailors because it prevented scurvy. The term limey, referring to some people born in England, has its derivation from this naval dietary caution. Although the lime was not known to Biblical peoples, there are many mentions of citron, a member of the lemon family.

Crust:
1 cup sifted flour
1/2 teaspoon salt
1/3 cup shortening
1/4 cup cold water

Filling:
6 egg yolks
1/8 teaspoon salt
1-1/2 tablespoons cornstarch

1-1/3 cups water
3 teaspoons grated lime rind
8 tablespoons lime juice
1-1/2 cups sugar
6 egg whites, beaten

Topping:
1 cup heavy cream, whipped
1/4 cup sugar

Crust: Sift together the flour and salt. With a pastry blender, cut in the shortening to a consistency of coarse sand. Add the water and toss lightly to form a dough which "cleans" the bowl when pushed into a ball. Roll out between pieces of wax paper to fit a 9 inch pie pan. Flute the edges and prick all over or line with foil and dried beans. Place in a preheated 450-degree oven for 10 to 15 minutes or until golden. Cool completely on a rack before filling.

Filling: In the top of a double boiler, over simmering water, combine the beaten egg yolks, salt, cornstarch, water, rind, and juice. Stir. Add half of the sugar. Turn the heat up so that the water boils gently and stir until the mixture is thick. Remove from heat and cool. Beat the egg whites, adding the remaining sugar gradually, until stiff peaks form. Fold into the cooled yolk mixture. Pour into the baked pie shell and place in a preheated 450-degree oven for about 5 minutes to set. Do not let it brown. Cool. Whip the cream, gradually adding the sugar. Cover the cold pie with the whipped cream. Refrigerate.   Serves 8.

Cakes

Cakes

Lekach
(Honey Cake)

This cake is traditional for Rosh Hashanah and festive occasions. The custom is attributed to the Biblical quotation from II Samuel 6:15. *"So David and all the house of Israel brought up the ark of the Lord with shouting and with the sound of the horn (shofar). . . . And he dealt among all the people . . . to every one a cake of bread, and a cake made in pan, and a sweet cake."*

Among the crypto-Jews of Latin America in the sixteenth century, *lekach* was sometimes served as a first course at weddings. The explanation for this custom, as given in *The Jews in New Spain* by Seymour B. Liebman, is that "honey cakes were eaten in memory of the honeycomb which the angel gave to Asenath, the oldest daughter of Potiphar, when she married Joseph."

4 cups sifted flour	1/3 cup margarine
1 teaspoon baking soda	4 eggs
3 teaspoons baking powder	1-3/4 cups honey
1 teaspoon cinnamon	3/4 cup strong coffee
1/2 teaspoon ground ginger	4 tablespoons brandy
1/2 teaspoon allspice	1/2 cup sliced almonds
1/2 teaspoon nutmeg	1/2 cup raisins
1 cup brown sugar	1/2 cup candied citron peel

Sift together the flour, baking soda, baking powder, cinnamon, ginger, allspice, nutmeg. Cream the margarine and add the sugar. Cream until light. Add the eggs, one at a time, beating after each addition. Add the honey. Combine the coffee with the brandy and add alternately with the flour mixture to the egg mixture. Fold in the almonds, raisins and citron peel.

Bake in 2 large loaf pans in a preheated 350-degree oven for 15 minutes. Turn down the heat to 325 degrees and bake for 45 minutes. This cake should be very slightly moist. It stores well in covered containers.

Tappuah Zahav
(Orange Cake)

The orange came to Israel via Persia and India. The word, "orange" is derived from the Persian *narang* and the Sanskrit *naranga,* both meaning "fragrant." The Spanish word *is naranja.* Josephus Flavius, a Jewish historian of the first century, called it the Persian apple. In Israel it is called *tappuah zahav,* golden apple or *tappuz.*

3 medium oranges	1-1/2 teaspoons baking powder
2 teaspoons cognac	2/3 cup sugar
7 egg yolks, beaten	7 egg whites, beaten
1 cup ground almonds	whipped cream
1 cup matzo meal	

Put the whole oranges in a pot with water to cover and boil gently for 1-1/2 hours. Drain. When cool enough to handle, put into a bowl and cut into chunks, discarding the seeds. Put the orange chunks into a blender and whir until finely chopped. Add the cognac. Beat the egg yolks and add the ground almonds, matzo meal, baking powder, sugar and orange pulp. Mix to blend thoroughly. Beat the egg whites until stiff and fold into the orange mixture. Pour into a well greased 9-inch springform pan. Bake in a preheated 400-degree oven for about 1 hours, or a little longer. This cake remains moist and almost like a pudding, but it should not be "wet." Garnish with whipped cream.   Serves 8 to 10.

Tishpishti
(Greek Honey Cake)

One of the most nostalgic and best-known of Yiddish folksongs is "Rozinkes mit Mandlen" (Raisins and Almonds). It has to do with a widow who is rocking her only son to sleep. Her lullaby predicts that he will earn his living by peddling raisins and almonds.

4 cups sifted flour	1 cup coarsely chopped almonds
1 teaspoon baking soda	1 cup raisins
2 teaspoons baking powder	whole almonds
1 teaspoon salt	
1 cup margarine	*Syrup:*
1-1/2 cups freshly brewed coffee	3 cups sugar
1/2 cup brandy	1/2 cup honey
1 cup honey	3/4 cup water
1 cup sugar	1/4 cup brandy
1 teaspoon cinnamon	juice of 1 lemon
1 teaspoon allspice	3 tablespoons orange blossom
	water (optional)

Combine the flour, baking soda, baking powder and salt.

Put into a saucepan and bring to a boil the margarine, coffee, brandy, honey, sugar, cinnamon, allspice. When the mixture has boiled, remove from the heat and stir in the flour mixture to form a smooth batter. Fold in the chopped almonds and raisins. Pour into a well-greased 9 x 13 inch baking pan. Press the dough evenly into the pan and score with a sharp knife into about 3 dozen diamond shaped pieces. Press an almond into each piece. Bake in a preheated 350-degree oven for about 40 minutes. Do not permit the cake to dry out. Cool for 5 minutes. Meanwhile, bring the sugar, water, honey, and brandy to a quick boil. Stir. Remove from heat and add the lemon juice and orange blossom water. With a sharp knife cut through the hot cake in the score marks. Spoon the syrup over the cake so that it is well covered and is absorbed between the pieces and around the edges. Return to the warm oven for 5 minutes. Remove, cool. Let stand overnight so that the flavor and texture can mellow.

Makes about 3 dozen pieces.

Pumpernickle Cake

Although probably apocryphal, a story is told of Napoleon's fateful campaign in Russia. Food for the French army had been exhausted and the troops subsisted by foraging or acquiring whatever was available from the peasants in the countryside. Even Napoleon's horse, Nicole, had little to sustain it. One day, one of the aides brought some bread into the camp and offered it to Napoleon. Upon seeing the heavy, dark Russian bread, and remembering the fine, white bread of his homeland, the General contemptuously said that it was only "bon pour Nicole," good for Nicole. The soldiers took to calling the black bread Bon Pour Nicole, which later, non-French speaking people corrupted to pumpernickle.

Pumpernickle is associated with Russian Jews although various kinds of dark bread are made in several parts of Europe.

2 cups dry pumpernickle crumbs
1/4 cup orange liqueur
1/4 cup finely chopped or
  ground pecans
5 egg yolks, beaten
1/2 cup crushed pineapple, drained
1/4 teaspoon nutmeg
1/4 teaspoon cinnamon
1/8 teaspoon ground cloves
Grated rind of 1 orange
5 egg whites beaten
1/8 teaspoon salt
1 cup sugar
1/4 cup rum
1 cup heavy cream, sweetened,
  whipped
1/2 cup candied cherries, chopped

Combine the crumbs and liqueur. Permit the crumbs to become saturated. Add the ground pecans. Reserve.

Beat the egg yolks and add the drained crushed pineapple and the nutmeg, cinnamon, cloves, and rind.

Add the salt to the egg whites and beat until foamy. Add the sugar, one tablespoon at a time, beating continuously until the egg whites are stiff and glossy. Stir about 3/4-cup beaten egg white into the yolk mixture. Fold the remaining egg whites and yolk mixture into the crumb mixture, alternately. Combine gently but thoroughly to insure a uniform batter. Pour into a well greased 9-inch tube pan. Bake in a preheated 350-degree oven for approximately 50 minutes or until the cake springs back when lightly pressed. When thoroughly cool, remove from the pan, sprinkle with rum and place in an airtight container, or wrap tightly in foil, place for 24 to 48 hours in the refrigerator. Serve garnished with the whipped cream into which have been folded the well-drained crushed pineapple and chopped candied cherries.   Serves 10 to 12.

Pastel de Castanas
(Chestnut Cake)

This Spanish cake is appropriate for use during Pesach since it requires no flour or leavening.

Vanilla is the fruit, or pod, of a variety of yellow orchid native to Mexico but now cultivated in several tropical areas. It is said that Cortez was introduced to it when he first drank the frothy *xocolatl* (chocolate), flavored with *tlilxochitl* (vanilla) with Moctezuma. Among the more constructive aspects of his conquering of Mexico are the foods which Cortez brought back to Europe from the New World. The vanilla bean was one of them. The Spaniards named it "vanilla", little scabbard, because of its shape.

1 lb. chestnuts	4 egg yolks, beaten
1/2 cup margarine	1/2 teaspoon salt
1 cup sugar (scant)	4 egg whites, beaten
1/2 teaspoon salt	2 tablespoons sugar
2 teaspoons vanilla	

Remove the outer shell of the chestnuts. Place nuts in lightly salted water to cover. Bring to a boil. Remove from the heat and let stand for 30 minutes. Remove the inner skins. Press the nuts through a sieve or whir in a blender to puree. In a saucepan, put the pureed chestnuts, margarine, sugar, salt, and vanilla. Cook over medium heat just until margarine is melted. Do not boil. Stir and set aside. When lukewarm, beat the egg yolks until light and creamy and add to the chestnut mixture. Combine thoroughly. Add the salt to the egg whites and beat until stiff but not dry. Fold the beaten egg whites into the chestnut mixture. Pour the batter into a well greased 9-inch tube pan in which the 2 tablespoons of sugar have been sprinkled. Bake in a preheated 375-degree oven for about 45 minutes or until an inserted toothpick comes out clean. Do not overbake. This cake has a moist, almost pudding-like texture. Serve with whipped cream, chocolate sauce or brandied fruit.

Serves 10 to 12.

Baklava
(Middle East Nut Pastry)

Baklava is the favorite dessert of the Middle East. Other desserts are made using the same dough and usually saturated with honey syrup.

"... take of the choice fruits of the land ...
a little balm and a little honey, spicery and
ladanum, nuts and almonds."

(Genesis 43:11)

1 lb. phyllo dough
3/4 lb. unsalted margarine melted
1-1/2 cups pistachio nuts, walnuts
   (or a mixture of both)
3 tablespoons sugar
1/2 teaspoon ground coriander

Syrup:
1/2 cup water
2 cups sugar
juice of 1 lemon

Unfold the dough and keep covered with a tea towel or a piece of plastic wrap because the dough dries out very quickly and becomes very brittle and difficult to handle.

Chop the nuts and mix with the 3 tablespoons of sugar and the coriander.

Grease a 9 x 13 baking pan. Line the pan with one sheet of the dough and brush with the melted margarine. Add another sheet of dough and brush with margarine. Brush each sheet of dough out to the edges. Repeat the process until half of the sheets have been used. Make a thick layer of the chopped nut mixture. Cover with the remaining sheets of dough, brushing each one with melted margarine. Tuck in the overhanging dough. With a sharp knife carefully score through the top layers of the dough to make diamond shapes. Brush generously with more margarine. Bake in a preheated 375-degree oven for about 45 minutes, or until the dough is golden and flakey.

Make the syrup ahead of time by combining the sugar and water and boiling for 20 to 25 minutes or until it coats a spoon. Remove from heat and add the lemon juice. Cool and refrigerate.

When the baklava is baked, remove from the oven and cut the pieces completely through. Spoon the cold syrup over the hot baklava; over the top and between the pieces and around the sides. Do not cover until completely cool. This may be made a day or two ahead of time.

Makes 12 to 15 pieces.

Al-Borak
(Fruited Layer Cake)

Al-Borak was name of the horse which carried Mohammed to heaven. An Imam, upon tasting this rich delicacy, proclaimed that he was transported to heaven and called the cake al-Borak. The large rock from which the horse is said to have sprung into heaven is enshrined in the center of the interior of the mosque called the Dome of the Rock in Jerusalem.

2-1/4 cups sifted flour
1/2 teaspoon salt
3 tablespoons sugar
3/4 cup shortening
1/3 cup water

Filling:
1 can pineapple pie filling

1 lb. *lekavh* (prune butter)
1 large can apricot halves
cornstarch
1 9-inch sponge cake layer, split
2 tablespoons brandy
1/2 cup coarsely-chopped
   pistachio nuts

Reserve about 6 apricot halves and 1/2 cup of syrup. Put the remainder in the blender and whir until the apricots are chopped but not pureed. Measure the chopped apricots into a saucepan. For every cup and a half of apricots allow 1 tablespoon of cornstarch. Dissolve the cornstarch in 1/4 cup water and add to the apricots. Stir and cook until thickened. Cool.

Sift the flour with the salt and sugar. With a pastry blender cut in the shortening until like coarse sand. Add the water and toss lightly with a fork. Form a ball of the dough and refrigerate for 30 minutes. Press the dough into a 9-inch springform pan, covering the bottom and the sides almost to the top of the pan. Put the pineapple filling in the prepared pan. Split the sponge cake layer and place one half over the pineapple. Sprinkle it with 1 tablespoon of brandy. Cover the cake layer with the lekvah. Place the other half of the cake layer over this. Sprinkle it with 1 tablespoon of brandy. Cover the cake with the chopped apricots. Trim the dough on the sides to about 1 inch above the apricots. Bend the top inch of dough over the apricots all around to make a border over the filling. Bake in a preheated 400-degree oven for 45 minutes or until the border is brown. Cool on a rack. Arrange the reserved apricot halves on the top of the cake. Dissolve 1-1/2 teaspoons cornstarch in 2 table-spoons water. Combine with 1/2 cup apricot syrup and cook over moderate heat until clear and thickened. Spoon over the top of the cake. Sprinkle with chopped pistachio nuts. When completely cool remove sides of pan.   Serves 10 to 12.

California Fruit Almond Cake

The first synagogue in San Francisco was established in 1850, the congregants having come, like so many others, in the gold rush to California in 1849. Some remained to help in the many aspects of California's development.

Crust:
1-1/2 cups flour
1/2 teaspoon baking powder
1/2 teaspoon salt
2 tablespoons sugar
1/2 cup margarine
1 egg yolk, beaten
2 teaspoons water
1/2 cup almond paste

Filling:
1/2 cup margarine

1/4 cup sugar
2 egg yolks
3/4 cup dried apricots, soaked
    overnight, chopped
3/4 cup chopped prunes
1/4 cup orange juice

Topping:
3 egg whites
1/3 cup sugar
1 teaspoon almond extract
3/4 cup ground almonds

Soak the chopped prunes and the soaked, chopped apricots in the orange juice for 2 hours. Sift the flour, baking powder, salt, and sugar. With a pastry blender cut the margarine into the flour mixture until it has the consistency of coarse sand. Stir the beaten egg yolk into the water and add to the flour mixture. Knead to a smooth dough. Press into a 9-inch springform pan to cover the bottom and about 1-1/2 inches of the sides. Spread the almond paste over the dough in the bottom of the pan. Set aside. Cream the sugar and margarine until light and fluffy. Add the egg yolks. Beat until thoroughly mixed. Add the chopped prunes and apricots, but not the liquid. Mix well and spread in the prepared pan. Beat the egg whites until almost stiff. Gradually add the sugar and almond extract. Continue beating until stiff. Fold in the ground almonds. Spread on top of filling, making a smooth, flat surface. Bake in a preheated 375-degree oven for 45 minutes.   Serves 8 to 10.

Baked Frosting Spice Cake

In Egypt, it was thought that hysteria could be cured by taking a mixture of cinnamon, cardamom, and cloves mixed with honey. Cinnamon drink vendors called out in the streets, *"Dolchin,* dolchin!" which was essentially cinnamon and hot water. This was drunk to "tone up the system."

2-3/4 cups sifted flour	2 egg yolks
1 teaspoon baking powder	1 cup milk
1 teaspoon baking soda	1 cup raisins
1/2 teaspoon salt	
1 teaspoon cinnamon	*Frosting:*
1/2 teaspoon ground cloves	2 egg whites
1/2 teaspoon ground cardamom	1/2 teaspoon salt
1 cup butter	1 cup brown sugar
2 cups brown sugar	1 cup coarsely chopped nuts

Sift together the flour, baking powder, baking soda, salt, cinnamon, cloves, and cardamom. Cream the butter and sugar until light and fluffy. Add the egg yolks, one at a time, beating well after each addition. Add the flour mixture, alternately with the milk. Combine thoroughly. Add raisins with the last flour addition of flour. Pour into a well greased 9 x 13 inch baking pan. Beat the egg whites with the salt, adding the sugar one spoonful at a time until completely combined and thick and foamy. Spread carefully over the entire surface of the cake. Sprinkle with the nuts. Bake in a preheated 375-degree oven for about 25 minutes.

Serves 12 to 14.

Flourless Chocolate Cake

The world owes an eternal debt to the Nahuatl Indians of Mexico who appreciated and used the bean of the native cacao tree, which they called *caca-huatl,* and from which they made a drink, *xocolatl.* The Spanish conquistadors, enchanted by the taste, took beans back to Spain with them. The exotic flavor, greatly in demand, was soon in use throughout Europe. Chocolate is said to be the favorite flavor in the world today.

There are some who cannot give up the discredited theory that the Mexican Indians stemmed from the so-called Lost Ten Tribes of Israel. The Mormon Church has had a standing offer of a million dollars for research leading to proof of that contention.

1/2 cup margarine	6 squares unsweetened chocolate,
2-1/2 cups confectioners' sugar	melted
8 egg yolks	1 teaspoon vanilla
8 egg whites	1 cup nuts, chopped
3/4 teaspoon salt	nut halves for decoration

Cream the butter and sugar until light. Add the yolks, one at a time, combining well after each addition. Add the melted chocolate. Mix well. Beat the egg whites with salt until stiff, but not dry. Fold gently into the chocolate mixture. Pour off 1/3 of the batter and refrigerate. Pour the remaining 2/3 into three 8 inch cake pans which have been greased, lined with wax paper and greased again and very lightly floured. Bake in a preheated 350-degree oven for about 15 minutes. Remove from the oven and cool completely. Turn out one layer on a serving dish and peel the paper off. Spread less than half of the refrigerated batter on the layer. Sprinkle with half of the chopped nuts. Repeat with the second layer. Add the third layer and spread the remaining batter on top. Decorate with the nut halves. Refrigerate for 2 hours before serving.

Serves 8 to 10.

Daiquari Cake

In the Canterbury Cathedral there are thirteenth-century stained glass windows, one of which depicts the figure of Moses and a female figure which represents the Synagogue, holding in her arm the Tablets of the Law. Jews lived in Canterbury until England expelled all Jews in the thirteenth century. At that time it was the third largest Jewish community in England. Cromwell permitted Jews to return after 1656. However, no Jewish community exists there now. The synagogue is now used as a church social hall. Leon-Hart rum, still made in Strasbourg, was the product of a Jewish firm, one member of which, Alderman Hart, was the mayor of Canterbury for three terms.

2 cups sifted flour	*Filling:*
2 teaspoons baking powder	1 (3 oz.) package vanilla pudding
1/4 teaspoon salt	1/2 cup rum
1/2 cup butter	1 cup milk
3/4 cup sugar	1/2 cup heavy cream, whipped
2 egg yolks	
2 teaspoons grated lime rind	*Frosting:*
2 tablespoons lime juice	6 oz. semi-sweet chocolate
1/2 cup milk	6 tablespoons butter
1/4 cup rum	pecan halves
1/2 teaspoon vanilla	
1/3 cup sugar	
2 egg whites	

Sift together the flour, baking powder, baking soda, and salt. Cream the butter and add the sugar gradually, beating until light and fluffy. Add the egg yolks, one at a time, beating after each addition. Add the lime juice. Stir well.

Combine the milk and vanilla extract. Blend into the batter, alternately with the flour mixture. Beat the egg whites until soft peaks are formed. Gradually add the sugar, beating until stiff. Gently fold the batter into the egg whites until smooth. Pour into 2 greased and wax paper lined 9 inch cake pans. Bake in a preheated 350-degree oven for 20 to 30 minutes. When completely cool, split to make 4 layers. Sprinkle each with 2 tablespoons rum.

Filling: Prepare pudding according to label directions, using 1 cup milk and 1/2 cup rum. Stir. Cover surface with a piece of plastic wrap and refrigerate. Whip the cream and fold into the completely cool pudding. Spread between the layers.

Frosting: Heat the chocolate over simmering water until almost completely melted. Add the butter and mix to blend. Spread on the cake and decorate with pecan halves.   Serves 10.

Passover Seder Cake
(Orange Layer Cake)

The Rhadanites were the great Jewish merchant adventurers of the ninth century. There are several theories concerning the origin of the name "Rhadanites." The most likely one is that they were "men of Rhaga" in Persia, since it is known that this city was the commercial metropolis of the area and that these Jews were from this location. The name "Rhaga" was somehow changed in writing to "Rhada" so that the people from that place were called Rhadanites. Be that as it may, the Rhadanite merchants sailed all over the known world of that time with the primary purpose of trading in spices. This did not prevent their also carrying from one place to another such cargos as furs, swords, and foodstuffs. Some of the foods which they carried from China and India to other parts of the world were cinnamon, rhubarb, and coconuts. From other places they brought apples and quinces or pomegranates and oranges.

Several factors conspired to bring an end to the complicated organization of world trade of the Rhadanite Jews. Internal conflict and the fall of the T'ang Dynasty in China broke off that country's communications with the West. The Christianization of the Slavonic countries and the fall of the Jewish kingdom of Khazaria eliminated the heads of state upon whose good will some of the trade routes depended. Also, the rise of Venice as the Mediterranean trade center caused decrees to be enacted to prevent or eliminate Jews as rivals.

The Rhadanites, during the time that they flourished, brought more than rhubarb and oranges to places which had not seen them before. They brought ideas as well as swords, books as well as spices, and they conveyed to the Christian world the fruits of Arab culture.

8 egg yolks, beaten
1-1/2 cups sugar
juice and grated rind of 1/2 lemon
grated rind of 1 orange
8 egg whites, beaten
1/4 cup matzo cake meal
3/4 cup potato starch
1/4 teaspoon salt

Filling:
2-1/2 tablespoons potato starch
1/2 cup sugar
1 cup orange juice
1/2 cup water
yolk of 1 egg, beaten
grated rind of 1 orange

Icing:
1 egg white
2 teaspoons orange juice
2 teaspoons grated orange rind
approx. 1-1/2 cups sifted
    confectioners' sugar

Beat together the egg yolks and sugar until light and creamy. Add the juice and rind of the lemon and the rind of orange. Beat the egg whites until stiff. Combine the cake meal, potato starch and salt. Into the egg yolk mixture fold alternately the beaten egg whites and the cake meal mixture. Bake in a 10 inch springform pan in a preheated 325-degree oven for about 1-1/2 hours. Remove from the oven and invert the pan and permit cake to cool. Turn over when cool and remove sides of pan. Cut the cake in half to make two layers.

Make the filling by combining the potato starch and sugar in a saucepan. Add the orange juice and rind and mix to dissolve the starch. Add the water slowly, stirring. Add the beaten egg yolk. Cook over low heat, stirring, until thickened. Do not boil. Cool. Spread between the cake layers. For the icing, beat the egg white until foamy. Add the orange juice and rind. Beat a few minutes. Gradually add the sugar, continuing to beat until thick enough to spread. Spread on top of the cake. Garnish with orange slices.   Serves 10 to 12.

West Indian Mocha Rum Cake

Rum was manufactured as early as 1647 by Portugese Jews who had fled to Barbados. The potent brew was first known as Kill Devil, then as Rum Boullion, and finally, as Rum. It was, at first, a by-product of the sugar refineries developed and worked by the Jews.

1-1/2 cups sifted flour	5 egg yolks
2 teaspoons baking powder	5 egg whites, beaten
3/4 cup cornstarch	2 tablespoons rum
1/2 teaspoon salt	2 tablespoons strong coffee
1-1/3 cups margarine	1 teaspoon vanilla extract
1-1/4 cups sugar	sifted confectioners' sugar

Sift together the flour, baking powder, cornstarch and salt. Cream the margarine and 1 cup of the sugar until light. Add the egg yolks, one at a time, beating after each addition, until fluffy. Add the rum, coffee and vanilla. Mix well. Beat the egg whites until soft mounds form. Gradually add the remaining sugar, continuing to beat until the egg whites are stiff. Fold into the egg yolk mixture. Fold the flour mixture into the batter, lightly but thoroughly. Pour into a greased 8 inch Turk's Head baking pan and place in a preheated 325-degree oven for about 1-1/2 hours. After cooling for 10 minutes, turn out on a plate which has been generously sprinkled with confectioners' sugar. Sprinkle more sugar over the cake when cool.   Serves 8 to 10.

Hawaiian Walnut Cakes

Israel Rosenberg, a resident of Hawaii in the nineteenth century, gave a Torah to his friend, King Kalakaua. The Torah is now preserved among the artifacts of Hawaiian royalty.

1-2/3 cups sifted flour	1 cup sugar
2-1/2 teaspoons baking powder	3 egg yolks, beaten
1/2 teaspoon salt	1/2 cup pineapple juice
3/4 cup coarsely chopped walnuts	2 egg whites, beaten
1 cup margarine	

Sift together the flour, baking powder, and salt. Add the nuts. Cream the margarine until light. Add the sugar, gradually, beating until fluffy. Add the beaten egg yolks and mix. Add the pineapple juice. Blend well. Add the flour mixture gradually, beating to a smooth batter. Fold in the stiffly-beaten egg whites. Fill 12 large, well-greased muffin cups. Bake in a preheated 375-degree oven about 20 minutes. When cool, glaze the little cakes with a thin icing made of confectioners' sugar, brandy, and grated orange rind.   Makes 12 large muffins.

Lemon Nut Cake

The Turk's Head pan was created in Vienna after the rout of the Turkish army there in 1618. The Viennese love of pastry caused them to express their joy in victory through creating special cookies and other delicacies to mark the occasion. One inventive baker created the Turk's Head pan in imitation of the draped turbans which the enemy wore. Cakes baked in this shape, and eaten with gusto, symbolized the fact that they "had the heads" of the Turks.

Vienna has been used, in recent times, as a stopover point for Soviet Jews en route to Israel. However, Arab terrorist threats against Austria caused the officials of that country to refuse further use of its facilities in the emigration procedures.

1 cup margarine	1/4 teaspoon salt
1 cup sugar	4 egg whites, beaten
4 egg yolks	
grated rind of 1 lemon	*Icing:*
1 cup ground pecans	1 cup sifted confectioners' sugar
2 tablespoons brandy	1 teaspoon milk
2 tablespoons lemon juice	1 tablespoon melted margarine
2 cups sifted flour	3/4 teaspoon ground ginger
2 teaspoons baking powder	

Cream together the margarine and sugar until very light. Add the egg yolks, one at a time, beating well after each addition. Add the rind and ground nuts. Mix well. Combine the brandy and lemon juice. Add to the yolk mixture alternately with the combined mixture of flour, baking powder, and salt. Blend thoroughly. Fold in the stiffly beaten egg whites. Pour into a well greased 8 inch Turk's Head pan. Bake in a preheated 350-degree oven for about 1 hour. Cool for 15 minutes and turn out on a plate sprinkled with confectioners' sugar. Sprinkle the cooled cake with confectioners' sugar or pour ginger icing over the top. Combine all icing ingredients to a smooth paste and pour over the cake.

Serves 8 to 10.

Della Robbia Cheese Cake

In the early part of the nineteenth century, Silvester Graham, an early health food enthusiast, put together what is today called graham flour. It was a combination of grains, largely whole wheat, used for baking and porridge. The most familiar use made of it today is as an ingredient of graham crackers.

Cream cheese is made in most countries, consequently, cheese cake is internationally known, although the kinds of cakes made with cheese differ widely. The type of recipe given here is particularly known and enjoyed in the metropolitan areas of the United States.

Crust:

1/2 cup ground nuts
1/2 cup graham cracker crumbs
2 tablespoons sugar
1 teaspoon cinnamon
1/3 cup butter, melted

Filling:
12 ozs. cream cheese
3/4 cup sugar
3 egg yolks
1 cup sour cream

3 tablespoons orange liqueur
2 tablespoons flour
2 tablespoons grated orange rind
3 egg whites, beaten

Topping:
Small can apricot halves
1 lb. pitted prunes
grapes, cherries or raisins
1 cup apricot syrup
1 tablespoon cornstarch
1/4 cup orange liqueur

Crust: Combine the nuts, crumbs, sugar, and cinnamon with the melted butter. Blend thoroughly. Press the mixture firmly into a generously-buttered 8-inch springform pan. Chill while preparing the filling.

Filling: Beat the cream cheese until soft. Beat in the sugar and the egg yolks, one at a time. Continue beating and add the sour cream, liqueur, flour, and orange rind. Beat the egg whites until very stiff and fold into the cheese mixture. Pour into the chilled crust-lined pan. Bake 1 to 1-1/4 hours in a preheated 275-degree oven or until the top of the cake is golden and the middle is just firm.

Topping: Drain the apricot halves very well. Soak the pitted prunes in hot water for two hours. Drain very well. With a sharp knife cut a thin slice from the side of each prune so that there is a flat side. Dissolve the cornstarch in the apricot syrup. Add the sugar and cook over low heat until mixture is clear and thickened. Add the liqueur and cool to lukewarm. When cheesecake is entirely cool, alternate an apricot half and a prune around the edge of the cake. Fill the spaces between with cherries, raisins or grapes to create a wreath effect. Spoon the cornstarch mixture over the fruit. Refrigerate.   Serves 8 to 10.

Sabra Cheese Cake

On the site of the battleground in Dublin where the Irish defeated the Danes in 1014 in the battle of Clontarf, there was established in 1718, a Jewish cemetery. The quarter-acre was leased to the Jewish community by the government for one peppercorn for a thousand years. This cemetery has not been used for almost one hundred years but headstones indicate that among others buried there are "Pencil" Cohen, who is credited with inventing the lead pencil and "Chocolate" Phillips, who was the first to manufacture chocolate in Ireland.

Both oranges and chocolate are produced in Israel. A delicious Israeli liqueur combines these flavors, which are just as pleasing as in this dessert.

Sabra is the Hebrew name of the edible cactus fruit. Native born Israelis are called sabras because, it is said, they are prickly on the outside and sweet on the inside.

Crust:	Filling:
1 cup graham cracker crumbs	3 eggs, beaten
1/4 cup sugar	1 cup sugar
1 teaspoon grated orange	3 (8 oz.) packages cream cheese
2 ozs. semisweet chocolate, grated	12 ozs. semi-sweet chocolate pieces
1/3 cup melted butter	1 cup sour cream
	3/4 cup butter
	2 tablespoons vanilla extract

Crust: Mix together the crumbs, sugar, grated orange rind, chocolate, and melted butter. Combine well and press into a heavily buttered 8-inch springform pan, evenly covering the bottom and about an inch of the sides.

Filling: Beat together the eggs and sugar until very light. Soften the cream cheese and cream it until it is fluffy. Add gradually to the egg mixture, beating to combine thoroughly. In the top of a double boiler, over simmering water, combine the chocolate and the butter. When the chocolate is melted and mixed with the butter, remove from heat and add the sour cream and vanilla. Mix. Add to the cheese mixture and mix until smooth. Pour the batter into the prepared pan and bake in a preheated 325-degree oven for 2 hours or until the center of the cake is firm. Cool on a rack and refrigerate overnight. Decorate with chocolate curls and whipped cream.   Serves 8 to 10.

Orange Raisin-Nut Cake

At an age when children today are starting their kindergarten experiences in "reading readiness," East European boys were sent to *cheder* (Hebrew School), to learn Torah. They were taught the Hebrew alphabet, then the Bible, by rote. From what we now know of attention span, we don't wonder that the *rebbe* or *melamed* (teacher) had some difficulty. However, some of the methods used then are now being rediscovered and called "behavior modification based on reward." After a child had mastered a segment of learning, the rebbe might tell him to close his eyes. When he opened them, raisins and almonds were scattered on the page he had learned. The rebbe always said that the angels left them because they were so pleased with the student's study of Torah.

2 cups sifted flour	2 eggs
1 teaspoon baking powder	1 cup chopped nuts
1 teaspoon baking soda	1 cup raisins
1/4 teaspoon salt	3/4 cup milk
1/2 cup margarine or butter	1 cup orange juice
1 cup sugar	1/2 cup sugar
grated rind of 1 orange	

Combine the flour, baking powder, baking soda, and salt.

Cream the margarine until light. Add the sugar gradually, beating until fluffy. Add grated orange rind. Add the eggs, one at a time, beating after each addition. Alternately, add the flour mixture and the milk, beginning and ending with the flour. To the last flour addition add the nuts and raisins. Mix well to blend. Pour into a greased 7 x 12-inch pan and bake in a preheated 375-degree oven for about 40 minutes. Dissolve the remaining sugar in the orange juice. While the cake is still hot, prick it deeply all over with a long-tined fork. Spoon the orange juice mixture over the cake slowly enough so that it is absorbed. Pour some around the edges of the cake after loosening from the sides of the pan. Use all of the orange juice.   Serves 8.

Saint Eustatius Fruit Cake

During the American Revolution, Saint Eustatius, one of the Dutch Caribbean Islands, was a very important center of trade. There was a prosperous Jewish community on the island, many members of which had relatives in Amsterdam. Active trading between the two places formed a large part of the business activity. Many American Jewish colonists who played a substantial role in financing Revolutionary efforts, had ties with Jews on Saint Eustatius. Originally these colonists traded with Saint Eustatius as a way to get kosher food from Europe. But during the war they sent messages with the captains of ships that were running the British blockade concerning needed supplies and armaments. They also sent the money to pay for these supplies. The islanders got the supplies and armaments from Europe, through Amsterdam. Of such enormous help to the Revolution was this relay service that the British had to find a pretext for destroying Saint Eustatius. So, in 1780, England declared war on Holland, but did not inform that country! Instead, Sir George Rodney, Admiral of the British Navy in the New World, simply attacked Saint Eustatius, a Dutch possession. He destroyed all the major buildings and institutions, all Jewish community and business records, and carried off one hundred ten Jewish men. Saint Eustatius never regained its economic prowess.

2-1/2 cups sifted flour	2 tablespoons dark rum
1 teaspoon baking powder	1-1/4 cups mashed bananas
1 teaspoon baking soda	2 cups candied pineapple,
1 teaspoon salt	slivered
1/2 teaspoon cinnamon	1 cup raisins
1/4 teaspoon nutmeg	1/2 lb. pitted dates, chopped
1/4 teaspoon ground cloves	1 cup broken pecans
3/4 cup margarine	
2 cups dark brown sugar,	*Glaze:*
firmly packed	1/2 cup strained orange juice
4 eggs	2 tablespoons dark rum
2 teaspoons grated orange rind	1/2 cup sugar
1/4 cup orange juice	pecan halves for decoration

Combine the flour, baking powder, baking soda, salt, cinnamon, nutmeg, and cloves.

Cream the margarine with the sugar until light and fluffy. Add the eggs, one at a time, beating well after each addition. Combine the mashed bananas with the orange rind, juice, and rum. To the egg mixture add, alternately, the flour mixture and the banana mixture. Blend well. Combine the pineapple, raisins, dates, and nuts. Mix with 2 tablespoons of flour. Add to the batter. Mix well. Grease and flour a 10-inch tube pan and pour in the batter. Bake in a preheated 325-degree oven for about 70 minutes, or until an inserted toothpick comes out clean. Remove from the oven and spoon the glaze over. Decorate with pecan halves.

Serves 16.

Persian Prune Roll

The reign of Nadir Shah of Persia in the eighteenth century was one of tolerance. He was opposed to Shia Islam and seriously pursued religious studies toward the goal of creating a universal religion. After his death, however, the Jews were again oppressed, made to wear distinctive garb, and finally, were forced, on pain of death, to convert to Islam. They were then called New Moslems and were still discriminated against, although made to attend prayer at mosques, follow Islamic laws, and make pilgrimages to Mecca. However, the majority of these forced converts remained secret Jews, maintaining, as far as possible, Jewish religious customs, even to the extent of praying in underground synagogues. Pilgrimages to Mecca often provided the opportunity to defect to Afghanistan, Turkestan, and Bukhara.

3/4 cup sifted flour
1/4 cup cornstarch
1 teaspoon cinnamon
1/2 teaspoon ground cloves
1/2 teaspoon mace
1/4 teaspoon salt
6 egg whites
3/4 cup sugar
6 egg yolks

Filling:
3 cups pitted prunes, chopped
1/4 cup water
1/2 cup sherry
2 teaspoons grated lemon rind
1/4 cup sugar

Topping:
1 cup heavy cream, whipped
1/2 cup sugar
1 teaspoon cognac

Sift together the flour, cornstarch, cinnamon, cloves, mace, and salt. Beat the egg whites until they hold soft peaks. Gradually beat in the sugar until the whites are very stiff. Beat egg yolks until light and creamy. In small amounts, fold the egg whites into the beaten yolks, just to combine. Very gently and gradually, fold in the flour mixture. Do not beat or overmix. Spread evenly in a 10 x 15-inch jelly-roll pan which has been greased, lined with wax paper, and greased again, and floured. Bake in a preheated 400-degree oven for 10 to 15 minutes or until very lightly colored. Do not overbake. Remove cake from oven and invert on a tea towel which has been generously sprinkled with sugar. Cut off the crisp edges after carefully peeling off the paper. Spread the entire cake with the warm filling and carefully roll up from the short end. Place seam side down and let cool completely. Just before serving, cover the cake with the whipped cream to which has been added the sugar and cognac. Sprinkle lightly with cinnamon.

Filling: Combine the chopped prunes and water in a saucepan. Simmer for 10 minutes. Add the sherry, rind, and sugar. Cover and let stand for 10 minutes. Drain off all the liquid and reserve 1-1/2 cups of the prunes. Puree the remaining prunes and the liquid in a blender. Combine with reserved prunes and mix well.   Serves 8 to 10.

Cookies

Cookies

Dutch Cream Cones

The Danes, who enjoy good food, particularly butter, cheese, and cream, suffered not only the expected interruption of their way of life during World War II, but increased their deprivation and danger voluntarily. During the Nazi invasion of Denmark, many Jews were hidden in the attics and cellars of Danish Christians. If they had been discovered, the Christians would have suffered the same fate as Jews. When danger seemed imminent, the Jews were moved at night to another house. Under the streets of Copenhagen are subterranean passages which, during this time, were used to smuggle Jews to safety.

1/3 cup butter, melted	raspberry jam
1/3 cup confectioners's sugar	1/2 cup heavy cream, whipped
1/2 cup sifted flour	2 tablespoons sugar
4 egg whites, beaten	1 teaspoon rum extract

Stir the sugar and flour into the melted butter until the mixture is smooth. Beat the egg whites until stiff. Fold into the butter mixture. Drop 1 tablespoonful of the batter from a measuring spoon onto a hot, well greased baking sheet. Drop only 3 or 4 at a time, leaving plenty of space between them. Spread each one into a rectangle about 4 x 5 inches. Bake in a preheated 400-degree oven for 5 minutes or until golden. Remove from the oven and quickly roll into cones while still hot. Repeat process until all the batter has been used. Whip the cream, adding the sugar and rum extract. Heat the raspberry jam and place 2 teaspoonful in each cone. Very gently smear it on the sides of the cones. Fill the large ends of the cones with the whipped cream, using a pastry tube or a spoon. Makes about 10 cones.

Jewels of the East

These and a large variety of other small sweets are sold in quantity in Spain and Portugal. The many pastry shops fill their windows with colorful displays of them. The Spanish and Portugese Jews brought these recipes to the Middle East where today many of these pastries are considered "native" to that area. This is especially true of those made with almonds or almond paste.

1 cup finely ground almonds	1 teaspoon brandy
1 cup sifted confectioners'	peel of 1/2 an orange,
sugar	finely chopped
1/2 cup orange juice	1/2 cup chopped pistachio nuts
1/4 cup water	

Mix together the almonds and sugar. Combine the water, orange juice, and brandy. Add enough of the liquid to the almond mixture to make a stiff paste. Knead the paste until it is smooth. Cover lightly and set aside for 15 minutes. Peel the orange very thinly, using just the colored part of the skin. Chop finely. Shell and skin the pistachio nuts and chop.

With dry hands, pinch off pieces of the almond paste. Form into balls less than an inch in diameter. Roll half of the balls in the chopped orange peel. Roll the remainder in the chopped pistachio nuts. Place in a covered container until ready to use.

These are as much a candy as a cookie. They make a colorful and delicious addition to a plate of assorted cookies.

Makes about 12 cookies.

Roumanian Truths

The Roumanians were said to twist the truth into odd shapes. Thus, these twisted cookies were called Roumanian Truths or Roumanian Twists. The same kind of cookie was known in the Middle East as Taratir-at-Turkman, or Turkish Hats.

2 cups flour	4 tablespoons sour cream
2 teaspoons baking powder	2 tablespoons brandy
1 teaspoon salt	oil
4 egg yolks, beaten	sugar

Sift together the flour, baking powder, and salt. Beat the egg yolks until thick and lemon colored. Add the sour cream and brandy. Blend thoroughly. Gradually add the flour. Knead on a floured board until the dough is blistery. Roll out very thinly. Cut into strips about 1 x 4 inches. Cut a slit in the middle of each strip and pull one end through.

Fry in deep oil until puffed and golden, turning once. Drain on absorbent paper and sprinkle with sugar. Makes about 3 dozen.

Macaroons

Macaroons are traditional during Pesach when matzo meal is substituted for the flour. Macaroons are mentioned in the nineteenth century book called "Masseket Purim" as one of the sumptuous dishes eaten by Jews who could afford them in Italy in the Middle Ages.

4 egg whites	1/4 teaspoon salt
1/4 cup cold water	1 tablespoon flour
2/3 cup sugar	2-1/2 cups commercial flaked
	coconut

Combine the egg whites and water and beat until stiff. Add the sugar gradually. Blend in the flour and salt lightly. Fold in the flaked coconut. Drop by the teaspoonful onto a lightly greased cookie sheet. Bake in a preheated 325-degree oven for 25 to 30 minutes, or until lightly browned.

Makes about 30 cookies.

Butterscotch Fingers

In 1654, the Portugese took Brazil from the Dutch and expelled the Jews who thought that they had found respite from the Inquisition. While in Brazil, David and Rafael Mercado invented the process and machinery for refining sugar. Leaving Brazil, they went to Barbados where they set up a sugar refining mill. It went so well that others were soon engaged in the business, not only in Barbados, but in other Caribbean islands as well. The slaves, whom Spain and Holland had been bringing to the West Indies from Africa since 1550, became the labor force. Holland, through its Dutch West Indies Company, for many decades was in control of the European sugar market. The entire sugar industry in the New World was developed and expanded by this group of Jewish merchants and exporters.

1/4 lb. butter	2 teaspoons baking powder
1 package light brown sugar	1/8 teaspoon salt
2 eggs	1 teaspoon vanilla extract
2 cups sifted flour	1 cup chopped nuts

Cream the butter and sugar until light and fluffy. Add eggs, one at a time, beating after each addition. Gradually add the combined flour, baking powder and salt. Mix well. Add the vanilla and chopped nuts. Mix.

Turn into a greased 9 x 11 baking dish and bake in a preheated 375-degree oven for about 25 minutes. Do not overbake. These should be slightly moist and chewy. While still warm cut into squares or bars. Sprinkle with sifted confectioners' sugar.

Hamantaschen
(Haman's Pockets)

About two thousand years ago in Persia, King Ahasueras took as his bride the lovely Jewess Esther. The perfidious Prime Minister Haman, tricked the King into signing a decree to put to death all the Jews in the kingdom on a date to be chosen by Haman. Haman selected the date by casting lots, *purim.* Esther, however, managed to avert the decree and Haman was hanged. Purim is the holiday during which these cookies, called Haman's Pockets (the Yiddish word for pockets is *taschen),* are eaten. Some say that the three-cornered cookies represent Haman's hat. The cookies are sometimes filled with poppy seeds and raisins.

4 eggs, beaten
1-1/4 cups dark brown sugar
1 cup butter, melted

grated rind of 1 orange
5 cups sifted flour
1 lb. lekvar (prune butter)

Beat the eggs. Beat in the sugar, melted butter, and orange rind. Continue beating until light and fluffy. Gradually stir in the flour. Divide the dough into fourths, forming each part into a ball, and chill for several hours. On a lightly floured board, quickly roll out one of the balls of dough to less than 1/4 inch thickness. Cut into 3 inch circles. Place the circles on a greased cookie sheet. Place a heaping teaspoon of the lekvar on each. Bring up the sides of the circle to form a tricorn, but leaving the filling exposed at the center. Pinch the edges of the dough together tightly. Continue with the remaining refrigerated dough until all has been used. Make in a preheated 375-degree oven for about 20 minutes.

Makes about 40 cookies.

Erste Sterne Cookies
(First Star Cookies)

It is a widely observed custom to break the Yom Kippur fast with coffee and cookies while the regular meal is being warmed or put on the table. These cookies are called Erste Sterne, or First Star Cookies because they are eaten only after the first stars appear, indicating the end of fasting.

1-1/2 cups sifted flour
3/4 cup ground almonds
1/4 cup sugar

3/4 cup butter
1/2 teaspoon vanilla extract

Place all the ingredients in a bowl and, with the fingertips, quickly work them together. Push the dough together into a ball. Break off egg size pieces and smear each on a board with the heel of the hand. Scrape it up and form a ball of all the dough. Refrigerate, covered, overnight. Break off teaspoon size pieces of dough and quickly roll into cigar shapes about 2-1/2 inches long. Place them on ungreased cookie sheets and flatten slightly. Bake in a preheated 450-degree oven for about 8 minutes or until very lightly colored. Remove from pans almost immediately and dredge in sifted confectioners' sugar. Handle carefully. Let cool completely.   Makes about 4 dozen cookies.

Israeli Fruit Bars

The origins of apricots are intermingled and confused with that of plums, but it seems that the early Chinese had both. In Israel, as in all the Middle East, apricots are commonly used. Apricot puree is dried and made into thin sheets which are rolled up. They are eaten either by tearing off pieces to chew or by melting in a little hot water for use in cooking or baking.

1 cup dried apricots	2/3 cup sifted flour
1/3 cup sugar	1/2 teaspoon baking powder
2 cups sifted flour	1/4 teaspoon salt
3/4 cup butter	1 teaspoon vanilla extract
3 large eggs	1 cup chopped nuts
1 cup brown sugar	sifted confectioners' sugar

Boil the apricots in water to cover for 8 to 10 minutes. Drain and, when cool, chop. Reserve. Sift together 2 cups of the flour with 1/3 cup of sugar. With a pastry blender, cut the butter into the flour mixture. Until the consistency of coarse sand. Press into the bottom and about 1/2 inch high on the sides of a greased 9x13 inch baking pan. Bake in a preheated 350-degree oven for about 15 minutes or until very lightly colored. While this is baking, sift the remaining flour with the baking powder and salt. Beat the eggs until very light and gradually beat in the brown sugar. Continue beating until thick. Blend the flour mixture, gradually and thoroughly, into the egg mixture. Stir in the vanilla. Fold in the chopped nuts and apricots. Spread over the baked layer. Return to the oven for about 30 minutes. Do not overbake. Cool to barely warm and cut into about 4-1/2 dozen bars. Roll in confectioners' sugar.

An older version of this recipe calls for dates (uncooked) instead of apricots. The finished bars are drizzled with a mixture of 1 cup of honey and 3 tablespoons rose water. This makes a very sweet concoction and probably should be cut into smaller bars. They are served with small cups of very hot, strong black coffee.

Kipfel

Austrians were hearty eaters in the days of the Empire, and eating was a special event—six times a day! Kipfel were eaten for breakfast, with midmorning or midafternoon coffee. Kipfel are very popular with American Jews, at any time of the day.

1 cup butter	*Filling:*
1/2 lb. cream cheese	1 cup chopped walnuts
2 cups sifted flour	1/2 cup chopped raisins
(or a little more)	1/2 cup sugar
1 teaspoon salt	2 teaspoons cinnamon

Sift into a bowl the combined flour and salt. With a pastry blender, cut the cold butter and cream cheese into the flour mixture until a very fine consistency is reached. Quickly work into a smooth ball. Refrigerate for an hour. Divide the dough into thirds. Leave 2/3 in the refrigerator. Between pieces of wax paper, roll out 1/3 of the dough into a 9 inch circle. Cut the circle into fourths. Divide each fourth into 3 wedges. On each wedge put some of the filling, made by combining all the filling ingredients. Roll each wedge from the wide end to the point. Curve into a crescent shape. Place on ungreased cookie sheets and repeat with remaining dough. Bake in a preheated 400-degree oven for 20 to 25 minutes, or until a pale gold.   Makes 3 dozen cookies.

The Peaks of Mount Sinai

Shavouth is the festival commemorating the giving of the Law to Moses on Mount Sinai. These little cakes are thought to have originated with the Jews of Spain and to have been dispersed with them to the whole Mediterranean area. They represent the mountain of Sinai topped with the tablets (walnut halves) of the Ten Commandments.

4 eggs, beaten	1/2 teaspoon salt
1/2 cup brown sugar	1/2 teaspoon cinnamon
4 tablespoons butter, melted	1/2 teaspoon nutmeg
2 tablespoons brandy	walnut halves
1-1/3 cups sifted flour	

Beat the eggs well and add the sugar, butter, and brandy. Continue beating until smooth. Sift together the flour, salt, cinnamon, and nutmeg. Add gradually to the egg mixture. Mix to form a soft dough. From walnut size pieces of dough, form cone-like peaks. Press a walnut half, upright, into the top of each. Bake on greased cookie sheets in a preheated 350-degree oven for fifteen minutes, or until golden.

Makes about 3 dozen cookies.

Mexican Wedding Cakes

When the Aztec goddess of flowers and love, Xochiquetzal, was stolen from Tlaloc, the rain god, by Tezcatlepoca, it is doubtful that these wedding cakes were served at the occasion of that union. However, in modern Mexico, where the majority of the population marks its proud Indian heritage, these cookies are traditionally served at weddings and other festive occasions, especially in rural areas.

At most Jewish weddings these are not featured, although they are served on occasions when cookies are appropriate.

1 cup butter	2-1/4 cups sifted flour
1/2 cup sifted confectioners' sugar	1/2 teaspoon salt
1 teaspoon vanilla extract	1 cup chopped pecans
	confectioners' sugar

Cream the butter and sugar until light. Add the vanilla. Sift together the flour and salt and gradually add to the butter mixture. When the dough is smooth add the chopped nuts and mix thoroughly. Make balls of about a teaspoon of dough each. Flatten them slightly in the palms of the hands and place on greased cookie sheets. Bake in a preheated 400-degree oven for 10 to 15 minutes, or until they just begin to color. Remove from the oven and while still hot roll in confectioners' sugar. When completely cool store in a covered container.

Makes about 3 dozen cookies.

Jodenkagar
(Jewish Cakes)

These cookies, widely made in Denmark, are also known in the Netherlands and Surinam. They are popular as tea cookies and especially served with wine on such occasions as a betrothal, circumcision, or holiday.

1 cup butter	3/4 cup sugar
3 cups flour	1 egg, beaten
1 egg, beaten	cinnamon
1 teaspoon vanilla extract	sugar
	finely chopped nuts

Rub the butter into the flour with the fingertips until the mixture is like fine sand. Add the egg and vanilla. Stir. Add the sugar and mix well. Knead lightly to blend all the ingredients thoroughly. Refrigerate for 30 minutes. Remove half the dough and roll out thinly. Cut into 2-inch circles. Brush with the beaten egg and sprinkle with cinnamon, sugar, and chopped nuts. Repeat with the remaining dough. Place on greased cookie sheets and bake in a preheated 425-degree oven for 5 to 7 minutes, or until very lightly browned around the edges.

Makes 3 to 4 dozen cookies.

Fragrance of Heaven Cookies

The word "cardamom" is derived from the Greek and means "spice plant." But cardamom is no ordinary spice. It is second only to saffron in cost. Sanskrit writings of four thousand years ago mention it as having "the fragrance of heaven" and the Vikings, discovering it in their early voyages to the spice centers of the East, brought it back to Scandanavia where it became a characteristic ingredient of Danish pastry and Christmas *glogg*.

Being native to India, its use and fragrance spread all through the Middle East and North Africa where some Jewish communities make these cookies as part of the Purim celebration. Others break the Yom Kippur fast by eating cookies made of the same kind of dough.

1-1/2 cups sifted flour	3 egg yolks
1-1/2 cups ground almonds	1-1/2 cups sugar
1 teaspoon ground cardamom	3 egg whites

Combine the flour, almonds, and cardamom. Beat the egg yolks until light and thick. Add the sugar gradually and continue beating until creamy and light. Add the flour mixture, a little at a time, beating continuously. Beat egg whites until stiff. Fold into the batter. Form into small balls and place on greased cookie sheets. Bake in a preheated 350-degree oven for about 25 minutes.   Makes about 40 cookies.

Victory Crescents

When Kara Mustafa and his Turkish hordes kept the city of Vienna under siege in 1618, the Viennese despairingly saw the possibility of their culture being overrun by the star and crescent. However, the Polish army came to the rescue and drove the invaders off. The people inside the city gates had been hoarding their small remaining provisions but, upon victory, used the last of their flour to bake cookies in the shape of crescents, which they gleefully devoured.

This recipe has been adopted by many people and is frequently served to Sabbath callers.

2 cups sifted flour
1/4 cup sifted confectioners'
  sugar
1/2 cup ground almonds
1-3/4 sticks butter, crumbled

1 teaspoon vanilla extract
3/4 cup raspberry or apricot
  preserves
confectioners' sugar

Sift together the flour and sugar. Add the ground almonds. Work the cold, crumbled butter and the vanilla into the flour mixture with the fingers. When well mixed, knead lightly until the dough holds together. Wrap in wax paper and chill for several hours. Roll out on a lightly floured board to 1/8 inch thickness. Cut into crescents with a cookie cutter. Bake on lightly-greased cookie sheets in a preheated 450-degree oven for 5 to 8 minutes, or until cookies are just beginning to color. When almost cool, heat the preserves. Put some preserves on half of the crescents and cover, sandwich style, with the other half. Sprinkle with confectioners' sugar, or dip the ends into chocolate frosting.

Makes about 40 cookies.

Mandelbrodt
(Almond Cuts)

The Hebrew word *"kiddush"* means "sanctification." Kiddush is recited on the Sabbath or a festival eve over a cup of wine immediately before the meal. Following a religious ceremony such as a *bar-mitzva* (the time when a boy reaches his religious majority), a wedding, circumcision or other joyous occasion, the blessings are said over wine and bread, and refreshments, called a kiddush, follow in order to afford an opportunity for the guests to participate in the sanctification of the event. *Mandelbrodt* and *lekach* (honey cake) are almost always served on such occasions.

1-1/2 cups sifted flour
  (approximately)
2 teaspoons baking powder
1/2 teaspoon ground coriander
1/4 teaspoon salt
2 eggs, beaten
3/4 cup sugar

3 tablespoons oil
1/2 teaspoon almond extract
1/2 teaspoon vanilla extract
1/2 cup coarsely chopped almonds
1/2 cup candied cherries,
  cut in half

Sift together the flour, baking powder, coriander, and salt. Beat the eggs well and gradually add the sugar, continuing to beat until thick and light. Add the oil and the extracts. Blend thoroughly. Add the flour mixture gradually and mix well. Fold in the almonds and cherries. The dough should be very soft but not runny. Add a little more flour, if necessary. Lightly grease a long, narrow baking sheet or a cookie sheet. With floured hands, form a loaf about 3 inches wide and 3/4 inch high. Bake in a preheated 375-degree oven about 40 minutes. Do not overbake. This should be slightly moist inside. Remove from the oven and cut into diagonal slices about 1/2 inch thick. Turn each slice with a cut side up. Raise the temperature of the oven to 400 degrees. Return the pan to the oven for 5 to 10 minutes so that the slices toast very lightly. The undersides toast more rapidly than the tops. Five minutes may be enough. These store well.   Makes about 2 dozen cookies.

Trovados

These filled cookies are served in North Africa by the Sephardim. They are usually included in the exchange of foods between a bride and groom in the weeks prior to the wedding. Their name probably derives from the Spanish word "trova," which means "love song."

3 cups sifted flour	*Filling:*
1 tablespoon sugar	**Combine the following:**
1/2 teaspoon salt	**1-1/2 cups finely chopped nuts**
1/2 cup butter	**1/2 cup sugar**
1/2 cup sweet red wine	**1/2 cup chopped raisins**
	1 tablespoon rose water

Sift the flour, sugar and salt together. Cut in the butter until the mixture has the consistency of coarse sand. Add the wine gradually and blend quickly. Refrigerate for 30 minutes. Divide the dough into four parts. Roll out one part at a time, leaving the others in the refrigerator. Roll out on a lightly floured board to about 1/8-inch thickness. Cut into 2-inch rounds. Place about 1 teaspoonful of the filling on each round and fold in half. Pinch the edges together. Repeat with the remaining dough. Bake in a preheated 375-degree oven about 25 minutes, or until faintly colored. Sprinkle with confectioners' sugar.

Makes about 2 dozen.

Oasis Squares

The Jewish tribes could not have survived the forty year wandering in the desert had it not been for the life-giving support of the oases. Settlements were established at some of them which later became cities, as in the case of Beer-Sheba.

3/4 cup sifted flour	2 eggs, beaten
1/2 teaspoon baking powder	3 tablespoons butter, melted
1/2 teaspoon salt	1 cup coarsely chopped dates
1 cup firmly packed brown sugar	1 cup nuts, coarsely chopped

Sift goether the flour, baking powder, and salt. Add the brown sugar. Mix well. Add the well-beaten eggs and melted butter. Blend well. Add the nuts and dates. Stir. Pour into a well greased 8 x 8 or 9 x 9-inch-square baking pan. Bake in a preheated 350-degree oven for 25 to 30 minutes. Cut into squares while warm. Roll in granulated sugar.

Makes about 3 dozen cookies.

Ghorayebah
(Bracelets of the Queen)

These cookies are sometimes served during the Purim holiday to represent the bracelets of Queen Esther. The nuts are the gems. Cookies made of this dough are common in the Middle East. A similar dough is used for cookies in Viennese baking.

1 cup unsalted butter	1/2 cup ground hazelnuts
1 cup sugar	chopped pistachio nuts
2 cups sifted flour	

Cream the butter until it looks almost white. Add the sugar gradually and beat until the mixture is very smooth and very creamy. Add the flour gradually until a dough is formed, then knead by hand as flour is added. The dough remains very soft. If it is too soft to handle, add just a little more flour. Roll in pieces about 5 inches long and 1/2 inch thick. Press ends together to make bracelets. Place on ungreased baking sheets. Sprinkle with the chopped pistachio nuts. Bake in a preheated 350-degree oven for about 25 minutes. Watch carefully. They should not brown at all. Even slight browning spoils the characteristic taste.

Makes about 40 cookies.

Asereth Dibrot
(The Ten Commandments)

These cookies, sometimes called Moses Biscuits, are served during the Shavuoth festival which commemorates the giving of the Ten Commandments to Moses on Mount Sinai. It was traditional in some countries, to begin the formal Jewish education of young children at this holiday. To sweeten the discipline required for this undertaking, the students were started on their way with cookies made in the shape of the Tablets of the Law. Each piece of nut represents one of the Commandments.

2 eggs, beaten	grated rind of 1 orange
1/2 cup margarine, melted	2-1/2 cups sifted flour
1/2 cup brown sugar	coarsely chopped nuts

Beat the eggs slightly. Beat in the margarine, sugar and rind. Continue beating until the mixture is fluffy and thick. Gradually stir in the flour. Chill for several hours or overnight. Roll out on a lightly floured board to 1/8-inch thickness. Cut into rectangles 2 inches long and 1-1/2 inches wide, cut the top of each rectangle like the top of a heart shape. The pieces which come off can be combined with the rest of the dough. Place the tablet shaped cookies on a greased baking sheet. Place 10 pieces of nuts on each tablet in two vertical rows of five pieces in each row. Bake in a preheated 350-degree oven for 15 minutes.

Makes 5 to 6 dozen cookies.

Desserts

Desserts

Yema Doble
(Cuban Syrup Boiled Pancakes)

On May 13, 1939, the liner *Saint Louis* left Hamburg with nine hundred thirty seven Jews aboard who were fleeing the death camps of Germany. All of these passengers held dearly bought Cuban visas and the ship was headed for Havana. While on the high seas, the *Saint Louis* captain was informed that the refugees would not be allowed to land in Cuba. A political struggle was in progress between the Immigration Minister and President Bru of Cuba, and the government would not recognize the visas issued by the Immigration Minister.

United States immigration was closed. Father Coughlin and other anti-Semitic voices were loud in the land of the free. The *Saint Louis* arrived in Cuban waters on May 27. It steamed north and south several times off the coast of Miami until June 7. Pleas to the Cuban and United States governments for permission to land fell on deaf ears. The ship headed back to Europe. Arrangements were finally made to land at Antwerp. There the passengers were given a choice of destination—Belgium, France, United Kingdom, or the Netherlands. Each of these countries offered haven to a proportion of the refugees.

The Freedom Flights of recent years have brought many Cuban Jews to our country. They have brought with them Cuban recipes which have become part of their tradition.

2 cups sugar	3 egg whites
1 cup water	2 tablespoons flour
2 teaspoons lemon juice	6 egg yolks
1 teaspoon lemon rind	2 tablespoons rum
1/2 teaspoon salt	

Combine sugar, water, juice, and rind. Cook until thick and syrupy. Pour off half and reserve. Beat egg whites with the salt until stiff but not dry. Sprinkle the flour lightly over the beaten egg whites and gently incorporate by folding into the egg whites. Beat egg yolks until very light. Fold carefully into the egg white mixture. Reheat half the syrup to a boil. Drop the egg mixture into it by the tablespoonful. Cook only 2 or 3 at a time. When the little pancakes come to the top, use two forks to remove them from the syrup. Fold them in half on a serving dish. When all are cooked, heat the remaining syrup, add the rum, and spoon over the pancakes.   Serves 6 to 8.

Veiled Country Lass

The grated chocolate of this Danish dessert is the veil covering the humble lass, rye bread. This is a variation of the more traditional noodle charlotte, made with layered noodles, apples, and jam.

2 lbs. apples	raspberry jam
1/2 cup sugar	1 cup semi-sweet chocolate,
4 tablespoons butter	grated
3 cups crumbled rye bread	1-1/2 cups heavy cream, sweetened
4 tablespoons sugar	and whipped

Peel, core and slice apples very thinly. Place in a skillet with 1/2 cup sugar. Over low heat, let the apples crystallize. Melt the butter in a small skillet and add the finely crumbled rye bread and the 4 tablespoons of sugar. Stir until the crumbs are crisp. In a buttered glass casserole or small skillet and add the finely crumbled rye bread and the 4 tablespoons sugar. Stir until the crumbs are crisp. In a buttered glass casserole or bowl, place a layer of crumbs, a layer of jam, a layer of apples, and a layer of grated chocolate. Repeat the layering, ending with crumbs. Let stand for several hours at room temperature to blend. Before serving cover with the whipped cream. Sprinkle generously with grated chocolate.

Flan

In France or England, a flan is a one-crust pastry filled with fruit, custard, or a savoury filling. In Latin America, flan is always this kind of custard dessert. In some countries of Latin America, flan is served on the occasion of a *bris* (circumcision).

2 cups sugar	2 teaspoons vanilla extract
8 eggs	8 tablespoons rum
2 large cans evaporated milk	

Put 1-1/4 cups of the sugar in a six cup ovenproof mold or baking dish. Place over heat, stirring constantly, until the sugar is liquid and golden. Tilt the pan so that the entire surface is covered with the carmelized sugar. Set aside to cool. Beat the eggs with the remaining 3/4 cup sugar until smooth. Gradually add the milk and vanilla extract. Mix thoroughly. Strain through a sieve into the sugar coated pan. Place the pan in a larger pan containing hot water which is one inch deep around the mold. Bake in a preheated 350-degree oven for about 1 hour or until a knife inserted in the center comes out clean. Cool and refrigerate. When ready to serve, turn out onto a flat dish which has a rim. Warm the rum and light. Pour it over the flan. Flan should be made several hours, or the day before, serving.   Serves 8 to 10.

Cheese Apple Betty

"Stay ye me with dainties, refresh me with apples;
For I am lovesick."

(Song of Songs 2:5)

4 cups cornflakes, slightly crushed	3/4 cup grated Cheddar cheese
3 cups peeled, thin apple wedges	3/4 cup chopped walnuts
1 cup brown sugar	1/2 cup melted butter
1 teaspoon nutmeg	1 tablespoon lemon juice

In a generously buttered baking dish, place a layer of crushed cornflakes, a layer of apple wedges, a sprinkling of the combined sugar and nutmeg, some of the cheese, and nuts. Repeat the layers, ending with cornflakes. Combine the melted butter and lemon juice and spoon over the top. Bake in a preheated 375-degree oven for 30 minutes or until ingredients have blended and the top is browned.   Serves 6.

Carrot Pudding

Athenaeus wrote the "Banquet of the Learned" (The Deipnosophists) in the third century. It is an account of a symposium of learned men. Their discussions ranged over many topics, but the subject of food seemed to concern them to a far greater degree than the others. Dephilus, one of the discussants, said of the carrot that, although it had food value, it was difficult to digest. He also noted that it prompted men "to amatory feelings."

Carrots are frequently used in Jewish cookery in everything from *gefillte* fish to *izimmes*. The round slices, perhaps because they look like coins, are eaten, especially at Rosh Hashanah, in hope of prosperity.

1/4 cup sugar
1/2 cup butter
2 eggs
9 tablespoons matzo meal
1 teaspoon baking powder
1/2 teaspoon salt
1/2 teaspoon nutmeg
1 teaspoon cinnamon
4 tablespoons cornstarch

1/2 cup sweet red wine
1/2 cup orange juice
1 lb. grated, raw carrots
1/2 cup chopped walnuts
1/3 cup raisins
grated rind of 1 orange
2/3 very well-drained crushed
   pineapple
1/2 cup brown sugar

Cream the butter and sugar. Add the well-beaten eggs. Combine the matzo meal, baking powder, salt, nutmeg, and cinnamon. Dissolve the cornstarch in the combined wine and orange juice. Add to the butter mixture. Gradually add the matzo meal mixture. Blend. Add the grated carrots, nuts, raisins, rind and pineapple. Mix well. Generously butter a heavy bundt pan and sprinkle with the brown sugar. Carefully spoon in the carrot mixture. Bake in a preheated 375-degree oven for about 45 minutes. Five minutes after removing from the oven turn the pudding out on a platter.

If potato starch is substituted for the cornstarch and the baking powder is omitted, this makes an excellent Passover dessert.   Serves 10 to 12.

Apfelpfannkuchen
(German Apple Pancake)

Reform Judaism had its birth in Germany. It was an effort, according to the Reformers, to more adequately meet the needs of modern Jews and to aid them to participate more fully in the national life and culture. German Jews became more fully integrated in their national life and aspiration than did the Jews of any other European country. The tragically ironic and catastrophic destination of the German Jews was Buchenwald, Auschwitz, or Dachau.

1-1/2 cups peeled, very thin
   apple wedges
3 tablespoons butter
3 tablespoons sugar
3 egg yolks
4 tablespoons cream

1 tablespoon brandy
5 tablespoons flour
1/8 teaspoon baking powder
salt
3 egg whites
3 tablespoons sugar

In a 10-inch casserole melt the butter and add the sugar and the apple wedges. Cook until the apples are transparent but still firm. Beat the egg yolks until light and add the cream and brandy. Combine the flour, baking powder and salt. Add gradually to the egg mixture and beat until smooth. Beat the egg whites until they make soft peaks. Gradually add the sugar and beat until stiff. Fold into the yolk mixture and pour over the apples. Place in a preheated 400-degree oven for about 15 minutes, or until set. Turn out on a serving plate, apples on top. Cut into wedges.   Serves 6.

Stuffed Ataif
(Filled Pancakes)

A more complicated recipe for *ataif* was traditionally made by Jews of North Africa as part of the wedding feast. The bride brought sweetmeats for the guests. Among the many kinds of tartlets, pastries, and pancakes, were ataif. The people in the procession going to the synagogue always had some of these sweetmeats to give to pedestrians whom they met on the way.

1 cup sugar	*Filling:*
1/2 cup water	**chopped nuts and raisins**
1 tablespoon lemon juice	**sugar and cinnamon**
1 tablespoon orange rind	
Commercial pancake mix	*Topping:*
oil for frying	**whipped cream**
	chopped pistachio nuts

Make a syrup by combining the sugar, water, lemon juice, and rind. Cook over low heat until it is thick enough to coat a spoon. Cool and refrigerate. According to package directions, make pancakes about 3 inches in diameter. Cook on one side only. Put a spoonful of filling on each pancake and fold over. Pinch the edges together. Fry the filled pancakes in deep, hot oil for 3 or 4 minutes, or until golden. Drain on paper towels. Drizzle cold syrup over the hot ataif. Cool slightly. Top with whipped cream and chopped pistachio nuts.

Coffee Charlotte

According to Scheha Beddin, an Arab author of the fifteenth century, the Mufti of Oden in the ninth century was the first to taste coffee. Despite the many legends concerning its origin, coffee is thought to have originated in Ethiopia. There is confusion about the origin of the word itself. The old Arabic word for wine was *kahwah*. Since Moslems were forbidden alcoholic beverages, the dark brew became the "wine of Islam." Another version claims that the bean was called *kaffa* because it was native to Kaffa, in the mountains of Ethiopa. However, as its use spread to Europe the pronunciation changed to conform to the various languages into which it was incorporated. It became known as *kava, coffa, kaffee, kaffie, cafe* and coffee.

12 ladyfingers
6 tablespoons cognac
2 tablespoons instant coffee
1/4 teaspoon salt
3/4 cups sugar

2 envelopes unflavored gelatine
3 cups milk
2 cups heavy cream, whipped
shaved chocolate
whipped cream

Split ladyfingers. Sprinkle the flat sides with 2 tablespoons of the cognac. Very lightly butter the bottom and sides of a 9-inch springform pan. Line bottom and sides with the ladyfingers, closely pressed together and against the pan. Cut ladyfingers even with the top of the pan. Use the pieces to fill in spaces on the pan bottom.

Combine the coffee, salt, sugar, and gelatine in a saucepan. Add milk and stir over low heat until sugar and gelatine are completely dissolved. Remove from heat and add the cognac and stir. Chill until the mixture mounds slightly when dropped from a spoon. Fold in the whipped cream. Pour slowly into the prepared pan. Chill overnight. Remove the sides of the springform and decorate the top of the charlotte with whipped cream. With a vegetable parer shave curls off a bar of semisweet chocolate which is at room temperature, and place on the charlotte.   Serves 8.

Yellow Rice and Cream

In the section of London called Old Jewry, there is a Milk Street. The name is a corruption of the English transliteration of the Hebrew word, *melech*, king. The original Melech Street is now Milk Street.

5 cups hot, cooked rice
   cooked with 1/4 teaspoon
   saffron in the water
1/2 cup sugar
1 (3-3/4 oz.) package vanilla
   pudding

1/2 cup apricot brandy
2 cups whipped cream
   sweetened
1-1/2 cups pistachio nuts, chopped
2 cups chopped dates
chopped pistachio nuts

To the hot cooked rice add the sugar, stir, and cool. Cook the vanilla pudding according to package instructions. Cool. Stir the rice mixture into the pudding. Add the apricot brandy, 1 cup nuts and the chopped dates. Stir. Fold the whipped cream into the rice mixture. Pile into 8 sherbert glasses. Sprinkle with chopped pistachio nuts. Chill.

Kataiyiff
(Noodle Pudding)

This is called *konafa* in parts of the Middle East but is known as *kadaif* in Greece and Turkey, and *kataiyiff* in Israel. It is another of the many ways to make noodle pudding, although the original kadaif dough is not identical with noodles.

1 cup sugar	1 lb. fine noodles
1/2 cup water	1 cup chopped dates or prunes
1 tablespoon lemon juice	2 cups slivered almonds or
2 tablespoons rose water	other nuts
	4 tablespoons melted margarine

Combine the sugar and water and cook until the mixture coats a spoon. Add the lemon juice and rose water. Stir. Cool and refrigerate.

Cook the noodles in salted water. Drain. Firmly pack half of the noodles into a well-greased baking dish. Spread the dates (or prunes) and 1 cup of the nuts over the noodles. Pack the other half of the noodles on top. Sprinkle on the remaining nuts. Spoon the melted margarine over the top. Bake in a preheated 375-degree oven for about 25 minutes. Remove from the oven and cut into squares. Immediately spoon the chilled syrup over the top and between the squares. Serve cold.

Serves 8.

Scaltsounia
(Almond Fritters)

Some authors say that the French word for fritter, *beignet,* comes from the Celtic word meaning "to swell." Fritters, dropped into hot fat, puff up and swell, a characteristic of this kind of dough or batter based food. These and similar fritters were made by Egyptian and Greek Jews to serve on special occasions.

2 cups flour	1/2 teaspoon ground cardamom
1 teaspoon baking powder	1-1/2 tablespoons cream cheese
3/4 teaspoon salt	milk
2 tablespoons butter	oil for frying
milk	*Syrup:*
1/2 cup sugar	1 cup honey
1 cup finely chopped almonds	1/4 cup boiling water
1 teaspoon cinnamon	1 tablespoon rose water

Sift together the flour, baking powder, and salt. With the fingertips, work in the butter. Add enough milk to make a soft dough. Roll out very thinly on a lightly floured board. Cut into 2 inch squares. Combine the sugar, almonds, cinnamon, and cardamom. Add the cream cheese and a few drops of milk to make a paste. Put a little of this mixture on each of the dough squares. Fold them over to make triangles. Moisten the edges and press the dough together. Fry in deep oil for about 2 minutes or until lightly browned. Drain briefly on absorbent paper and dip immediately into a syrup made by combining the honey, boiling water and rose water. Place on a serving dish. Makes about 40.

Baltasares de Nueces y Naranja
(Walnut-Orange Crepes)

The walnut, known in Greece and Judea in early Biblical times, was introduced into Europe by the Romans. The Romans invaded much of the world and, happily, walnuts have irrevocably invaded our culinary repetoire.

Crepes:
3/4 cup milk
3/4 cup water
3 egg yolks
2 tablespoons sugar
3 tablespoons cognac
1-1/2 cups sifted flour
6 tablespoons butter, melted
3/4 cup finely-chopped nuts

Filling:
1/4 lb. unsalted butter, softened
1/4 cup sifted confectioners' sugar
3 tablespoons orange liqueur
1/3 cup orange juice

Sauce:
1 cup orange marmalade
1/2 cup orange juice
1/4 cup orange liqueur

Crepes: Blend all the ingredients in the blender, except the nuts. Add those when blending is finished. For crepe making procedure see page 96.

Filling: Cream softened butter with the confectioners' sugar. Beat until smooth. Gradually add orange liqueur and blend. Add orange juice a teaspoon at a time, beating continuously so that mixture has a creamy consistency. Spread the orange-butter mixture on each crepe and fold into fourths. Place in a flat baking pan. Cover with foil in which holes have been punched with a large-tined fork. These can be made a few hours ahead of time and warmed in a 200-degree oven for 10 to 15 minutes prior to serving.

Sauce: In a saucepan, mix orange marmalade with the juice and simmer over low heat until thoroughly blended. Remove from heat and add liqueur. Stir. Serve warm over the crepes.   Makes about 10 crepes.

Chocolate Rum Dessert Waffles

Waffles were brought to this country by the Dutch. The word itself stems from an old Dutch form, meaning "honeycomb." The waffles were so named because of the honeycomb appearance caused by the griddle indentations. Some Dutch Jews make waffles as the "pancakes" traditional for Chanukah. Waffles were mentioned in poems dating from the twelveth century when these delicacies were made and sold by vendors on the streets. On religious holidays or feast days they were sold in churchyards.

Waffles:
2-1/2 cups sifted flour
4 teaspoons baking powder
1/2 teaspoon salt
1/2 cup sugar
1/4 cup cocoa
2 egg yolks, beaten
2 egg whites, beaten
3/4 cup milk
3/4 cup rum

1/2 teaspoon vanilla extract
1/3 cup butter melted

Chocolate Rum Sauce:
4 squares unsweetened chocolate
2 tablespoons butter
2 tablespoons white corn syrup
7 tablespoons sugar
1/2 cup milk
1/4 cup rum
pinch of salt

Sift together the flour, baking powder, salt, sugar, and cocoa. Combine the well beaten egg yolks, milk, rum, and vanilla extract. Add to the flour mixture. Beat until smooth. Add the melted butter and blend. Fold in the stiffly beaten egg whites. Bake in a moderately hot waffle iron.

Sauce: Combine over hot water the chocolate and butter. When melted add the corn syrup and sugar. Blend. Add the salt, milk, and rum. Cook, stirring, for 10 to 15 minutes.

To serve, place pistachio ice cream on each waffle and pour the chocolate rum sauce over. Makes about 10 waffles.

Melon Delight

"And I will turn the captivity of My people Israel,
And they shall build the waste cities, and inhabit them;
And they shall plant vineyards, and shall drink the wine thereof;
They shall also make gardens, and eat the fruit of them.
And I will plant them upon their land,
And they shall no more be plucked up,
Out of their land which I have given them,
Saith the Lord thy God."

(Amos 6:14)

1 medium, ripe honeydew
   melon
1 pint fresh raspberries
3 ripe peaches, thinly sliced
1/3 cup sugar

1 tablespoon lime juice
1/4 teaspoon salt
3 tablespoons rose water or
   orange liqueur

Cut the melon into melon balls, saving all of the juice. Add the raspberries and thinly sliced peaches. Mix the lime juice, sugar and salt together and pour over the fruit. Mix and refrigerate for 2 hours. Thirty minutes before serving, add the rose water or orange liqueur. Mix gently. Serve in sherbert glasses plain, with whipped cream or as a topping over cake.   Serves 8 to 10.

Polacsinta
(Hungarian Walnut Pancakes with Chocolate Sauce)

In the Coratian part of Yugoslavia, there is strong evidence of Hungarian culinary influence, a reminder that Croatia was once a province of Hungary. Among the dishes usually considered typically Hungarian are found these delicate crepes, filled with jam or fruit or sauced with chocolate.

The first Jews to come to Croatia did so with the invading Turks, but they have now disappeared. The Czechs, Yugoslavs, and the Hungarians brought *polacsintas* to America.

Crepes:
4 eggs
1 cup cream
1 cup sifted flour
1 tablespoon brandy
1/2 teaspoon sugar
pinch of salt

Walnut Filling:
2 cups walnuts, coarsely chopped
4 tablespoons sugar
1 cup milk (scant)
1 cup apricot preserves
1-1/2 tablespoons rum

Chocolate Sauce:
6 oz. semisweet chocolate
1/4 cup water
1 egg yolk, beaten
1/4 cup milk
1/2 teaspoon flour

Crepes: Put all ingredients into a blender and whir for a few seconds. For crepe making procedure see page 96.

Filling: In a small saucepan combine the nuts, sugar, and milk. Bring to a boil, stirring. Cook for 2 minutes over moderate heat. Remove from heat and reserve. Combine the apricot preserves and rum over low heat and warm, stirring to blend.

Sauce: In the top of a double boiler combine the chocolate and water. Melt the chocolate and stir to blend in the water. In a bowl, beat the egg yolk with the milk and flour. Stir into the chocolate mixture and stir over the hot water until thickened. Do not reheat.

Spread each crepe with the apricot-preserve mixture. Put a spoonful of the nut filling on each crepe and fold over. Place in a shallow, buttered baking dish and place in a 150 to 200 degree oven to keep warm. Pour sauce over just before serving.   Makes 8 to 10 crepes.

Framboise en Poires
(Raspberries on Pears)

Napoleon's attitude toward the Jews of France resulted in restrictive and discriminatory laws against them. Champagny attempted to change Napoleon's attitude by calling his attention to the Jewish contribution in agriculture and their refinement of some of the fruit species and of their abilities in the arts and sciences. He spoke of their loyalty and bravery in war and mentioned those who had been decorated for courage with the Order of the Legion of Honor. But this only resulted in a moratorium on payments of debts owed to Jews and calling Jewish representatives to defend the moral character of the Mosaic laws.

2-1/2 cups water	1 teaspoon cornstarch
2-1/2 cups sugar	1 tablespoon cold water
1-1/2 teaspoons vanilla extract	3 tablespoon Kirsch
4 ripe pears, peeled	toasted slivered almonds
and halved	whipped cream
1-1/2 (10 oz.) packages frozen,	
sweetened raspberries, thawed	

In a saucepan, combine the water and sugar. Boil 7 minutes to make a syrup. Add the vanilla and pear halves. Cook over low heat until the pears are tender. Cool the pears in the syrup. Drain and chill.

Puree the half package of raspberries through a strainer. Dissolve the cornstarch in the tablespoon of water and combine with the raspberry puree and drained juice from the remaining package of raspberries. Cook over low heat until slightly thickened, about 3 to 5 minutes. Combine with the remaining package of raspberries. Mix and chill. When ready to serve add the Kirsch and spoon the raspberry sauce over each pear half. Garnish with the whipped cream and toasted almonds.

Serves 8.

Index